Books are to be returned on or before
the last date below.

7 – DAY
LOAN

LIVERPOOL JOHN MOORES UNIVERSITY
Aldham Roberts L.R.C.
TEL. 051 231 3701/3634

LIVERPOOL JMU LIBRARY

3 1111 01098 3086

Qualitative research for the information professional

A practical handbook

Qualitative research for the information professional

A practical handbook

SECOND EDITION

G. E. Gorman and Peter Clayton

with contributions from

Sydney J. Shep and Adela Clayton

facet publishing

© G. E. Gorman and Peter Clayton 1997, 2005

Published by
Facet Publishing
7 Ridgmount Street
London WC1E 7AE

Facet Publishing is wholly owned by CILIP: the Chartered Institute of Library and
Information Professionals.

G. E. Gorman and Peter Clayton have asserted their right under the Copyright, Designs
and Patents Act, 1988 to be identified as authors of this work.

Except as otherwise permitted under the Copyright, Designs and Patents Act, 1988 this
publication may only be reproduced, stored or transmitted in any form or by any means,
with the prior permission of the publisher, or, in the case of reprographic reproduction, in
accordance with the terms of a licence issued by The Copyright Licensing Agency.
Enquiries concerning reproduction outside those terms should be sent to Facet
Publishing, 7 Ridgmount Street, London WC1E 7AE.

First published 1997
This second edition 2005

British Library Cataloguing in Publication Data
A catalogue record for this book is available from the British Library.

ISBN 1-85604-472-6

Typeset from authors' disks in 10/12 pt Aldine 401 and Chantilly by Facet Publishing.
Printed and made in Great Britain by MPG Books Ltd, Bodmin, Cornwall.

Contents

Tables, Figures, and Research scenarios

About the authors

G. E. Gorman BA MDiv STB GradDipLib MA ThD FCLIP FRSA is Professor of Library and Information Management in the School of Information Management at Victoria University of Wellington, New Zealand, where his principal research and teaching interests are in the areas of research methods, collection development, collection management, evaluation studies and professional education. His books have been published in the UK, the US and Australia, with translations in Russian, Korean, Chinese and Thai. He is founding general editor of the *International Yearbook of Library and Information Management* for Facet Publishing, editor of *Online Information Review* (Emerald), associate editor of *Library Collections, Acquisitions and Technical Services* (Elsevier), reviews editor of the *Australian Library Journal*, and is actively affiliated with a number of other journals. He is also engaged in information-related development projects in Vietnam, Thailand and Lebanon, and is managing a major bequest for the education of Vietnamese information professionals. He is actively involved in IFLA, especially as chair of the Regional Standing Committee for Asia and Oceania and member of the IFLA ALP Advisory Board.

Peter Clayton BA DipLib GradDipArts InfStudies MA PhD AALIA AFAIM MACE is Associate Professor in Information Management and Program Director for Information Studies at the University of Canberra, Australia, where as well as research methods his research and teaching interests include information service management, academic applications of internet technology, collection development and postgraduate education. Dr Clayton has published well over 100 items, including more than 20 monographs and research reports. With G. E. Gorman he published *Managing Information Resources in Libraries: Collection Management in Theory and Practice* (London: Library Association Publishing, 2001). His other published titles include *Implementation of Organizational Innovation: Studies of Academic and Research Libraries* (San Diego: Academic Press, 1997), and *Academics Online: A Nationwide Quantitative Study of Australian Academic Use of the Internet* (with Ann Applebee, Harry Bruce, Celina Pascoe and Edna Sharpe; Adelaide: Auslib Press, 1998). He has been editor of *Australian Academic & Research Libraries* since 1997. He has held various offices in the Australian Library and Information Association, including President of the ACT Branch and of the University, College and Research Libraries Section.

Sydney J. Shep HonsBA MA MA PhD is Senior Lecturer in Print and Book Culture at Victoria University of Wellington, New Zealand, and the Printer at the University's Wai-te-ata Press, a letterpress teaching, research and fine press printing facility. She teaches for the Library and Information Management programme as well as in Media Studies, specializing in books, print and historical research. Dr Shep has published widely on topics in New Zealand print culture, typography, design, and paper history, and was awarded a Marsden Fund grant from the Royal Society of New Zealand in 1998. She designs and edits *SHARP News* as well as the *Bulletin* of the Bibliographic Society of Australia and New Zealand, and is Pacific editor for the International Association of Paper Historians electronic newsletter. In 2003 she was awarded a New Zealand National Tertiary Teaching Award for Excellence in Innovation.

Adela Clayton BA AALIA is a reference librarian in the Research Centre of the Australian War Memorial in Canberra. Her previous positions have included Director, Curriculum Resources Centre, University of Canberra, and Distance Education Librarian, University of South Australia. She has had wide experience as a reference librarian in state, public and academic libraries and has published several previous bibliographies.

Preface to the second edition

I asked him how his research was going. He said quite well, he had collected quite a lot of paradise references already. He took a notebook out of his shirt pocket and ran through the list: Paradise Florist, Paradise Gold, Paradise Custom Packing . . . . He had spotted these names on buildings or the sides of vans or in newspaper advertisements. I asked him if it wouldn't be simpler to look up the Honolulu telephone directory under 'Paradise', and he seemed rather offended. 'That's not the way we do fieldwork,' he said. 'The aim is to identify totally with your subjects, to experience the milieu as they experience it, in this case to let the word "Paradise" impinge on your consciousness gradually, by a slow process of incrementation.' I inferred that it would be improper for me to pass on any Paradise motifs I happened to come across, but he seemed prepared to stretch a point, so I told him about Paradise Pasta and he wrote it down in his little book.[1]

In his inimitable way, David Lodge paints a picture of the classic qualitative researcher that is both true to form and light-hearted. This, we trust, sets the tone for this volume – formative and informative, but not self-important or without a sense of the absurd. One of the great disappointments in our lives as researchers is the unbearable pomposity of so many other researchers, who can be immodest, opinionated, jargon-driven, narrowly focused and utterly without any awareness of the fun that can be derived from research. For some reason this applies more to those in the qualitative mould than their counterparts in quantitative research. Consider, for example, the ethnographer who specializes in participant observation of information seekers – surely he must see some wonderful vignettes of absurdity in information organizations, but how often are we regaled with these tales? Research is a serious business, but we need to keep it in perspective and to realize that, for most of our colleagues, it is not of ultimate significance. Rather, we have a mission to show information professionals that research is something that is inherent in our work, that it can be done in a spirit of simplicity and modesty, and that it can make a significant difference to how well we provide that service that is the essence of the information professions.

Key features of the second edition

The critical and commercial success of the first edition of this work (1997) has prompted the publishers – rather more urgently than its authors, it must be said – to completely revise and update it. All references in existing chapters have been updated, newer readings including online sources suggested where relevant, and research scenarios amended as appropriate, but the key features of this new edition are its two completely new chapters:

- Chapter 2, Evaluating qualitative research
- Chapter 14, Human resources in knowledge management: a case study.

In addition, Dr Sydney J. Shep has taken on the challenge of revising Chapter 10, on historical investigation. In so doing she has turned it into her own distinctive presentation while acknowledging the earlier version by Professor Lyn Gorman. Also, inclusion of the chapter on evaluation, in particular, addresses what we subsequently came to see as an omission from the first edition.

Readers (and libraries) who own the first edition should not rush to weed it yet. The earlier chapters on historical investigation by Professor Lyn Gorman and 'Sensemaking in the electronic reference centre', the case study by Mary Lynn Rice-Lively, remain relevant and useful, if now inevitably a little dated. Similarly, in updating the Bibliography Adela Clayton has had to omit much earlier material still of value and recorded in the first edition.

Like its predecessor, this book has several characteristics worth highlighting. First, it is aimed specifically at researchers and practitioners in information organizations, whether libraries, archives, knowledge management centres, records management centres or any other type of information service provider. The intended audience includes those who may be in training as research workers or information professionals. Thus the content, tone and examples are geared to this audience, and not to social scientists in general. Second, the work is unashamedly in the 'how-to-do-it' mould, with only passing attention to the historical and theoretical prolegomena characteristic of many qualitative research texts. The intention is purely practical – to help readers learn how to conduct qualitative investigations in information organizations. Purists and those of precious sensitivities will object to this, but in our experience learning to be a qualitative investigator requires minimal knowledge of the theoretical aspects of this mode of enquiry, just as one may know little about the internal combustion engine but still be a very competent and safe automobile driver. Third, to facilitate its use as a learning tool the text contains in each chapter a number of aids to understanding: focus questions at the beginning, information-specific 'research scenarios' to exemplify procedures and practice, and suggestions for further reading. Finally, it is our strong belief that research, perhaps more than any other university-level, practice-based discipline, is learned by example. Accordingly, the text contains numerous references to published research relevant to the information professions that readers should use to extend their understanding.

Terminology

For many new to the field of qualitative research, one of the confusing aspects is the apparent fluidity in terminology, with each discipline seeming to invent its unique term for 'qualitative research' – some call it interpretive research, others ethnography or case study research, and still others field research. In this text we seek to introduce some order or hierarchy to the use of terms by treating 'qualitative research' (defined on page 3) as the generic approach, 'case study' (defined on page 47) as the manifestation of this generic approach, and 'fieldwork' (defined on page 64) as the means by which a case study is conducted.

Overview of the chapters

The opening chapter, 'The nature of qualitative research', seeks to set the framework for understanding this method of investigation by addressing four questions: What is qualitative research? What are its distinctive features? How does it differ from the quantitative framework? How does it contribute to information work? Through a detailed definition it is shown that qualitative research incorporates a number of distinctive features that make it both different from quantitative research and give it potential for significant contributions to information work. This chapter also addresses a number of practical issues, including choice of topic, types of data to be collected, and the various methods used in qualitative research.

Arguably Chapter 2, 'Evaluating qualitative research', could have been placed much later in this volume, as assessment of the quality of completed research is the final stage of the research process. But all competent research builds upon previous work: which previous work may be replied upon? The criteria which apply to qualitative studies clearly differ from those more familiar to us in quantitative studies. Tests of statistical significance are clearly inappropriate, for example. Starting with the importance of critical evaluation of any piece of published work, this chapter suggests criteria for the assessment of qualitative research and how these might be applied to one's own work.

In the third chapter, 'Qualitative research design in information organizations', some time is spent describing the process of qualitative investigation as a recursive movement across stages, or developmental progression up an ever-narrowing pyramid. This chapter also introduces four investigative methods appropriate for qualitative research in an information setting (observation, interviewing, group discussion and historical study), and concludes with some ethical considerations.

Chapter 4, 'Case studies in information organizations', then describes the case study approach in its various manifestations (organizational, observational, interview and life history). In addition, some attention is devoted to the important aspects of research known as reliability and validity. By understanding the methods introduced in Chapter 3 and the case study approach described in Chapter 4 the researcher should be in a position to move on to more specific details of qualitative research practice, and these are the focus of the remaining chapters.

Chapter 5, 'Laying the foundations for fieldwork', describes the preparation for fieldwork in an information setting. It begins by defining fieldwork, discusses how it fits into the overall framework of qualitative research and the case study approach, describes the researcher's role and the concepts of experience-near and experience-distant. It then concentrates on the four steps that constitute the first stage in a qualitative investigation: considering the research focus and choosing a topic, stating the problem and formulating research questions, reviewing the literature, and establishing a theoretical framework. In each of these four steps guidelines are offered to help the reader work through the process.

In the sixth chapter, 'Beginning fieldwork', attention focuses on the two steps that make up the second stage in the qualitative research process: selecting locations and subjects, and formulating a research plan. Deciding where to base your investigation and who will be your sources of data are crucial factors in the success of a qualitative study, so these points are dealt with at some length. Likewise, the formulation of a research plan provides a blueprint for all that follows, so this aspect of investigation must be understood clearly before undertaking fieldwork.

Chapters 7 through 9 then discuss each of the three data-gathering methods most commonly employed by information workers during fieldwork: observation, interviewing and group discussion techniques. Chapter 7, 'Observation', opens with a brief discussion of the third stage in the research process, which we call focused activity and which constitutes the remainder of investigative work in qualitative investigations. In the balance of the chapter the principal focus is on unstructured observation, on the observer's position *vis à vis* participation in what is being observed, and on the actual observation process. At the conclusion of this chapter we hope that you will have a reasonable grasp of the procedures involved in observing.

Similarly, in Chapter 8, 'Interviewing', the discussion concentrates on the characteristics of interviewing in information settings and on the specifics of recording interview data. Again, the intention is that you have a basic understanding of how to collect data by means of interviews. In Chapter 9, 'Group discussion techniques', we seek a similar result with regard to the two major approaches to group-centred data-gathering: focus groups and the nominal group technique (NGT). Both approaches have much to offer the investigator in an information organization.

The tenth chapter, 'Historical investigation', by Dr Sydney J. Shep, returns to the most traditional of all qualitative investigative methods among information professionals. Although we are seeing the refinement of other techniques and the introduction of new approaches, history has an enduring role in qualitative research, especially in an organizational context. Accordingly, this chapter discusses characteristics of historical sources of information, their identification, location, use and interpretation. It concludes with advice on writing history, and on integrating historical elements into a qualitative study.

Having in these chapters discussed ways in which data may be gathered in the qualitative mode of research, Chapters 11 and 12 then turn to the key aspects of recording and analysing fieldwork data. In Chapter 11, 'Recording fieldwork data', note-taking techniques are described in some detail, with particular attention to the problems of error and bias and to the conversion of field notes into full notes. Because each data-gathering procedure has unique features, each of these is dealt with specifically in the context of data recording: observation, interviewing and group work. The information and procedures presented in this chapter supplement the basic overview of data recording offered in the earlier chapters.

When the data have been gathered and recorded the researcher turns to analysis, the topic of Chapter 12. Here, following an overview of the analytical process, a distinction is made between preliminary field analysis and later, more detailed analysis, with emphasis on the latter – all important techniques for understanding data gathered from information organizations Particular attention is devoted to coding, content analysis, ethnographic data analysis and memoing, all valuable means of teasing out themes and trends in information-based research. Also, the increasingly important role of computers in qualitative data analysis is treated at some length, for these are as much a boon to qualitative as to quantitative investigators.

When the data have been gathered, recorded and analysed it is time to write the 'story' that emerges, and there are certain conventions regarding the writing of qualitative research reports. These are addressed in Chapter 13, which discusses the writing process, followed by matters of structure, style and readership. This is all done in full recognition of the reality that different contexts require different methods of presentation, so the discussion seeks to be indicative rather than prescriptive. The chapter concludes with suggestions on writing for publication, a desirable conclusion to any worthwhile qualitative investigation.

Chapter 14, entitled 'Human resources in knowledge management: a case study', is intended to serve as a 'model report' of a qualitative investigation in an information setting, in this instance human resources policies in a knowledge management firm. Not only does this chapter serve as an exemplar, but it also offers concrete examples of principles and procedures described in the preceding chapters. In this it should be regarded as having an integrating and clarifying function, and anyone new to qualitative investigation is strongly advised to study Chapter 14 in conjunction with the various research scenarios in other chapters – learning by example is especially helpful in qualitative research.

Finally, the Bibliography, prepared by Adela Clayton, is a selective, annotated guide to qualitative research in an information setting. It is intended to guide readers to fuller discussions of topics and procedures dealt with in the text. It is not a comprehensive listing but rather representative and indicative. It lists materials of three types: items *about* qualitative research in information settings, descriptions of particular qualitative methods, and reports *of* qualitative research in information organizations. The last group, in particular, is only a selection from what is available, and readers are encouraged to search for additional examples of reports in their areas of interest.

Acknowledgements

Readers will have noted that both a chapter and the Bibliography have been prepared not by the principal authors but by associates who are expert in specific aspects of qualitative investigation. Thus Chapter 10, 'Historical investigation', has been revised by our friend and colleague, Dr Sydney J. Shep. She, an experienced historian, is far better placed than either of us to tackle this topic. Similarly, Adela Clayton's searching skills are evident in her work which concludes this book.

Three chapters in the first edition of this work were written by our colleague in the Graduate School of Library and Information Science at the University of Texas-Austin, Dr Mary Lynn Rice-Lively. Although she has not contributed to this new edition, it will be apparent that in preparing it we owe her a debt of gratitude which we happily acknowledge. Similarly, we would like to acknowledge the work of Professor Lyn Gorman who contributed the chapter on historical investigation in the first edition.

While these and others have contributed in various ways to *Qualitative Research for the Information Professional: A Practical Handbook*, all errors and infelicities remain those of the principal authors. With a view to improvement in content and presentation, either of us would be pleased to receive comments, criticisms and suggestions from users of the work. As you read this volume, heed the advice of W. H. Auden:

> Thou shalt not sit
> With statisticians nor commit
> A social science

G. E. Gorman writes

While both Dr Sydney J. Shep and Adela Clayton have improved the content of this volume through their own additions, the most valuable contribution has been that of my co-author, Peter Clayton. I wish, in particular, to acknowledge his Job-like patience when a multitude of extenuating circumstances caused unconscionable delays in the preparation of this edition. Equally important has been the sometimes gentle, sometimes frustrated nagging of our masters at Facet Publishing, especially Rebecca Casey and Helen Carley. With colleagues like these, who needs a guilty conscience?

This second edition remains dedicated to my former supervisor, Dr A. J. Shinkfield, retired headmaster of the Collegiate School of St Peter in Adelaide. But I also wish to doff my cap to those past students who have 'caught the bug' and realize the value and pleasure of doing good quality research – you know who you are, and may you continue to flourish!

Peter Clayton writes

This was the revision which seemed fated never to be finished. My wife Adela and I even spent several months in Wellington, New Zealand, hoping to complete both this and a related volume; however, although we did see G. E. Gorman from time to time, there never seemed to be the opportunity for sustained work on it which we really needed. Only the persistent nagging of our publisher has finally resulted in its delayed appearance. However, as access to useful information over the internet has continued to improve, perhaps this delay has resulted in better and more comprehensive coverage of some topics, and increased the chances that the volume will remain sufficiently up to date for several years to come.

As with the first edition, I would like to dedicate this work to my postgraduate students, past and present. I hope that they have learned as much from me as I from them.

G. E. Gorman and Peter Clayton

Note

1   These words are from the diary of the lapsed priest-turned-lecturer, Bernard Walsh, and refer to Dr Roger Sheldrake, an academic whose field of research is tourism, in David Lodge's *Paradise News* (London: Penguin, 1992), p. 163.

1 The nature of qualitative research

FOCUS QUESTIONS

- What is qualitative research?
- What are the distinctive features of this method of investigation?
- How does it differ from quantitative research?
- How can qualitative research contribute to information work?

This chapter presents an overview of qualitative research and its place in information work from a practical perspective. To achieve this we work through some definitions and a touch of theory, but this discussion is tempered with practical examples of research that should enhance your understanding of theoretical perspectives. What are the important features of qualitative research? How do these features distinguish qualitative from quantitative enquiry? In addition, we offer several reasons for undertaking qualitative research in information agencies, and why it should be considered by more information professionals when they undertake research.

What is qualitative research?

Qualitative research is not alien to information work. Rather, it is something that every information professional does instinctively almost every working day. In the case of one author, this approach to problem solving started as soon as I began my career. When I finished my librarianship course at University College London, I went to work as an assistant librarian in a research library. Although this library employed about six professionals and more than a dozen para-professional and clerical staff, it was managed along very traditional lines, with the chief librarian assuming responsibility for almost everything.

From the first day I noticed that the librarian actually opened all the post himself. This was no mean feat, given our usual delivery of three very full postal bags each morning and a further bag or two in the afternoon. This librarian would spend up to two hours each morning opening envelopes and book packs, sorting items into appropriate piles. Meanwhile, the serials librarian would wait patiently for her morning's work, the secretary would wait impatiently for the correspondence, and the rest of us would get on with such important professional tasks as shelving books, sharpening pencils and making cups of tea.

With growing unease I observed this peculiar post-opening ritual for a number of days, wondering why such an obviously inefficient system was allowed to continue. I watched how other staff behaved with varying degrees of impatience or mirth and decided in my youthful naïvete 'to do something about it'. First, I observed over a two-week period how long the librarian spent opening the post, and how much time others wasted waiting for him to finish. I also interviewed those who were willing to talk about the situation, and listened to them present ideas about ways in which it might be improved. I put the observation data and interview results together into a memo describing what I saw, and summarizing staff views about a range of options for altering work procedures.

However imperfectly it might have been done, this was my first taste of applied research, and it was based not on quantitative methods of data collection and analysis but on something we all do most of the time by instinct – observe behaviour, develop a sense of place and atmosphere, discuss ideas informally with colleagues, listen to conversations, and then create structures of reality based on what we see and hear. In other words, we conduct qualitative research all the time. In my case, the fact that the librarian was incensed by the memo and accused me of undermining his authority, of creating dissent among the staff and of not knowing my place as an assistant librarian, is neither here nor there. How one presents the results of even the simplest research is another issue, one that will be discussed in Chapter 13. The point of this vignette is to demonstrate that we all engage unconsciously in data gathering and analysis within a qualitative frame-work very often during our professional lives.

A definition of research

Research is an inquiry process that has clearly defined parameters and has as its aim the: discovery or creation of knowledge, or theory building; testing, confirmation, revision, refutation of knowledge and theory; and/or investigation of a problem for local decision making.[1]

This is a common definition of research in general, and one that is entirely appropriate to information work. Such definitions abound, with almost every text on research in information work offering its own definition. Unfortunately, when one turns more specifically to qualitative research, a precise definition becomes somewhat more elusive. In fact, asking a qualitative researcher to define this field is as productive as asking an information manager to define information manage-ment. In the library science literature, for example, about the best one can find is Sandler's somewhat vague statement that 'qualitative research methods . . . are loosely defined as those techniques which contribute to the in-depth description and understanding of experiences and interactions occurring within libraries.'[2] While this is a start, such a definition really begs more questions than it answers.

Glazier's view that the most fruitful approach to understanding qualitative research is through a series of negative statements is more helpful:

It is not procedures that predominantly rely on statistical analysis for inferences. It is not a set of procedures that rely predominantly on quantitative measures as a means of data gathering. It is not a set of preliminary data-gathering procedures intended to be used as a device for determining what non-qualitative methods should be employed for a project.[3]

Having said what qualitative research is *not*, Glazier fails to proceed with a statement of what it *is*; in this he shares a trait common to many qualitative researchers – an inability or unwillingness to define qualitative research. In a practical handbook such as this, however, we cannot avoid the issue, so we offer the following as a working definition of our topic.

A definition of qualitative research

Qualitative research is a process of enquiry that draws data from the context in which events occur, in an attempt to describe these occurrences, as a means of determining the process in which events are embedded and the perspectives of those participating in the events, using induction to derive possible explanations based on observed phenomena.

This rather complex definition incorporates a number of features that makes qualitative research distinct from quantitative research. Before discussing it in detail, we need to indicate the major assumptions underlying the definition – with apologies to those seeking a detailed discourse on qualitative research theory.[4]

The key *assumption* made by qualitative researchers is that the meaning of events, occurrences and interactions can be understood only through the eyes of actual participants in specific situations. An investigator cannot know in advance what such phenomena mean to those being studied. Rather, the only genuine way of knowing is to become part of the subjects' world, thereby better understanding the meanings they attach to events. The ultimate goal of qualitative research is to understand those being studied from their perspective, from their point of view. Although the researcher thus intervenes in the reality of those being studied – and therefore distorts that reality to some extent – this distortion can be minimal and, indeed, can be far less than in other methods of research.

Qualitative research is one of two main types of investigation employed in the social sciences, the other being quantitative research, that is, research which focuses more on numerical or statistical data. The quantitative model, which has dominated research in information work for many decades, comes closer to the 'scientific' approach to data collection and analysis. It falls within what one might call the *positivist paradigm*. Followers of this approach view the world as a collection of observable events and facts that can be measured. The qualitative approach, on the other hand, lies within the *interpretivist paradigm*, which focuses on social constructs that are complex and always evolving, making them less amenable to precise measurement or numerical interpretation.[5] Such generalizations do, of course, tend both to oversimplify the complex issues involved and to understate the areas of overlap, interaction and complementarity between the two approaches.

In the following sections some of the distinctive features of qualitative research are presented, followed by a brief comparison with similar features in quantitative research. Tables 1.1 and 1.2, which summarize the key characteristics of each approach, and Research Scenarios 1.1 and 1.2, which provide examples of what is usually meant by qualitative and quantitative enquiry, should be of special help.

What are the distinctive features of qualitative research?

We need to go back to our definition of qualitative research. Here, the key words or phrases are 'context', 'describe', 'process', 'perspectives of those participating', 'induction'. Table 1.1 summarizes the distinctive attributes of qualitative enquiry.

Context

Qualitative research draws data from the context or environment in which events occur. Put another way, qualitative research is contextual in that it uses the natural setting in which events occur as an 'observation post' from which data are gathered. In quantitative research there is a tendency for real life to be regarded as a quasi-experimental, controlled environment in which the researcher manipulates variables. In a qualitative research model, on the other hand, the researcher does not remain remote and detached from events but actually enters the context or situation, collecting data and – an important point, this – enhancing these raw data collected first-hand through the insights gained from actually being on site.

Table 1.1 Summary of the qualitative mode of enquiry[6]

Assumptions	Social construction of reality
	Primacy of subject matter
	Complexity of variables
	Difficulty in measuring variables
Purpose	Contextualization
	Interpretation
	Understanding participant perspectives
Approach	Theory generating
	Emergence and portrayal
	Researcher as instrument
	Naturalistic
	Inductive
	Pattern seeking
	Looking for pluralism and complexity
	Descriptive
Researcher role	Personal involvement and partiality
	Empathetic understanding

In the words of Roger Sheldrake, David Lodge's superb characterization of a qualitative researcher quoted in the Preface, 'The aim is to identify totally with your subjects, to experience the milieu as they experience it . . . .' Thus a researcher investigating staff relations in a library might gain significant insights from participating with staff in their tea breaks, attending their meetings, listening to casual discussions in the cloakroom. Knowing the time and place in which events occurred and words were exchanged can help inform the content of what was said, adding a richness and depth not otherwise available.

Description

Qualitative research attempts to describe occurrences. Using tape recorders, video cameras, notes on paper, photographs, personal records of participants, diaries and memos, this type of research proceeds anecdotally to describe what happened at a specified time and place. Such description tends not to be quantitative, but rather verbal narrative by the participants themselves. To this narrative the researcher, having entered the context personally, can add observations about physical aspects of behaviour, descriptions of settings, and other characteristics of the environment. It is the written word that dominates in this world, and lengthy verbatim records of conversations by the participants themselves are used to ensure that the 'flavour' of events is included in the research. The researcher intervenes only to add additional information not apparent in the anecdotes of the participants.

Note the emphasis on verbal narrative, the written word and verbatim records – this is the essence of qualitative investigation. It is based on the view that the meaning we attach to reality is socially constructed, then expressed in language by the person. Language for the qualitative researcher is the lynchpin between reality and self, which may be shown schematically thus:

Reality – is constituted by facts, which are reflected by
⇓

Language – which reflects facts and expresses meanings created by
⇓⇑

Self – creates meaning, which may be expressed by language as a medium[7]

Therefore, the task of the qualitative researcher is to understand the meaning that people create in context and then to describe and interpret that meaning.

Process

It is not so much the end result of an event, the final construction of that event or activity, that concerns qualitative researchers as the process, the entire event itself. In the words of Czarniawska,

It is the process of construction that is interesting rather than the constructs themselves – a point that escapes many researchers, who, after solemnly stating that 'reality is socially constructed' . . . , proceed to study the reified results of a construction process that is never revealed.[8]

Because of its emphasis on the context in which events occur, qualitative research is ideally placed to understand the process of events – how ideas become actions, the reactions to those actions, and so on – and the various components of the process. For example, a university library might be concerned about poor student participation in its reader education programmes. With its focus on process the qualitative approach to problem solving can be employed to examine the attitudes of reference staff engaged in reader education towards students from specific classes or ethnic groups, and how these attitudes are reflected in the behaviour of staff during training sessions with the students. By looking at the entire educational process, investigators might find that staff disapproval of certain types of students has become embedded in the whole training ethos, thereby making students feel unwelcome.

Instead of focusing on just one component of the process (staff profiles or teaching methods or training packages or student backgrounds), the qualitative researcher is able to develop fuller and richer understanding through immersion in the entire activity. Putting context and process together allows one to have a grasp of the 'natural history' of events, which is why this approach is often referred to as 'naturalistic enquiry'.

Participation

What do those involved in a particular process think? Qualitative researchers seek to understand what people believe, how they feel, how they interpret events; and the researchers try to record and describe these beliefs, feelings and interpretations accurately. Because qualitative investigators are determined to portray the perspectives of their participants with absolute accuracy, they often provide some opportunity for participant involvement in or comment on what is being recorded and said about them. Thus in our study of a university library's reader education programme, it would be entirely in order to show a videotape of a training session to both students and librarians as a means of confirming the researcher's interpretations of student–librarian interactions. To derive the full meaning from a context and process it is essential that the participants' perspectives be respected and reported as fully as possible. This means that the views of all participants must be included, and that the researcher be fully sensitized to the subtle nuances and often obscure meanings of participants' words and actions.

Induction

Putting it all together, that is, the context, the description of occurrences, understanding of the process and presentation of participant perspectives, is no easy task. Research is not merely the reporting of events; rather, the context, description, process and participant perspective must be analysed in a meaningful and coherent manner. In qualitative research this is done primarily by the process of induction, using a 'bottom-up' approach after data have been collected. In quantitative research, one usually starts with certain assumptions, questions or hypotheses and looks for data that will support or deny them.[9] By contrast, often the qualitative researcher collects evidence and uses this to develop an explanation of events, to establish a theory based on observed phenomena. This is sometimes referred to as 'grounded' theory, as the theory is based on the data found on the ground, or built 'from the ground up'. The researcher begins by collecting, observing and studying as widely as possible, and uses this broadly based approach to data acquisition and interpretation to help understand emerging concerns and to offer specific analyses of those concerns.

It is only natural that the assumptions, purpose, approach and techniques of qualitative research at this point appear somewhat complex. After all, most of us have been trained to think in the neater categories of quantitative research. There, the methods often assume primacy, relationships are measured, and causal explanations (about what causes things to happen) are made. Qualitative research can be a far more flexible and much less concrete way of seeking understanding, but this is not to say that it is amorphous or without distinctive features and boundaries. In fact, the key features and characteristics of qualitative research can be distilled into a set of four statements.

- Researchers collect data within the natural setting of the information they are seeking, and the key data collection instruments are the researchers themselves.
- The data are verbal, not numerical.
- Qualitative researchers are concerned with the process of an activity, not only the outcomes of that activity.
- Qualitative researchers usually analyse their data 'rationally' rather than statistically. The outcomes of much qualitative research are the generation of research questions and conjectures, not the verification of predicted relationships or outcomes. [10]

To illustrate how these characteristics might come together in a qualitative research project, consider Research Scenario 1.1, which presents a notional project involving reader education for university undergraduates.

RESEARCH SCENARIO 1.1

INFORMATION LITERACY EDUCATION IN AN ACADEMIC LIBRARY[11]

This is a field investigation of the management of information literacy programmes in university libraries from the perspective of first-year undergraduates. Data are gathered from the undergraduates' perspectives and from programme management situations in different libraries, in a process that involves uncovering the undergraduates' agendas and analysing underlying theoretical constructs.

To become part of the student group the researchers, young postgraduate students, enrol in information literacy programmes at selected universities; by thus taking the role of students the researchers are able to learn first-hand about student perspectives. So that the researchers are treated like any other students, library personnel are asked by the project director to ignore the fact that researchers are part of the undergraduate group. Indeed, the library instructors may not even have met the postgraduate researchers.

During the instructional sessions, the researchers remain part of the student group and do not associate with library staff. If questioned by undergraduates, the researchers emphasize their student status, and they participate fully in all discussion sessions, instructional activities and assignments. During the sessions the researchers make observational notes under the guise of taking classroom notes. In this way the researchers are able to understand undergraduate behaviour in the wider context of participant goals, cultural standards, social influences and behaviour settings.

So far we have assumed that 'qualitative research' is a single, unified approach to gathering, analysing and interpreting data. Not so – just as 'quantitative research' includes many different ways of collecting and analysing data, so there are numerous traditions of qualitative research. Most of these have arisen out of the unique requirements of specific disciplines (education, sociology, psychology and anthropology in particular) but since then have spread to other fields, including information work. Thus the information professional will come across a host of unique terms when reading qualitative literature relevant to information work – 'holistic ethnography' and 'communication ethnography', for example. Rather than discuss the distinctive features of these various schools here, we refer you to Marshall and Rossman, *Designing Qualitative Research.*[12]

How does qualitative research differ from quantitative research?

Because the quantitative mode of enquiry is more familiar to most information professionals (although not necessarily more popular), it may help to clarify the distinctive features of qualitative research by summarizing certain aspects of the quantitative alternative. The key features of quantitative research in Table 1.2 can be compared with the features of qualitative research in Table 1.1 (page 4). It should be realized, however, that this comparative approach assumes a polarity with which not everyone agrees. Czarniawska, for instance, maintains that:

A troublesome convention in these matters insists on a separation at this point between 'quantitative' and 'qualitative' methods, with the second belonging 'obviously' to the realm of the interpretive paradigm. The opposite procedure is to claim that the interpretive approach can use quantitative techniques (and why not?) and that meanings can be counted (but what for?). The point is not to demonstrate that interpretation may be a variation of the positivist paradigm. The difference is in perceiving the language of numbers as 'natural' (and therefore standing unequivocally for the referents in reality), and in treating it as conventional, along with literary language. From this last perspective, the choice between numbers and words is a communicative choice, no less, no more.[13]

Keeping this warning in mind, especially the 'communicative choice' aspect, is important as we seek to characterize the differences between qualitative (interpretive) and quantitative (positivist) methods.

Table 1.2 Summary of the quantitative mode of enquiry[14]

Assumptions	Objective reality of social facts
	Primacy of method
	Possible to identify variables
	Possible to measure variables
Purpose	Generalization
	Prediction
	Causal explanation
Approach	Hypothesis based
	Manipulation and control
	Uses formal instruments
	Experimentation
	Deductive
	Component analysis
	Seeking norms and consensus
	Reducing data to numerical indices
Researcher role	Detachment and impartiality
	Objective portrayal

Context

Like qualitative research, quantitative research is interested in context, but the quantitative researcher often focuses upon only a few, selected contextual factors thought to be of importance or relevance. Sometimes these are tested in a quasi-experimental environment. At other times, participants are asked to report on the presence or absence of these factors. For example, a researcher investigating staff relations in a library might test relationships between variables by collecting data from subjects, typically by a survey, but generally such data would not be supplemented by researcher participation in the work context. The researcher seeks to remain detached from events and rarely enters the context as a player, for fear of influencing the outcome.

Description through norms and numbers

Both quantitative and qualitative modes of enquiry attempt to describe occurrences. The former uses numerical representations to quantify occurrences, while the latter uses words to present anecdotal descriptions. The quantitative researcher is looking for patterns in events, for normative behaviour (that is, behaviour that participants think 'should' take place) and for causal relationships among variables. For such purposes numerical and statistical approaches tend to be most useful. Hence, for the quantitative researcher a single event tends to be just one of many being measured and quantified. Conversely, for the qualitative researcher a single event may be data-rich, and this richness is best teased out by the descriptive use of language.

Results rather than process

It is the end result of processes that more often concerns quantitative researchers, who hope that variables can be identified and their relationships measured. As noted, in qualitative research the whole process is of potential interest. For example, the proposed study of student participation in reader education programmes would be approached quite differently by the quantitative researcher. The process would be divided into its components (staff, teaching methods, training packages, students), and relationships between variables related to these components might be tested. This would help identify reasons for poor student participation. However, it could be argued that such an approach artificially compartmentalizes components that are integrated in practice. A qualitative approach to the same study would prefer to seek understanding through immersion in the full process.

Deduction rather than induction

Whereas qualitative researchers often use the 'bottom-up' approach known as induction when analysing data, their quantitative counterparts usually rely on deduction. That is, they begin with certain assumptions (questions, hypotheses) and then look for data to support or contradict these assumptions. At the risk of over-simplifying, the quantitative researcher is more likely to be predictive, beginning with theory and then collecting evidence; the qualitative researcher is more likely to be interpretive, tending to begin with evidence and then building theory.

Perhaps this is the place to repeat the point that, in order to make the very real distinctions between qualitative and quantitative research more apparent, we have stressed some of their differences rather than the many similarities. In some current research there has been a coming together of these two approaches, as both have much to offer. Our aim has been to characterize, rather than caricature, these differences. In many contexts, of course, the similarities and complementary qualities will be very much more important than their differences – just as would be the case if we were talking about the differences between men and women, rather than schools of research.

To conclude this discussion of the features of qualitative research, and how these often differ from their quantitative equivalents, it should help to see how each method might investigate the same problem. This is done in Research Scenario 1.2, which is purposely simplified to heighten the distinctions between quantitative and qualitative methods.

RESEARCH SCENARIO 1.2

QUANTITATIVE AND QUALITATIVE STUDIES OF JOB SATISFACTION IN ARCHIVAL ORGANIZATIONS

The purpose of this study was to determine whether middle managers in archival organizations are deriving job satisfaction from their employment. In the quantitative approach 100 middle managers were selected at random from a range of archival institutions in a major city. They were asked to complete a questionnaire consisting of two questions. The first asked, 'How long have you been in your present position?' The choice of responses was:

1 [ ] more than 5 years
2 [ ] 5 years or less

The second question asked, 'How satisfied are you with your job?' The choice of responses was:

5 [ ] very satisfied
4 [ ] satisfied
3 [ ] neither satisfied nor dissatisfied
2 [ ] dissatisfied
1 [ ] very dissatisfied

By averaging the responses of all archivists to the second question, the average score was found to be 3.6; however, when the results were separated according to length of employment, it was found that those who had been employed for a shorter period (5 years or less) had an average score of 4, whereas those employed longer had an average score of 2.4. This survey was useful because it pointed out that (1) an overall job satisfaction of 3.6 left some room for improvement in the long term, but that (2) in the meanwhile the longer-serving managers required special attention because of their strong dissatisfaction (2.4). This allowed the archives to identify both a problem requiring immediate solution, and one requiring less immediate attention.

In the qualitative approach to the same problem, 30 middle managers were selected at random from a range of archival institutions in a major city. Each of these managers was interviewed in person by the researcher, who asked how long they had worked in their present job and how they felt about the job. The managers replied to these questions without being given predetermined response categories. During the interviews they were also asked to discuss why they were satisfied or dissatisfied, and from this it emerged that lack of continuing education opportunities was a major source of complaint among those who had served longest. Subsequent investigation revealed that most of the archives had cut their budgets for three consecutive years, with continuing education allowances being the first to suffer. This result gave senior management information that might be useful in improving job satisfaction among middle managers.

In this very much simplified example, the qualitative approach gave at least a partial explanation for job dissatisfaction among a small number of staff, as well as some in-depth information that could be used by those in authority to address the problem. The quantitative approach, on the other hand, has the potential for providing a greater breadth of data across a larger population.

The value of mixed methods

Remember that painting such clear distinctions between quantitative and qualitative approaches to research can be misleading, if not downright inaccurate. It should never be assumed that the qualitative approach is inherently superior to the quantitative, or vice versa. Both have strengths and weaknesses that we must recognize, and we must work to these in constructing our research, always adopting the methods best suited to answering the research questions we are posing: 'Sometimes quantitative methods and data will be required to answer the questions we have asked; sometimes qualitative methods and data will be required; sometimes both will be required . . . .'[15]

'Sometimes both' – a view now held by most experienced researchers. Before we commend this view, a note on terminology is in order. Previously 'triangulation' was a term used by many writers, including the authors of this text, to mean 'multiple research strategies'. This was not universally accepted, however; Burgess for one argued that 'the term triangulation appears to imply the notion of three points of view within a triangle. . . . Accordingly, I suggest the term *multiple strategies* to allow the researcher to use a range of methods, data, investigators and theories within any study.'[16] In place of triangulation, and the misunderstanding to which Burgess alludes, the phrase 'mixed methods' seems to have become the preferred terminology – certainly this is used in major texts by Creswell and Punch for example, and the mixed methods approach has been the subject of important monographs by Brannen, Brewer and Hunter, and others.[17]

Whatever we choose to call it, the fact is that competent researchers today realize that confining an investigation to a particular investigative approach does not yield the fullest understanding of a phenomenon. In a mixed method study multiple methodologies are used. Ideally, these will be both qualitative (perhaps both observation and interviews) and quantitative (perhaps descriptive statistics related to specific activities and work performances).

The purpose of mixing methods is twofold. First, when two or more methods are employed, the researcher is able to address different aspects of the same research question, thereby extending the breadth of the project. According to Hittleman and Simon, 'one procedure used by qualitative researchers to support their interpretations is triangulation, a procedure for cross-validating information. Triangulation is collecting information from several sources about the same event or behavior.'[18] This improves the quality of the research; obviously, conclusions arrived at by using several different means are more likely to be correct, and accepted as such.

Second, by employing methods from different research paradigms (positivist and interpretivist), the researcher is able to compensate for inherent weaknesses in each approach. For example, the qualitative paradigm allows the researcher to have detailed understanding of the perspectives of those involved in events; but it is also 'vulnerable to the criticism that it tends to limit the scope of the data-collecting process, resulting in a micro-level perspective and in reductionist conclusions'.[19] By triangulating data-collecting methods, especially by using a quantitative method in conjunction with a qualitative method, the researcher is able to draw on the unique strengths of each – thus providing both macro- and micro-level perspectives in a single project.

An interesting early example of mixed methods in information science research was provided by Dervin, in a project which used both quantitative and qualitative methodologies in studying information seeking.[20] Since her work in the early 1980s, mixing methods has become much more commonplace in library and information research generally, and researchers would no longer be surprised by such descriptions of multiple strategies as the following:

> Several methods of data collection were used. Personal interviews were conducted with the reference department heads. The operations of the two reference departments were observed by the researchers, and the policy documents were analyzed. A questionnaire allowing for structured, open-ended responses was constructed and used for the interviews.[21]

A word of warning – it is not simply a matter of combining methods to produce more robust results. This belies the complexity of the issue. Are we just combining findings or results from two types of research in a single project? Or are we combining data during the analysis to produce more complex and richer findings? Or perhaps we are combining methods, data and findings in a full mixed method enquiry. Punch concludes that 'there are many models for combining the two approaches, and no one right way. How they are combined should be determined by the reasons for doing so, set against the circumstances, context and practical aspects of the research.'[22]

How can qualitative research contribute to information work?

In libraries and other information agencies the demand for accountability and assessment in its various guises has in the past led to the entrenchment of many quantitative methods of investigation. While this 'counting' approach is fine as far as it goes, for many information professionals it does not go far enough in helping to understand the meaning behind the figures, or in addressing issues that are not readily quantified (user satisfaction, for example, or the state of staff morale). A more qualitative approach to information issues and problems has the benefit of presenting new answers to old problems, or at least different perspectives derived from potentially richer data. This approach also might be said to provide broader insights not only into existing issues and problems, but also into so far unexamined areas of information work.

More specifically, qualitative research methods and data analysis techniques can contribute to libraries and library operations in a number of respects. They:

• are attuned to growing complexity in an information environment that requires flexibility and variability in data analysis
• facilitate the use of triangulation to enrich research findings
• are responsive to the need for libraries to fulfil their service imperative
• are suited to the non-quantitative background of many information professionals
• fit the social nature of libraries.

Responding to complexity in the information environment

Information professionals operate in a complex environment and are under increasing pressure to deliver goods and services efficiently. Competing providers, ranging from large corporate information services to small independent information brokers, not to mention internet providers, are more than willing to offer alternatives to traditional, institutional information provision, and what they offer in terms of digitized information is highly attractive to many information consumers. This means that problems arising in the delivery of information and services must more than ever be dealt with swiftly and conclusively if the library-based information professional is to maintain an edge.

Flexibility in any approach to problem solving permits information professionals to understand complex organizational and social phenomena more clearly. Indeed, this is a particular strength of the qualitative approach, which, with its interpretivist focus, permits a more flexible understanding of complex and evolving social constructs. Furthermore, its 'bottom-up' approach to local problems and issues allows complexities to be elucidated by those who are directly involved, rather than studied from a distance by remote researchers who may not be aware of the subtle nuances and hidden currents in a particular situation.

In the past we tended to rely on a single means of research-based problem solving, that of the positivist, quantitative researcher. While this remains a valid approach, information professionals are now aware that it is but one among many, and has no natural right to be the preferred methodology. In fact the best option is for a range of approaches that will allow flexibility in understanding problems and offering multiple insights into their solution. If the information professional has at hand an armoury of research techniques, ranging from the most controlled statistical approach useful in assessing collection use to the most fluid, contextually driven participatory approach useful in understanding staff relations, then the odds are that a research response to environmental complexity will be more appropriate. Increasing the range and variety of our research techniques can only be to our advantage – and, indeed, Martin has argued that the use of non-traditional methodologies can help us overcome the blindspots caused by 'mono-method monopolies'.[23]

Fulfilling the service imperative

The overriding task of an information professional is to provide the best possible services to a range of users, and a knowledge of qualitative research assists in fulfilling this task in several ways. First, knowledge of research, both quantitative and qualitative, helps information professionals facilitate the work of researchers in both academic and special libraries.

> If the librarian has some cursory knowledge of the researcher's field and of the research methods used, the librarian is in a position to be part of the researcher's network. In this role, the librarian may foster growth of the researcher's network by referring one researcher to another. By being a generalist, the librarian can also counsel the researcher concerning access points to research in the researcher's field and in related areas.[24]

Second, and more broadly, knowledge of qualitative research also has the potential to improve service to users of all types because qualitative methods are particularly suited to the user service point interfaces in libraries and other information agencies. As the name implies, qualitative methods are often considered ideal for assessing the *quality* of a service provided, when that is of more importance than its frequency or cost. The techniques discussed in the following chapters, especially observation and interviewing, are highly appropriate research methods for researching information-gathering behaviour of users, user education programmes, reference service performance, relations between users and staff and a host of other service-related functions. To the extent that these methods are used to gain insight into our performance, then they can be said to contribute to the service imperative of our organizations.

Matching the background of information professionals

Many practitioners have long bemoaned that fact that research in information work remains largely the provenance of academics in library and information science, whereas in such a practical and service-oriented profession much should be done by those at the coal face, practitioners involved in day-to-day work with information, information systems, users and organizations. There are, however, compelling reasons for this gap between practitioners and research. To begin with, it is well known that most recruits to information work have an arts background, and in the arts the positivist, quantitative mode of thinking is not the norm. At the same time these recruits have been led to believe, by example if nothing else, that quantitative methods of investigation are the norm in information work. How many times do students or practitioners say 'I hate research', when they really mean 'I hate statistics' or 'I can't do maths' or 'Tables and figures fill me with dread' – all features of the positivist approach to research.

By taking a more qualitative, interpretivist view and encouraging this more naturalistic approach to research, we hope to encourage many highly competent, insightful professionals to adopt a research-oriented, problem-solving mentality. In this respect, qualitative research relates more closely to what is happening in the profession today and speaks in terms that people can understand. In future, both students and practitioners may be less prone to say 'I hate research', and more prepared to try it for themselves.

Fitting the social nature of libraries

For decades in the past information work was viewed as a profession in the positivist tradition, and libraries as 'laboratories' in which quantitative survey techniques were the best, and often the only, way to collect data for (primarily statistical) analysis. The 'scientific' methods of quantification were regarded as much more credible and appropriate than the apparently less scientific methods employed by many social researchers. Even today the pages of most library and information management journals publish relatively few articles with a qualitative focus. While it has become increasingly clear to more thoughtful researchers in recent years that organizational settings do not always meet the requirements of quantitative research with regard to sample size and representativeness, quantitative research continues to be the norm, which leads one to question how often the results are meaningful in a statistical sense.

It is thus appropriate for information professionals to look at alternative means of investigating problems. Furthermore, information agencies are service organizations involving social realities and individuals who work within these realities; they are places rich in meaning created by these individuals, and in which group and individual behaviour is an important factor. Given this service orientation and social nature of information agencies, and the resulting existence of such subjective factors as motivation and behaviour, it is only natural that qualitative research and its search for meaning be adopted as an appropriate investigative paradigm. By complementing the traditional quantitative approach with thoughtful qualitative studies we can only improve our organizations, our service to clients, and our profession.

Review of Chapter 1

This opening chapter has sought to provide a basic understanding of the nature and design of qualitative research by answering four key questions: What is qualitative research? What are the distinctive features of this method of investigation? How does it differ from quantitative research? How does qualitative research contribute to information work?

In the opening overview of qualitative research it was suggested that five key words emerge from a comprehensive definition of the topic; these are context, description, process, participation and induction. Putting these terms together results in a research method that is distinctly different from the standard quantitative approach adopted in much information research.

Indeed, qualitative research contributes to information work in a number of ways that give it at least as much value as the quantitative approach. Specifically, it is responsive to complexities in the information environment, it contributes to mixed methods as a means of enriching research findings, it aids information professionals in fulfilling the service imperative, and in approach and method it suits the background of many information professionals better than quantitative methods.

Where to now?

Because almost all research builds upon previous research, Chapter 2 discusses how you might assess published qualitative research. Before going on to read that chapter, however, you may wish to test your understanding of this first chapter by reviewing the focus questions – as suggested in the Preface. After that, you might wish to turn next to the final chapter of this volume, which provides an example of a qualitative research investigation. Then see if you can answer the following questions:

- Could this project have been conducted as a quantitative study? If so, how?
- Did triangulation or mixed methods figure in the study? If so, how complementary were the methods?
- As the researcher in this project, what difficulties would you expect to have encountered?
- What conclusions were drawn? Do you think they justified the effort expended in the project?

Further reading

If you would like to read additional material on the content of this chapter, of all the items suggested in the notes and bibliography we suggest you start with J. D. Glazier, 'Qualitative Research Methodologies for Library and Information Science: An Introduction'. In *Qualitative Research in Information Management*, eds. J. D. Glazier and R. R. Powell (Englewood, CO: Libraries Unlimited, 1992), pp. 1–13; and B. Sutton, 'The Rationale for Qualitative Research: A Review of Principles and Theoretical Foundations', *Library Quarterly*, **63**, October 1993, pp. 411–30. Both are now more than a decade old, but they are classic scene-setting works that have not been overtaken by events.

U. Flick, *An Introduction to Qualitative Research* (Thousand Oaks, CA: Sage Publications, 2001) offers a newer and more generic introduction to qualitative research, and is a useful complement to this text. Much more comprehensive is the collection of 16 essays edited by A. M. Huberman and M. B. Miles, *The Qualitative Researcher's Companion* (Thousand Oaks, CA: Sage Publications, 2002); in the context of this chapter, Huberman and Miles' Part 1, with chapters on theory building, validity, ethnography and realism, organizational ethnography and 'Real Men Don't Collect Soft Data', by S. Gherardi and B. Turner, is especially recommended at this juncture.

On mixed methods generally perhaps the most accessible discussion is in J. W. Creswell, *Research Design: Qualitative, Quantitative and Mixed Methods Approaches*, 2nd edn (Thousand Oaks, CA: Sage Publications, 2003). Also worth reading is N. Fielding and M. Schreier, 'Introduction: On the Compatibility between Qualitative and Quantitative Research Methods', *Forum: Qualitative Sozialforschung/Forum: Qualitative Social Research*, **2** (1), 2001, http://qualitative-research.net/fqs. This introduction to an issue of *Forum* devoted to the relationship between quantitative and qualitative research includes insightful and useful comments on their interrelationships, integration, triangulation and related matters.

Notes

1   P. Hernon, 'The Elusive Nature of Research in LIS'. In *Library and Information Science Research: Perspectives and Strategies for Improvement*, eds. C. R. McClure and P. Hernon (Norwood, NJ: Ablex Publishing Corporation, 1991), pp. 3–4.

2   M. Sandler, 'Qualitative Research Methods in Library Decision-Making'. In *Qualitative Research in Information Management*, eds. J. D. Glazier and R. R. Powell (Englewood, CO: Libraries Unlimited, 1992), p. 174.

3   J. D. Glazier, 'Qualitative Research Methodologies for Library and Information Science: An Introduction'. In Glazier and Powell, op. cit., p. 6.

4   A 'practical handbook' such as this is not the place for theoretical discourse, which is presented in some detail in any number of larger works. Perhaps the most accessible studies of qualitative research that include reasonably detailed discussion of theory are the several works by A. L. Strauss, including the following: B. G. Glaser and A. L. Strauss, *The Discovery of Grounded Theory: Strategies for Qualitative Research* (Mill Valley, CA: Sociology Press, 2000 [first published by Sage, 1967]); A. L. Strauss, *Qualitative Analysis for Social Scientists* (Cambridge: Cambridge University Press, 1987); A. L. Strauss and J. Corbin, *Basics of Qualitative Research: Grounded Theory Procedures and Techniques* (Newbury Park, CA: Sage Publications, 1990).

5   This discussion is based on the distinctions between quantitative and qualitative research made by C. Glesne. However, it has to be said that these distinctions are perhaps too clear cut and certainly unfairly biased against the quantitative paradigm, which is never so mechanistic as they suggest. See C. Glesne, *Becoming Qualitative Researchers: An Introduction*, 2nd edn (New York: Longman, 1999).

6   Ibid.

7   This perception is based on the insightful discussion by B. Czarniawska, *Narrating the Organization: Dramas of Institutional Identity* (Chicago: University of Chicago Press, 1997), pp. 57–9.

8 Ibid., p. 63.

9 Not everyone accepts this antithesis between the deductive approach in quantitative research and the inductive method employed in qualitative investigations, and some would argue that hypothesis testing can be undertaken in both types of research. See, for example, S. I. Miller and M. Fredericks, 'The Confirmation of Hypotheses in Qualitative Research', *Methodika*, **1**, 1987, pp. 25–40.

10 These points are taken from D. R. Hittleman and A. J. Simon, *Interpreting Educational Research: An Introduction for Consumers of Research*, 2nd edn (New York: Merrill, 1997), pp. 43–4.

11 This notional library project is based on a secondary school classroom project reported by Hittleman and Simon, Ibid., p. 44.

12 C. Marshall and G. B. Rossman, *Designing Qualitative Research*, 2nd edn (Thousand Oaks, CA: Sage Publications, 1995).

13 Czarniawska, op. cit., p. 63.

14 Based on Table 1.1 in Glesne, op. cit., p. 6.

15 K. F. Punch, *Introduction to Social Research: Quantitative and Qualitative Approaches* (Thousand Oaks, CA: Sage Publications, 1998), p. 241.

16 R. G. Burgess, *In the Field: An Introduction to Field Research*, Contemporary Social Research Series, 8 (London: Allen and Unwin, 1984), p. 146.

17 Punch, op. cit. Chapter 11 deals with mixed methods. See also Chapter 11 of J. W. Creswell, *Research Design: Qualitative, Quantitative and Mixed Methods Approaches*, 2nd edn (Thousand Oaks, CA: Sage Publications, 2003). Among the monographs devoted to mixed methods, see especially J. Brannen, ed. *Mixing Methods: Qualitative and Quantitative Research* (Aldershot: Avebury, 1992) and J. Brewer and A. Hunter, *Multimethod Research: A Synthesis of Styles* (Newbury Park, CA: Sage Publications 1989). Of particular value are three papers in J. Brannen (ed.), *Mixing Methods: Qualitative and Quantitative Research* (Aldershot: Avebury, 1992) dealing with this issue: J. Brannen, 'Combining Qualitative and Quantitative Approaches: An Overview', pp. 3-37; M. Hammersley, 'Deconstructing the Qualitative–Quantitative Divide', pp. 39–55; and A. Bryman, 'Quantitative and Qualitative Research: Further Reflections on Their Integration', pp. 57–78.

18 Hittleman and Simon, op. cit., p. 232.

19 R. Grover and J. D. Glazier, 'Structured Participant Observation.' In Glazier and Powell, op. cit., p. 108.

20 B. Dervin, et al., 'Measuring Aspects of Information Seeking: A Test of Quantitative/ Qualitative Methodology', *Communication Yearbook*, **6**, 1982, 549–69.

21 E. Sjolander and R. Sjolander, 'A Strategic Analysis of the Delivery of Service in Two Library Reference Departments', *College & Research Libraries*, **56** (1), 1995, 61-2.

22 Punch, *op. cit.*, p. 250.

23 J. Martin, 'Breaking up the Mono-method Monopolies in Organizational Analysis'. In *The Theory and Philosophy of Organizations: Critical Issues and New Perspectives*, eds. J. Hassard and D. Pym (London: Routledge, 1990), pp. 30–43.

24 R. Grover, 'Qualitative Research in Library and Information Professional Education'. In Glazier and Powell, *op. cit.*, p. 194.

2 Evaluating qualitative research

FOCUS QUESTIONS

- Why is evaluation of qualitative research necessary?
- What are the differences between the evaluation of qualitative research and quantitative research?
- Are there criteria specific to qualitative research which should be used in its evaluation?
- How might the evaluation of other people's research affect the conduct of your own?

Regardless of whether we are likely to undertake a research project of our own, these days almost all professionals will encounter qualitative research reports in the professional literature. Unless one is simply to accept that everything published is, in fact, credible – certainly too reckless an assumption for either of us – then some criteria have to be applied to sort the genuinely groundbreaking from the routine, the competent from the flawed. For quantitative research this is, if not easy, at least comparatively straightforward; there are many well-established rules to follow, and guides to their application.[1]

No such well-established rules or universally recognized guides exist for qualitative research. This chapter proposes some that are gaining wide acceptance and suggests how they might be employed.

The importance of evaluation

There are many reasons why an information professional needs to be able to evaluate the quality of qualitative research reports. Perhaps the most apparent is to be able to read one's own professional literature intelligently and quickly – there is no need to waste time reading inadequate work. If you are a manager, should you rely on the findings and recommendations of studies which appear to have been conducted in organizations similar to your own? Few would wish to consider major changes to policies, services or procedures if the study recommending them was itself flawed. For the novice researcher, since research is acknowledged to be cumulative in nature, it is necessary to know whether or not it is safe to rely on earlier work. If you do accept something that is, in fact, dubious, not only will your work be built on inadequate foundations – and hence far more likely to encounter problems – but also if they know or suspect the weaknesses in the work you cite, more expert readers will be inclined to dismiss your own work as similarly flawed.

Criteria for evaluating research

Of course, some of the criteria you would use for qualitative research are the same as those that apply to any research. Over 20 years ago in a standard text on research Busha and Harter suggested a set of criteria for the evaluation of research:

1 What are the conclusions of the research? Does the study answer the research question posed?
2 Is the methodology adequate for the research problem under investigation?
3 Have assumptions been explicitly identified, and are they reasonable and acceptable?
4 Are the instruments or indexes used by the investigator adequate reflections of the conceptual variable of the study?
5 If a test or experiment was conducted as a part of the research, are the results sufficiently conclusive so that the hypotheses can be accepted as tentative, theoretical knowledge or put to practical use?
6 Can conclusions of the study be generalized to a larger population?
7 Are the conclusions linked to other assertions so that findings can be incorporated into existing theory?
8 What was the hypothesis or research question?
9 Was the hypothesis of social or theoretical significance and was the problem stated so that it can be solved?
10 What were the independent and dependent variables of the research?
11 Did investigators appear to be aware of any intervening variables, and, if so, how did the researchers account for them?
12 What are the theoretical implications of the research? Did the researcher appear to be aware of them?
13 Were graphic or tabular formats appropriately used to display pertinent data?
14 If sampling procedures were used, were they adequately explained in the research report?
15 If the investigator claimed to have selected a random sample, was it actually chosen so that each member of the population had an equal chance of being selected?
16 Was the methodology explained in an understandable manner so that it can be easily replicated?
17 What techniques (statistical or others) were used to analyse quantitative or qualitative data? Were these techniques appropriate for the investigation?
18 Did the investigator conduct a literature search prior to the project's initiation? If so, was the study then related to past, similar investigations?
19 Did the investigator make recommendations for future study?
20 Was the research report written in a factual, straightforward, honest, and lucid

manner, and was it free of incorrect grammar, spelling errors, and emotionally laden words and phrases? [2]

We have added numbers to these criteria to point out those relevant to any form of research. Check them again yourself, and identify those that you think do not apply principally to quantitative research, but equally to qualitative research. Those we consider clearly universal are numbers 1–3, 7–9, 12 and 16–20. (Some of the others – such as 6, generalizability – could be applied to some qualitative research but seem more applicable to quantitative studies. With generalizability a properly drawn random sample should be representative of the population, for instance – not a situation that commonly occurs with qualitative research.)

Assessment criteria for qualitative research

In Figure 2.1 we set out some of the questions you might ask when reading any qualitative research report. While some of these are clearly related to the general criteria listed by Busha and Harter, we have chosen to present them in the order in which you would expect to encounter them in a typical research report. Much like academic theses, research reports do typically adopt a standard, expected format – even if sometimes greatly abbreviated in order to fit the word limits of a standard journal article.

Perhaps it seems less important that a research report that meets all these criteria should also be well and clearly written, but actually in qualitative research a clear and direct presentation style is of special importance. This is, in fact, one of the principal differences between quantitative and qualitative research. In quantitative research, a turgid, overlong or overly brief report, or one dense with statistics, can still persuade the persevering reader if it is apparent that all the usual methods were employed to assure its reliability and validity. A badly written and presented study, which nevertheless drew an appropriate random sample, surveyed it using a standardized instrument and then applied recognized statistical tests to the findings may still convince (even if far from a pleasure to trudge through). In contrast, a qualitative study that fails to place its subjects in context adequately by necessity cannot draw upon standardized interview schedules or focus group questions; therefore it may be charged with subjectivity in the choice of examples presented, as it cannot rely on such simple, formal defences to assert its integrity. It must persuade at a broader, more general level.

Centuries ago – long before the standard criteria we now routinely apply to qualitative research were developed – universities used to teach an important discipline called rhetoric. At the heart of rhetoric was the concept of presenting an argument in a form that would persuade the hearer to accept it. The rhetoric of scholarship fulfills the same purpose: it is a formalized discourse, designed to convince the reader to accept it. Unless a reader can be persuaded that a study has been properly and conscientiously executed, he or she is unlikely to do so. Scholars function in a social system in which there is general agreement on the types of topic

Abstract
- Is information about the major aspects of the research noted – its purpose, subject(s), method, findings and conclusions?
- Is the abstract brief and clearly written?

Introductory sections
- Is the purpose of the research explained and its importance noted? Is this a purpose that can be studied in an unbiased way?
- Are any assumptions or limitations noted?
- Is its theoretical basis presented?
- Has relevant previous work in the area been drawn upon, and related to the present study?

Methodology
- Is the use of a qualitative approach discussed and justified? If not, should it have been?
- Are the researchers' own assumptions and biases presented? How have the researchers attempted to prevent their presence from affecting the data they collected?
- Is there a clearly expressed research question or focus to the study?
- Are the subjects or groups or data sources involved clearly described, and are they appropriate for a study of this nature?
- Is the context of the study sufficiently well described that its relevance to other situations can be assessed?
- Is the way the research was carried out clearly described? Are samples of the forms used or questions asked or coding decisions taken included, perhaps as appendices? Do you think you or another researcher could replicate the research, and if you did would you expect to reach similar conclusions?
- Are there data presented drawn from different perspectives, or obtained from different techniques? This might include data from interviews and documents and from researcher observations; as noted in Chapter 1 the use of multiple data sources is usually referred to as 'triangulation' or 'mixed methods'.

Findings
- How have the researchers organized and presented their data?

- Are the processes used for identifying patterns and key ideas clearly described, and do these appear likely to have arisen from the data themselves?
- Is there any suggestion that only the data that support the propositions advanced in the study have been presented, or given prominence? Are findings that do *not* support the author's approach discussed?
- Are examples of the data obtained included? These might include extracts from interview transcripts, or excerpts from documents, or summaries of group discussions. Do these appear to have been selected to show the full range of opinions or perspectives, and do they include at least some unexpected or contradictory elements?
- If the study involved active participants, has any effort been made to have them check the accuracy of the findings as reported? This might involve members of the organization reading draft chapters or reports, or reporting back to an organization in some formal way.

Discussion and conclusions
- Do the discussion and conclusions directly relate to the research questions or research focus of the study?
- Do the discussion and conclusions accurately reflect the data gathered and presented in the preceding sections?
- Is there any attempt to generalize to the wider environment without taking into account the particular circumstances of the context of the study?
- Are any interesting or unexpected findings discussed?
- Is there any attempt to add to our theoretical understanding of the topic?
- Is there any attempt to add to our practical understanding of the topic?
- Are any recommendations made clearly based upon the findings, and do they seem reasonable?

Figure 2.1 Questions to ask of qualitative research studies

regarded as acceptable for study, agreement on the function of theory in underpinning research, agreement on the ways research should be undertaken, and agreement on the ways in which work may be presented. For quantitative research, much of the last two of these is formalized through long practice. The presence of expected components such as the drawing of an appropriate random sample thus function at a deeper level, by assuring the reader that the author knows the rules and has adhered to them. Lacking such explicit rules, qualitative studies have to persuade in part through simple, clear language and readily comprehended and as readily defensible procedures. The avoidance of value-laden language or description will play an important part in such persuasion. Having said this, we expect that, as qualitative research continues to develop, and as more excellent qualitative studies are published, there will in time come to be standard, expected components that most qualitative research reports mention and which serve a similar function to their quantitative counterparts. What might these components be?

Evaluating qualitative research
Reliability

When something produces consistent results it can be called reliable. Thus a clock is said to be reliable if it tells the time correctly. But this is a more interesting example than it seems: time is context sensitive, so local time depends upon where you are. It is also possible to have the wrong time, reliably. One of us is married to someone who likes to have clocks set a little fast so she is less likely to be late; unfortunately, she *knows* that the clocks are fast, so this is not particularly effective. (Reliability is dealt with in greater detail in Chapter 4.)

In qualitative research, because it is frequently the researcher who acts as 'instrument' or data gatherer, it is difficult to establish the reliability of the researcher. However, if the researcher notes his or her own assumptions and biases so that these may, if necessary, be discounted; fully and carefully explains the data-gathering procedures used; keeps thorough notes; and uses multiple sources of data to verify observations, then we are more likely to accept these data as reliable. Marshall and Rossman suggest what research consumers should look for are that the researchers:

- provide details of their method so its adequacy and logic can be determined, and there is an abundance of evidence
- provide evidence of their qualifications as participant observers
- make their assumptions clear
- state what their questions were, and the study seeks to answer those questions and generate further questions
- use preliminary days of the study to generate a focus for the study
- are present in the research context for an adequate period of time, and the researchers observe a full range of activities over a full cycle of those activities
- collect data from multiple sources
- save their data for reanalysis.[3]

Any study that meets most of these criteria is likely to produce consistent, and hence reliable, results.

Data analysis

Just as no one would present an undigested mass of quantitative data, so too qualitative researchers have to analyse their data so that they can understand and interpret it before it can be presented in the form of a research report. The researcher is not only the data-gathering instrument, but is also responsible for the organization and presentation of the data. Because this is in part an intuitive process, 'Research consumers should expect qualitative researchers to fully explain their analysis methods so that the logic of their decisions can be followed and evaluated.'[4] This might involve discussion of field note-taking procedures, details of data arrangement and storage, and where appropriate the categories and clusters of concepts or terms that were used to make sense of these data. Even in a paper that primarily presents the results of a qualitative study, one would expect to see some reference to this process – in a journal article, possibly in the form of a citation to the full report of the study.

Validity

Data analysis, carefully executed and as carefully reported, is one of many factors that may contribute to validity. Validity refers to the extent to which something actually measures what it is intended to measure. Obviously if a procedure is unreliable, it cannot produce valid results; however, like the time on a clock deliberately set fast, something can be reliable but still not valid (the correct time is not shown). Validity is built upon reliability, then, but asks the question, 'Are these findings credible?'

Like reliability, validity in qualitative research has been traditionally asserted by documenting all of the steps taken in the hope of assuring it. These might include:

- Triangulation, the collection of data from several different sources or by employing several different methods.
- The full documentation of data, including a 'chain of evidence' so that that appropriate reference can be made to particular transcripts, documents, events and other data sources in the event any are challenged.[5]
- Logical connections between what is examined and the conclusions drawn from these data.
- The conscious and deliberate inclusion of data that might not support the thesis being argued or interpretation being drawn.
- A preparedness to entertain alternative explanations of phenomena observed, even if these alternatives are then discounted.
- Self-reflection on the part of the researchers, where they attempt to allow for their own perceived prejudices and biases.[6]
- What Guba has called 'member checks': the review of draft reports by participants and/or independent observers who can confirm that the report gives a fair impression of a situation or event.[7]

• An awareness of limitations in both data obtained and the generalizability of a study.

In a seminal paper Guba has suggested that these terms, reliability and validity, are so tied to quantitative research that unless we are to risk qualitative research being judged by inappropriate criteria, we should instead refer to *repeatability* and *credibility*.[8] He points out that much quantitative research (he prefers the term 'rationalistic') makes a series of assumptions:

• that there is a single reality which can be investigated
• that the researcher can be truly independent of the object being studied
• that generalizations can be made which are essentially context-free.

None of these apply to qualitative research, where there may be multiple realities, investigation invariably influences a situation and the course of events, and context is of crucial importance. In qualitative research, in discussing consistency, if some observation were to be repeated under the same, or similar, circumstances, we should refer to repeatability rather than reliability; and to determine whether something is likely to be 'true', rather than speak of validity (or internal validity), we should prefer the term credibility. He goes on to suggest that in discussing whether findings are likely to be applicable elsewhere, we should avoid mention of generalizability (or external validity) and instead talk about transferability; and finally that, since in qualitative research it is usually impossible to be truly objective or neutral, we should instead aim for confirmability: not that the observer be independent, but that any investigator would come up with the same or similar data under equivalent conditions.

All of this led Guba to propose a series of actions qualitative researchers can take to increase the credibility, transferability, dependability and confirmability of their work (see Figure 2.2). To read this table, each row can be understood as a sentence. For example, in the top row the sentence is 'Inquiry can be affected by factor patternings, which produce effects of noninterpretability, to take account of which during the study we use prolonged engagement, persistent observation, peer debriefing, triangulation, collect referential adequacy materials and do member checks. After completing the study we establish structural corroboration (coherence), in the hope that these actions will lead to credibility and produce findings that are plausible.'

These actions are thus the direct equivalents of the use in quantitative research of control groups and randomization (for internal validity), random sampling (for generalizability), replication (for reliability) and appropriate distance of the researcher from the investigation (objectivity). Their value here, and the reason we have referred to them in this chapter, is that they provide a checklist of what to look for when reviewing a qualitative research report. To take just the first, has the researcher used prolonged engagement with his or her project? (For full details of each of Guba's proposed strategies we suggest you consult his work directly.) It is,

Inquiry can be affected by:	Which produce effects of:	To take account of which we:		In the hope these actions will lead to:	And produce findings that are:
		During	After		
Factor patternings	Non-interpretability	Use prolonged engagement Use persistent observation Use peer debriefing Do triangulation Collect referential adequacy materials Do member checks	Establish structural corroboration (coherence)	Credibility	Plausible
Situational uniqueness	Non-comparability	Collect thick descriptive data Do theoretical/ positive sampling	Develop thick description	Transferability	Context relevant
Instrumental changes	Instability	Use overlap methods Use stepwise replication Leave audit trail	Do dependability audit (process)	Dependability	Stable
Investigator predilections	Bias	Do triangulation Practice reflexivity (audit trail)	Do confirmabililty audit (product)	Confirmability	Investigator-free

Figure 2.2 The naturalistic treatment of trustworthiness [9]

however, important to note Guba's qualifications about these steps: in contrast to quantitative methodology, with naturalistic enquiries 'about all one can say is that to take these steps increases the probability of the study's trustworthiness'.[10]

By now you will have noted that in this volume we have continued to refer to reliability and validity, generalizability and objectivity, for these are still the terms most researchers use. However, in seeking to assess these in a qualitative study, it is Guba's set or criteria, or ones very much like them, that should be used. The well-accepted quantitative criteria – random selection of samples and so on – are simply irrelevant here.

Critical evaluation of published studies

It is important that you do not spend too much time in reading and evaluating prior work. Some beginners appear to postpone actually starting their own projects by unnecessarily reading in depth all the previously published work they come across. To avoid this, Hittleman and Simon [11] suggest that research consumers read research reports in three phases: pre-reading, reading, and post-reading. In the *pre-reading* stage you ask, What do I already know about this topic? What is it that I wish to gain from reading this report? In this phase you read the title and perhaps only the first sentence of the abstract, then look at each of the main headings. Those who have come across various speed-reading techniques will recognize this approach.

In the second phase, *reading*, you systematically read only those parts of the report which you have identified as relevant to you. Here you are looking only for the information you had identified as important: information that will enable you to confirm, modify or add to what you already know. Finally, in the last phase of *post-reading* you ask, Have I discovered what I was looking for in this report? At this point you would probably wish to write a short (two or three sentence) summary of what you have gained from your reading. Of course you would also note a complete citation for it and, unless you have a photocopy, record where you obtained it in case you need to access it again. (Perhaps unexpectedly, it is also important to note briefly works which prove *not* to be of any value. Because of this, they are readily forgotten, and it is all too easy, on seeing them cited elsewhere, to obtain another copy – only to discover these were items previously seen and dismissed.)

When reading a published qualitative research report, there is a series of questions that you might usefully ask of it:

1 What are the *assumptions* on which it is based? Occasionally assumptions are explicitly stated, but more frequently they are only implied. One assumption that almost all studies make is that the particular methodology they employ was appropriate – was it? What other assumptions does the study you are examining make?

2 Are there any *terms* that have been – or should have been – defined? Sometimes terms that are not rigorously defined appear to be used in different ways at different stages of a report: has this happened? At other times authors appear to use different terms as if they were synonyms, possibly to vary their writing style; if such related terms have been used, have they been given different shades of meaning?

3 What was the *research question* or questions, or problem statement, or perhaps the focus of the research? Has this been clearly spelt out, or does it have to be inferred? Does the report then address this question or questions? Sometimes studies actually have a very much more narrow focus than their authors appear to believe.

4 Was the chosen *methodology* adequately described, and did the researcher follow the method correctly? No one expects the equivalent of the methodology chapter in a thesis to appear in a journal article, but what little is said should assure the informed reader that the researcher knew what was expected and appears to have done this.

5 Do the findings appear *reliable*, or repeatable? Is there reference to a fuller description of the study elsewhere?

6 Do the findings appear *valid*, or credible? How has this credibility been established? Both reliability and validity have, of course, been discussed in greater detail above.

7 How closely does the study follow the recursive research *process* so typical of

qualitative studies (see Figure 3.2 on p. 37)? Can all parts of the model be identified or inferred: is there – or is it apparent that there has been – a literature review, a theoretical framework, a research plan and so on?

8 What seems likely to be the *impact* of this study: does it appear to be generalizable to circumstances beyond the immediate context in which it was undertaken? Does it add to our knowledge in some way, so contributing to the theory base of the information professions? Does it indicate whether future work in a similar area could be better executed, thus adding to the sophistication of the methodologies commonly employed? Does it contribute in some practical way to better professional practice? Does it confirm previous studies, perhaps establishing that findings in one context apply equally in another (for example, in a different country, or different type of information service)? Or does it appear to contribute very little indeed, just another me-too study enabling someone to gain a higher degree, or notch up another publication on the way to some hoped-for academic promotion.

Note that these questions are *not* much the same as those one might ask of a quantitative study. With qualitative research, questions about hypotheses, independent and dependent variables, sample selection and so on are simply not relevant or useful.

In the information professions most research has necessarily a strong applied focus – practitioners, in particular, are keenly interested in doing their jobs more effectively. But while some basic research investigates phenomena with no evident practical utility (famously, before the Second World War physicists thought investigating the structure of the atom just such basic research), studies in our area do frequently complement their applied value with some basic investigation. This is, of course, typical of research in the social sciences.

RESEARCH SCENARIO 2.1

LIAM'S THESIS

Liam is very fortunate. He's doing a Masters degree by research thesis in the area of knowledge management and his boss, Marie, is very supportive. She's suggested that he study their own organization and that, if he does, he can count a large part of the time he spends on it as work. He will also receive some assistance with photocopying, travel, and so on.

Liam has now been working very solidly at his project for six months. He is still at the literature review stage and seems to be stuck there. Each journal article takes him at least two full days to read, sometimes as long as a week, and each suggests additional interesting issues he feels he really should be following up in his own research. He is starting to feel he is drowning in all of the pieces of paper and the notes he has made on them, yet has not even properly started. His progress is so slow that, because he keeps on coming across new citations and additional material, he now has a far larger pile to read before he can begin his fieldwork than he did three months ago, and the mound of unread material is increasing far more quickly than the little group of items he has read (some of which he knows he will need to re-read).

Meanwhile, Marie is becoming impatient: she wants this project to get underway, and to be able to make a series of recommendations to senior management.

- What do you think Liam's problem might be?
- Has he more than one problem?
- Could you advise him how to overcome his difficulties?
- And do any other potential problems occur to you?

We suggest you consider your response *before* reading our text below.

In Chapter 5, 'Laying the foundations for fieldwork', we discuss the need to 'read around' in the literature before beginning a qualitative research project. In the Research Scenario 2.1 above it seems possible that Liam has not read enough in the area of knowledge management before attempting to begin his own study. Alternatively, perhaps he lacks self-confidence and is being unduly cautious. It seems at least as possible, however, that so far he has failed to find a focus for his study and simply does not know what will turn out to be relevant, and what irrelevant. Lacking a focus, he has to read everything with equal care – and there will never be sufficient time to do that with any project.

From the description given above it seems that Liam may not be very organized in his note-taking either (he is 'drowning in all the pieces of paper and the notes he has made on them'). Some of the guidance we note in Chapter 5 could be of assistance here.[12]

At a more fundamental level, Liam faces a conflict between the demands of his study and the demands of his work. The academic study needs to proceed cautiously as he builds up his confidence and finds his focus, but his work wants answers – and not necessarily carefully considered, scholarly answers – as soon as possible. This conflict seems unlikely to diminish. If Liam's research suggests that Marie's preferred strategies may not be optimal, will he be tempted (or feel pressured) to modify or qualify his conclusions and recommendations? We would not regard this potential for conflict as a reason necessarily to avoid a workplace-based study; in view of the support available to Liam on balance this may well have been his best choice. However, every choice brings with it advantages and disadvantages, which need to be considered and taken into account.

Finally, in both undertaking and presenting his work, Liam will need to be conscious of the need to take every possible step to avoid the potential for bias, and to be seen to have taken these steps. This will go directly to perceptions of the validity or credibility of his work. He should consider adopting several or all of the strategies we list elsewhere with regard to validity. In subsequent publication, one further strategy he might adopt could be to conceal the real name of his organization, for example, if he feels the need to criticize some aspects of its operation or management.

Applying the lessons of evaluation to one's own research

By now it must be obvious that all of the questions which you might ask of a piece of published qualitative research can equally well be asked of your own work. What is, perhaps, less obvious is how difficult this can be: all of us find it much harder to see our own work objectively (precisely the point we made above about the need for self-reflection on the part of qualitative researchers). Beyond question, it is easiest to review one's own work critically when it is still at the planning stage and one is not yet passionately committed to it in its present form. There is an additional advantage to reviewing it then, too: it is not too late to modify it, to build in additional checks and balances, or additional data-gathering approaches. Here, too, we would especially recommend working through Guba's checklist (Figure 2.2):

- Have I included all of the steps which are possible?
- Can I justify not undertaking those steps which do not seem possible?
- Can I involve other people, including respondents, in some way to improve the validity or credibility of my work?
- Will my record keeping be complete and accurate?

Review of Chapter 2

Noting first the importance of being able to evaluate published qualitative research, this chapter has described some of the general criteria used to evaluate research of all kinds before suggesting assessment criteria for qualitative research studies. The concepts of reliability or repeatability, and validity or credibility were then discussed in detail. Guba's series of actions qualitative researchers can take to increase the credibility, transferability, dependability and confirmability of their work were then presented. Following a short discussion of how to go about reading a published work, a series of questions was suggested which would facilitate its assessment. Finally, the relationship of this to planning one's own qualitative study was noted.

Where to now?

After reading a chapter like this, the obvious thing to do is to go out and select a piece of published qualitative research of interest to you. Working through each section of this chapter in turn, ask:

- Does each section of the report answer the questions in Figure 2.1, questions to ask of qualitative research studies?
- What steps have been taken to help assure the findings appear reliable or repeatable? Marshall and Rossman suggested eight characteristics research consumers could look for: how many of these appear? If they do, are they sufficiently well described for you to find the study persuasive?

- What steps have been taken to help assure the findings appear valid or credible? Here, we suggested a further eight criteria.
- Finally, in eight more points we suggested you look for the assumptions, definitions and so on in any published study (some of these overlapping with questions of reliability and validity).

This is not an easy task, even for those who have asked such questions before. We find that it is often in discussion of published studies that some of their weaknesses become apparent – hence the value of teaching postgraduate research students in small groups rather than singly. If this is not possible for you, perhaps in a work-based study there will be an opportunity to discuss the strengths and weaknesses of previous studies in the area with some more experienced colleagues working on the same project.

A more challenging alternative is to find a study with both qualitative and quantitative components:

- Are the two approaches equally well described?
- How have the authors addressed the very different requirements for establishing reliability and validity?
- Do the separate qualitative and quantitative components complement each other, and do you find the conclusions and recommendations, if any, more persuasive than if only a single methodological framework had been adopted?

Further reading

Most works that discuss the evaluation of research concentrate upon quantitative approaches – as, for example, do P. C. Stern and L. Kalof in their excellent *Evaluating Social Science Research*, 2nd edn (New York: Oxford University Press, 1996). Much of the other literature on evaluation takes a similar perspective – for example, P. D. Leedy, *How to Read Research and Understand It* (New York: Macmillan, 1981).

Given that we chose only to include selected excerpts from Guba's seminal article, 'Criteria for Establishing the Trustworthiness of Naturalistic Enquiries', this is well worth seeking out – even if not always easy reading (*Educational Communication and Technology Journal*, **29** (2), 1981, pp. 85–6). Guba and Y. S. Lincoln develop these ideas further, especially in relation to programme evaluation, in 'But Is It Rigorous? Trustworthiness and Authenticity in Naturalistic Evaluation' (*Naturalistic Evaluation*, **30**, 1986, pp. 73–83). However, you may prefer to start with a short, readable and very much more up-to-date article available in full text form on the web: N. Golafshani, 'Understanding Reliability and Validity in Qualitative Research', *The Qualitative Report*, **8** (4), 2003, pp. 597–606, www.nova.edu/ssss/QR/QR8-4/golafshani.pdf.

Notes

1 See, for example, P. C. Stern and L. Kalof, *Evaluating Social Science Research*, 2nd edn (New York: Oxford University Press, 1996); D. Wynar, *Syllabus for Research Methods in Librarianship* (Denver, CO: University of Denver, Graduate School of Librarianship, 1962), pp. 129–30.

2 C. H Busha and S. T. Harter, *Research Methods in Librarianship: Techniques and Interpretation*. (New York: Academic Press, 1980), pp. 27–9. A well-written, straightforward introductory text on the evaluation of research is P. D. Leedy's, *How to Read Research and Understand It* (New York: Macmillan, 1981). While this focuses primarily on quantitative methods, Chapter 7 does deal with the basics of reading historical research.

3 C. Marshall and G. B. Rossman, *Designing Qualitative Research*, 2nd edn (Thousand Oaks, CA: Sage Publications, 1995).

4 D. R Hittleman and A. J. Simon, *Interpreting Educational Research: An Introduction for Consumers of Research,*. 2nd edn (Upper Saddle River, NJ: Merrill, 1997), p. 231.

5 R. K. Yin, *Case Study Research: Design and Methods*. rev. ed, (Newbury Park, CA: Sage Publications, 1989), pp. 102–3.

6 This permits reasonable assessment of research which is avowedly partisan in approach. See, for example, P. Lather 'Issues of Validity in Openly Ideological Research: Between a Rock and a Soft Place', *Interchange*, **17**, 1986, pp. 63–84.

7 E. G. Guba, 'Criteria for Establishing the Trustworthiness of Naturalistic Enquiries.' *Educational Communication and Technology Journal*, **29** (2), 1981, pp. 85–6.

8 Ibid.

9 Ibid., Table 3, p. 83.

10 Ibid., p. 88.

11 Hittleman and Simon, op. cit., Chapter 3.

12 See especially H. M. Cooper, *Integrating Research: A Guide for Literature Reviews*, 2nd edn, Applied Social Research Methods, 2 (Newbury Park, CA: Sage Publications, 1989).

3 Qualitative research design in information organizations

FOCUS QUESTIONS
- What is the process that qualitative research follows?
- What initial questions should be asked when designing a qualitative investigation?
- What methods are commonly employed in qualitative research?

The qualitative research process in information settings

If we watch experienced qualitative researchers in information settings, we might notice that they sometimes appear to proceed without any plan, stumbling from one observational event or setting to another, taking notes at random and not steering a clear course through contexts, data or variables. There is both truth and falsehood in this appearance. At the outset it must be stated quite categorically that qualitative researchers do design their research – or perhaps 'adopt a broad research strategy' might be a more appropriate description. That is, they do not necessarily have a clearly set out, step-by-step design as we would expect to find in a quantitative research project. Rather they have a set of theoretical assumptions and traditional means of data collection that provide a general framework and set of parameters within which they operate.

Beyond that, however, qualitative researchers seek to be totally open to the setting and subjects of their study, allowing these to inform the process and to modify general research plans. In other words, within the established parameters of qualitative research, the researchers allow their plans to evolve as they come to know the subjects and settings more intimately – the act of conducting the research provides the final structure of that research, and detailed procedures can be described only afterwards.

As a rule, textbooks on research methods speak of research as a series of clearly defined stages: planning, design, implementation, analysis, conclusions (see Figure 3.1). This linear process applies most directly to quantitative studies in which step-by-step, detailed planning is essential for a variety of reasons – although even here the reality is often that the research does not proceed in such neat steps, even if it is written up in this way.

Qualitative research, on the other hand, tends to be represented as a cyclical process or as a series of overlapping stages. Marshall and Rossman, for example, offer a 'Wheel of Fortune' model of the research process with 14 key points on the

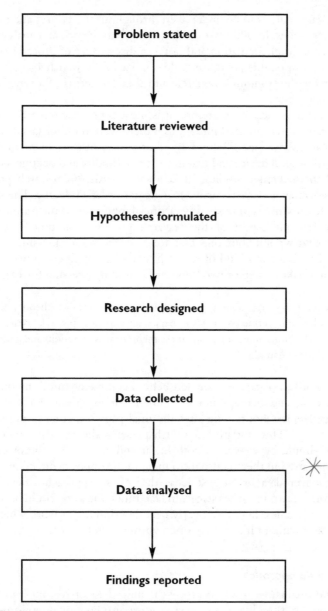

Figure 3.1 The linear research process

wheel, while Mellon presents a model of eight stages, of which five overlap.[1] The importance of these alternative models is that they show qualitative research proceeding in a non-linear, iterative manner. For example, because the qualitative researcher allows the subjects in part to determine the direction research takes, this requires data analysis to be undertaken throughout the project and not just in the concluding stages. In other words, decisions about design and analysis might well occur during implementation and not as a discrete set of procedures. While it is likely that most qualitative research does indeed follow such a pattern, it may still be easier for the beginning researcher to think in terms of a series of steps that follow each other.

As a learning exercise, therefore, it is most appropriate that the newcomer to qualitative research proceed initially *as if* there were more or less discrete steps or activities to follow (see Figure 3.2) – but always bearing in mind that this is a purely pedagogical device and that in the field, fluidity and openness to change are essential in qualitative studies. In Bradley's words, 'in research practice, these activities overlap and are recursive to a greater or lesser degree. The identification of separate activities is in many ways artificial, but it serves the purpose of focusing attention on one aspect of the research process at a time.'[2] An interesting alternative viewpoint, but one that follows this notionally linear approach, is presented by Berg as a kind of research 'two-step': with every two steps forward the research takes a step or two backward before progressing further:

> In the proposed approach you begin with an idea, gather theoretical information, reconsider and refine your idea, begin to examine possible designs, reexamine theoretical assumptions, and refine these theoretical assumptions and perhaps even your original or refined idea.[3]

In other words, no stage is really left behind completely until the final report has been written, and perhaps not even then, for experienced researchers tell of spending sleepless hours long after the final page has gone to press, wondering 'what if . . . .' Thus Figure 3.2, which presents the broad stages of qualitative research, should be viewed as both linear and recursive – the process certainly moves forward, but there is also movement in the opposite direction as succeeding stages uncover data or suggest ideas that revise approaches decided upon or conclusions drawn in earlier stages. In fact, much the same could be said for many quantitative studies: here too, overly neat descriptions of work which proceeded logically and without hiccups are often written in retrospect.

The pyramid approach

While the qualitative research process is indeed recursive, moving forward and back throughout the life of a project, it must also be moving toward a finite end, building steps toward a conclusion at each stage. Thus another way to visualize the process is as a three-stage pyramid (see Figure 3.3) that begins with preliminary preparation, moves into broad exploration and then concentrates on a set of focused activities. The researcher's objective is to work up the pyramid, from generalities at the base to specific details at the pinnacle, from preliminary 'scratching about' to a final, concrete product. Or in other words, you start with a

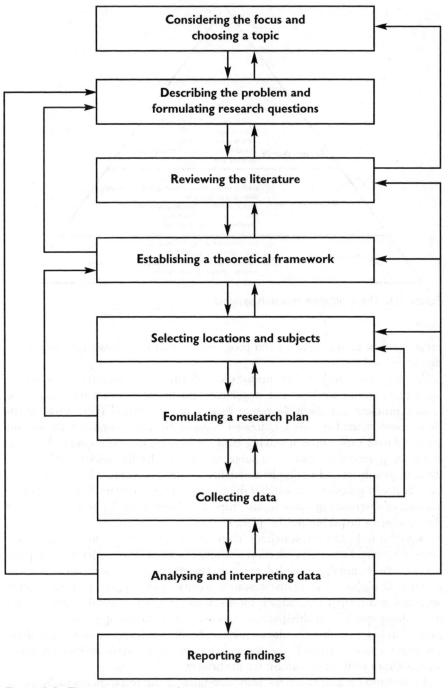

Figure 3.2 The recursive research process

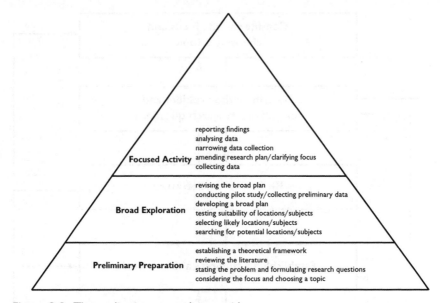

Figure 3.3 The qualitative research pyramid

broad, general field of interest and progressively narrow it down till you reach a tightly focused study.

At the base 'preliminary preparation' forms the foundation on which subsequent stones are laid. The major components of this first stage are: topic choice, problem statement, literature review and theoretical framework. When these components have been addressed sequentially and recursively, the second stage, a broad exploration involving field activity, begins with a general casting about for potential locations and subjects, followed by the selection of a likely location or subject and testing its suitability for the case study. Having selected a case for investigation, the researcher then engages in preliminary data collection as a means of determining a provisional shape and direction of the project, and from this develops a broad but flexible plan.

With this in hand the researcher is then able to move into the third main phase, focused activity. Here data collection continues in accordance with the broad plan, but the plan is usually amended as more data come to light – this is where the essential flexibility of qualitative research becomes most apparent. As the plan is amended and further data added, the focus of activity is generally clarified and made more specific. At this point data collecting is narrowed to specific topics, themes and ideas within the site or subject. Finally, with this more focused data-collecting activity in hand, the researcher concentrates data analysis on those aspects felt to be most significant for the project.

In designing a qualitative research investigation the researcher actually poses and answers a series of questions about the topic, the problem, the data for study and analysis and so on. The remainder of this book is designed to help you learn how to ask and answer these questions, beginning briefly in this chapter and presenting more detail in subsequent chapters.

First questions

In thinking about research design it is important to consider the major issues first, and resist the temptation to speed on to practical matters which are probably of more interest. To do so would be like writing a paper or book without first having a detailed outline – it may proceed well at first, but eventually you are likely to lose sight of the goal because time has not been spent preparing the way adequately. We have seen many incomplete postgraduate projects that suffered from just this lack of initial focus.

One way to settle the major issues of research is to ask three basic questions about what should be studied, and how:

- What should be the focus?
- What events or circumstances should be studied?
- How should these be studied?

The most basic question has to do with the research topic: what should be the focus? The more experienced the researcher, the less important this question of what should be studied, for most of us develop at least a *de facto* answer based on our past research projects, natural inclinations, available research funds, job requirements and similar factors. Blaise Cronin, for example, maintains that 'I have never had to look for a research problem: ideas for research tumble naturally out of workplace experiences, literature immersion, and routine intellectual trading. The things I do, read, hear, and say provide the inspiration for my personal research.' [4] However, for the less fortunate among us, and for the 'unblooded' researcher, the question of what to study often looms significantly as the first major obstacle to be navigated. A topic may be suggested from your reading, or from discussion with colleagues or supervisors; it may arise from a situation in your workplace, or from research done by others.

However a topic insinuates itself into your conscious thought, there is one essential which, if lacking, spells certain death from the outset: the topic must be one that is exciting, or at least interesting to you, for otherwise it really is almost impossible to sustain interest in research over the long term. Furthermore, you must be certain that the topic is intrinsically worthwhile, and ensure that you can get access to the data. Practical aspects such as these are discussed fully in Chapter 5, as part of a detailed description of topic choice.

The first two questions ask 'what', and the final asks 'how'. That is, having settled on a topic and what is to be investigated, the researcher then asks, how is it to be done? Four methods of qualitative research are commonly applied in information settings:

- Observation
- Interviewing
- Group discussion
- Historical study.

Observation and interviewing appear to be most used today, but group discussion and historical study are also important. In the first edition of this work we described a fifth technique, content analysis, as sometimes used as a qualitative technique but more commonly associated with quantitative research and complex statistical analysis.[5] Several years on, the increasing volume and importance of internet-based research of all kinds has somewhat changed this. As Mann and Stewart point out, 'the communicative power of the internet may be harnessed to further qualitative research.'[6] It is not considered as a separate qualitative research method in this volume, except to suggest that content analysis and the historical method are closely allied (see Chapter 10) and that content analysis can have a role in the data analysis stage of a research project (see Chapter 12). Those working in the information professions hardly need to be told that ever-increasing access to the internet has affected almost everything we do.

In this chapter, each of the four principal methods is introduced briefly. Fuller discussion of their application appears later: observation in Chapter 7, interviewing in Chapter 8, group discussion methods in Chapter 9 and historical study in Chapter 10. Those more interested in assessing other people's qualitative research than in planning and executing their own, might prefer to turn back to Chapter 2, about evaluating qualitative research, if you have not already read this, and then return to these later chapters.

Four methods of qualitative investigation
Observation

Observation studies typically involve the systematic recording of observable phenomena or behaviour in a natural setting. While observation may not tell the researcher very much about the stated attitudes or self-perceptions of subjects, it does provide useful insights into *unconscious* behaviour and how this might relate to self-perceptions of those involved in an event. By observing data about behaviour in specific contexts the researcher is able to uncover patterns of behaviour that both reflect otherwise hidden attitudes or views and unconsciously affect participants. A classic observation study is Harris and Michell's investigation of reference staff behaviour. Here observation is employed as a means of determining patterns of behaviour, contextual factors affecting behaviour and interactions between subjects. The observed behaviour patterns reveal previously unknown or unsuspected realities about library users and services.[7]

In libraries and information agencies the observation of behaviour, whether unobtrusive, participant or structured, is a common method employed by qualitative researchers. However, the fact that this method is so often chosen should not be confused with simplicity, because the effective observation of practices and procedures can prove exceptionally difficult. To begin with, the attempt must be to achieve deeper understanding of an event, process or phenomenon. Furthermore, *general* objectives must be established before final observation so that one avoids recording a considerable amount of unwanted data – but bearing in mind that the final objectives may not emerge until the data analysis stage much later in the project. Finally, the bias that occurs when a researcher is introduced into an otherwise 'natural' environment must not be overlooked. Few people can ignore a stranger sitting in a corner, both watching and taking notes. Observation as a data-gathering technique is discussed fully in Chapter 7.

Interviewing

Individual and group interviewing can obtain detailed, in-depth information from subjects who know a great deal about their personal perceptions of events, processes and environments. As a valuable adjunct to observation, interviews also have the potential to offer balance and corroboration where observed phenomena are complex or involve a number of factors. Interviewing may be done in a variety of ways, from highly formal and structured (appointments, set questions) to casual and non-directive (in the staff room, anecdotal), and each approach has its advantages. The structured situation allows you to collect data on carefully controlled topics, but participants may be somewhat constrained by the formality of the setting. The casual conversation, on the other hand, may encourage candour on the part of participants, but also makes it difficult to elicit information about topics on a set agenda.

Interviewing as used in qualitative research offers two important advantages. First, the person being interviewed is encouraged, by the use of open-ended questions or by non-directive listening, to highlight self-perceived issues or relationships of importance. This can be of inestimable value in understanding contexts and creating links that are such key aspects of qualitative research. Second, dialogue between researcher and subject allows the interaction to move in new and perhaps unexpected directions, thereby adding both depth and breadth to one's understanding of the issues involved. Such self-perceptions and enhanced understanding may be achieved in no other way, making this a cornerstone in qualitative research. Interviewing is also the subject of Chapter 8, which offers a more detailed discussion of this important data-gathering method.

Group discussion

Although interviewing, along with observation, is probably the most popular qualitative research technique, it is certainly not cast in concrete. One of the most exciting developments in qualitative research has been the introduction of focus groups as part of the researcher's armoury. These typically consist of six to 12 somewhat homogeneous participants (that is, for example, individuals from the same managerial level in a organization, or similar types of client) who are encouraged to interact about a particular topic. The researcher or facilitator joins the group and uses discussion and participant interaction as a way of collecting data on the topic. It is the interactions between group members, as well as those between the group and the researcher, that allow data to emerge. Although the use of focus groups does not have a long history in information research, it has been employed successfully in relation to a number of issues ranging from user studies to the design of physical facilities. Drabenstott offers a particularly useful introduction to this method from the standpoint of information research.[8]

A related method is nominal group technique (NGT). This gathers a similar number of participants – though here these may be a group in name only, hence the name given to this method. Unlike a focus group, a nominal group need not be homogeneous. Participants take part in a structured group process which results in a list of items they themselves have suggested, using their own words, and have then ranked in order of importance. The technique has often been used as a preliminary stage preceding a survey, and provides a good example of one way in which qualitative and quantitative approaches can complement each other.

Both focus groups and nominal group technique (discussed more fully in Chapter 9) offer the researcher the advantage of obtaining group perspectives on a research problem. This can be of particular value in examining an organization, which by definition consists of a group of people working together, as most other methods, qualitative and quantitative, obtain data from individuals.

Historical study

Although the historical method is often overlooked in qualitative research texts, it certainly embodies most of the characteristics of qualitative methodology. History is a major component in understanding human behaviour and human organizations, and such understanding is the underlying *raison d'être* for qualitative research.

Once upon a time, the historical approach was probably the best-established method of research in librarianship. That place has no doubt long since been usurped by the ubiquitous survey, but a knowledge of historical research is self-evidently essential for archivists and records managers. Within the various functions of libraries and archives history plays a significant role. The most obvious of these is collection development, in which collection strengths and weaknesses are firmly anchored in historical realities.

Organizations exist in an historical continuum, so organizational case studies are both historical and qualitative. To understand an organization you must also understand its historical roots, its evolution over time. This is best accomplished with reference to the historical record: the documents of its administration, budgets, policies, personnel records and institutional histories. In addition the knowledge of those who have lived within an organization for a considerable period is important, so written records need to be supplemented with personal interviews. The historical method, in other words, relies on documentary evidence plus first-hand observation. There is a full discussion of the historical method of qualitative research in Chapter 10.

Ethical considerations

Whatever research method is chosen for a qualitative study, ethical considerations will be as important if not more important than those arising from quantitative research. All research subjects have ethical rights: to be consulted, to give or withhold consent, and to confidentiality. However, we would argue that these rights apply with even greater force in much qualitative research, as:

- the researcher typically investigates his or her subjects in some depth, frequently being given access to highly personal information
- many of the approaches used in qualitative research elicit information that could potentially compromise either the person or the organization, which could be open to misuse
- the personal relationships that successful qualitative researchers build up with their subjects rely on mutual trust and respect, sometimes even friendship.

Hence, qualitative researchers have a special responsibility to all those who assist them with their investigations, both as individuals and organizations. There are several questions which any investigator must be able to answer.

Should subjects be knowingly involved?

One school says that participants must always be voluntarily and knowingly involved, but this may be more applicable in situations where 'harm' might befall them. This is sometimes less of an issue in qualitative research in information organizations, because there is less potential for harm. A second consideration here is that voluntary participants may be exposing us to a limited range of insights, which we should supplement with data from unwitting subjects. In addition, as noted above, there are many occasions on which behaviour differs when people know they are under observation.

On the other hand, covert research may be a violation of the rights of those being observed, and the researcher may be involved in an illegal act. Think, for example, whether it is legal to record a telephone conversation between yourself and another person as part of your investigation without first informing the other person. In our area, research that relies on or uses data illegally obtained has to be suspect.

Informed and implied consent

Sometimes a person we perceive to be a volunteer is actually someone who has been told by a superior to participate. In most institutionally sponsored or institutionally based research, consent must be ensured in writing. An informed consent slip contains a written statement that potential participants understand that they are participating, and that the process has been explained, that confidentiality will be assured, and that they have agreed to take part. When a subject agrees to be interviewed or take part in a discussions that person's consent to taking part in the interview or discussion is implied.

Organizational consent is normally obtained at the beginning of a study when access is negotiated. This issue is dealt with more fully in Chapter 6.

Confidentiality and anonymity

In most qualitative research confidentiality (concealment of individual identity) is the issue, not anonymity (subjects remaining nameless). Because we know the names of our participants, it is essential that they be assured of confidentiality. Give pseudonyms, and make sure the setting is not identifiable. Lists of names and places must be treated as confidential documents so that others do not gain access to them, and such lists should not be kept any longer than is necessary.

Codes of ethics

There are many codes that qualitative researchers in the information professions may need to take into account. Has the organization that you are studying a code to which you must conform, possibly obtaining formal ethics clearance first? Many local education authorities, for example, require ethical clearance before researchers can enter their schools. Research in a school library will require just such approval. If you are undertaking your research as part of a higher degree, it is more than likely your university will also have a code of ethics and require you to obtain formal approval for your project, or be able to demonstrate that your research is outside its scope.

Beyond these institutional codes there are also professional statements, such as the recently updated code of the Chartered Institute of Library and Information Professionals (CILIP), 'Ethical Principles and Code of Professional Practice for Library and Information Professionals' (see www.cilip.org.uk/about/code.html), which provide general standards of behaviour to be followed by any information professional. This can be taken to include anyone who conducts research in information organizations.

Ethical considerations need to be considered as part of initial research design, because it is at this stage that a project may most easily be adjusted to take account of legitimate concerns about the interests of those who will be participating in your research. Later on, it may be difficult or even impossible to make substantial changes to a study that has inadvertently breeched ethical guidelines, forcing the study to be abandoned.

Review of Chapter 3

This chapter has discussed the design or shape of qualitative research, suggesting that it is less a linear progression of steps than a recursive series of stages in which information and discoveries constantly inform preceding stages. This produces movement that is at once backward and forward. But the design can also be viewed as pyramidal, in which the researcher works from broad generalities to a specific focal point.

However one views the shape of qualitative investigation, there are important initial questions to be asked when designing a project. What will be the research topic, the data to be viewed or collected and the method of investigation? Four qualitative methods may be especially suitable for information research: observation, interviewing, group discussion and historical study.

Finally, this is the stage at which any ethical considerations need to be considered. For many studies formal project approval may be required before beginning.

Where to now?

Once again, we suggest you review the focus questions that appeared at the start of this chapter. Then you might turn again to the final chapter in this volume, and answer the following questions:

- What qualitative research methods were employed in this study?
- Do you think these were the most appropriate methods? Why?

Whether one uses observation, interviewing, group discussion, historical study or a combination of techniques, the most commonly recognized means of applying these methods in qualitative research is by means of the case study. For this reason, it is necessary to know something of case studies before progressing to a detailed discussion of qualitative research in the field, and the case study approach is introduced in the next chapter.

Further reading

There is an immense literature on all the topics covered in this chapter – and, indeed, covered by this book as a whole. It is all too easy to become overwhelmed, confused, or both. However, rather less of this literature focuses upon research design as such. Two titles we have found useful are C. Marshall and G. B. Rossman, *Designing Qualitative Research*, 2nd edn (Thousand Oaks, CA: Sage Publications, 1995), and C. A. Mellon, ed., *Naturalistic Inquiry for Library Science: Methods and Applications for Research, Evaluation and Teaching* (Westport, CT: Greenwood Press, 1990). Those who are hoping to undertake an internet-based study should look at C. Mann and F. Stewart, *Internet Communication and Qualitative Research: A Handbook for Researching Online* (Thousand Oaks, CA: Sage Publications, 2000).

Each of the particular qualitative methods mentioned above – observation, interviewing, group discussion and historical study – is discussed in more detail in coming chapters. We suggest that you defer examination of this wider literature until you have read the appropriate chapter here.

Notes

1   C. Marshall and G. B. Rossman, *Designing Qualitative Research*. 2nd edn (Thousand Oaks, CA: Sage Publications, 1995), p. 17; C. A. Mellon, ed., *Naturalistic Inquiry for Library Science: Methods and Applications for Research, Evaluation and Teaching* (Westport, CT: Greenwood Press, 1990), p. 25.

2   J. R. Bradley, 'Choosing Research Methodologies Appropriate to Your Research Focus'. In *Applying Research to Practice: How to Use Data Collection and Research to Improve Library Management Decision Making*, ed. L. S. Estabrook (Urbana-Champaign: University of Illinois, Graduate School of Library and Information Science, 1992), pp. 99–100.

3   B. L. Berg, *Qualitative Research Methods for the Social Sciences*, 2nd edn (Needham Heights, MA: Allyn and Bacon, 1995), p. 16.

4   B. Cronin, 'When Is a Problem a Research Problem?' In *Applying Research to Practice: How to Use Data Collection and Research to Improve Library Management Decision Making*, ed. L. S. Estabrook (Urbana-Champaign: University of Illinois, Graduate School of Library and Information Science, 1992), p. 118.

5   For a discussion of content analysis, see B. Allen and D. Reser, 'Content Analysis in Library and Information Science Research', *Library and Information Science Research*, **12**, 1990, pp. 251–62.

6   C. Mann and F. Stewart, *Internet Communication and Qualitative Research: A Handbook for Researching Online* (Thousand Oaks, CA: Sage Publications, 2000), p. 3.

7   R. M. Harris and B. G. Michell, 'The Social Context of Reference Work: Assessing Effects of Gender and Communication Skills on Observers' Judgments of Competence', *Library and Information Science Research*, **8**, January 1986, pp. 85–101; B. G. Michell and R. M. Harris, 'Evaluating the Reference Interview: Some Factors Influencing Patrons and Professionals', *RQ*, **27**, Winter 1987, pp. 95–105.

8   B. Hutton and S. Walters, 'Focus Groups: Linkages to the Community', *Public Libraries*, **27**, Fall 1988, pp. 149–50; see also D. J. Leather, 'How the Focus Group Technique Can Strengthen the Development of a Building Program', *Library Administration and Management*, **4**, Spring 1990, pp. 92–5; K. M. Drabenstott, 'Focused Group Interviews.' In *Qualitative Research in Information Management,* eds. J. D. Glazier and R. R. Powell (Englewood, CO: Libraries Unlimited, 1992), pp. 85–104.

4 Case studies in information organizations

FOCUS QUESTIONS
- What is the case study approach, and what types of case studies are applicable in information settings?
- What are reliability and validity, and how can these be achieved in a qualitative research project?

The case study approach

In the introduction it was stated that this book uses the terms 'qualitative research', 'case study' and 'fieldwork' in specific ways, each bearing a working relationship to the other terms rather than being synonymous with them. Up to this point we have been discussing qualitative research as a type of investigation in information work, seeking to describe its unique characteristics and distinctive features. We now need to talk about the particular type of qualitative research known as the case study. In this book we define a case study as follows:

> an in-depth investigation of a discrete entity (which may be a single setting, subject, collection or event) on the assumption that it is possible to derive knowledge of the wider phenomenon from intensive investigation of a specific instance or case.[1]

The 'case study approach' thus refers to application of specific qualitative research methods in a specific setting. The process of application, or fieldwork, is discussed in the following chapter. Because the case study approach is, for the most part, limited to a single setting, subject or event, it projects an aura of containment in space and time that appeals to those faced with the daunting task of first-time investigation. However, it must be recognized that concentrating on a single site or event is in no way inferior to (and certainly no easier than) more complex techniques, for it requires a depth of investigation that is both rigorous and thorough – a single site case study is not synonymous with superficiality.

In the actual practice of qualitative research, 'case study' is a blanket category that applies to a number of research types, each of which has particular benefits and procedures. These are described in some detail by Werner and Schoepfle.[2] In the context of information work there are several types most likely to be employed by researchers: observational case studies, interview case studies, organizational case studies, life history case studies, and multi-site and comparative case studies. In all of them the various methods of qualitative research are applicable – do not make the mistaken assumption that case study is synonymous with observation or interview only. One of the most persuasive arguments supporting the full range of qualitative methods being applied in case studies is Smith's powerful essay on qualitative case study research in education. In it he argues that case study research should employ a range of methods – historical, documentary, ethnographic – in order to derive the most benefit from cases.[3]

Observational case studies

In an observational case study the primary data-gathering method is participant observation in a single information agency, with the focus generally limited to a particular aspect: a particular place in a library (such as the reference area, the staff room or the stacks), a specific group of individuals (such as technical services staff, undergraduate users or collection managers), or a specific activity (such as user education programmes, acquisitions procedures or online searching for users). Most observational studies in libraries combine these aspects in some way – for example, in 'The Effects of Training Reference Librarians in Interview Skills: A Field Experiment' Dewdney studied a specific activity (communication behaviour) of a specific group (public librarians) in relation to a particular setting (reference section).[4] The primary focus is on the present situation, although it may well be necessary to include some historical background to the setting, showing how the distinction between case study types often blurs in practice.

In reality the researcher in an observational case study focuses on one component of an organization, which artificially isolates that component from its context. Although the competent qualitative researcher takes account of how that component is related to the entire organization as a functional entity, the reality is that the focus must remain narrow in order for the research to be viable. Therefore, the most suitable option is to concentrate on a physical unit or place, activity or group that forms a natural entity, and that both participants and researcher view as having distinctive unitary existence within the organization. To determine such a 'natural' unit the researcher must be very familiar with the organization and how it functions. The ideal physical setting is one that people use repeatedly in a similar way; the ideal activity is one that recurs as a regular part of an organization's overall procedures; and the ideal group is one that either shares in a specific function or shares common demographic or functional characteristics (for example, age or gender, professional level within the unit, or reasons for using the service).

In terms of subjects in an observational study, the group aspect is most important. You might look for groups that consciously share a common identity (first-year undergraduates in arts or engineering, for example, as distinct from first-year undergraduates in general). Sociologists distinguish between people who simply share characteristics and people who, on the basis of shared characteristics, share a sense of group identity. It is those who share group identity that make the best subjects for observational case studies. Subjects who simply share common traits but do not identify with a group based on these traits tend to be studied more effectively by means of interviews, which provide an opportunity to probe motivation, ask questions and so on. Whether the researcher will be able to observe or will need to interview emerges only through knowledge of the subjects. For example, reference librarians in a particular library clearly share a professional trait, but it may be that these librarians rarely meet as a unit and work independently on a roster. Therefore, this would probably not be a good unit for observation, because it lacks cohesiveness. On the other hand, through individual interviews the researcher would be able to elicit common ideas, issues and problems from members of this disparate group.

Interview case studies

As just suggested, there are times when interviewing is more appropriate than observation; when this forms the dominant means of data collection, the result can be said to be an interview case study. This type of study is in some respects a hybrid: it shares many characteristics of the observational study in terms of its focus on place, group or activity; but it is also closely related to the life history case study, which, in fact, relies heavily on interviewing for data collection. Generally an interview case study uses data collected from a series of individual interviews between researcher and subject, but there is increasing interest in the use of focus groups (discussed in Chapter 9) as a source of data. The latter method can be useful when interviewing individuals who are unwilling to talk without peer support or who feel threatened by an interviewer, or where the free flowing exchange of ideas can help spark additional observations. It is also useful when group discussion is likely to contribute substantially to the researcher's understanding of an issue.

Like observation, interviewing is a flexible process. To begin, the researcher will have prepared a number of questions before the interview, but additional questions will arise during the interview and the responses of subjects should be allowed to drive the process forward. All questions should be regarded as tentative and never cast in their final form until the research results have been written. As questions evolve through the process of interviewing, it may be necessary to return to earlier interviewees in order to ask them questions that did not emerge until later. It is often important to elicit the same information from all subjects in order to develop the broadest possible understanding of a topic.

Interviewing is a structured process in which the researcher is able to ask questions about what cannot be seen or observed. Using 'who', 'what', 'where' and 'when' questions, the researcher is able to collect factual data about a past event. In addition, by asking 'how' and 'why' questions the researcher is able to collect explanatory data that contribute to understanding the meaning of phenomena from those involved directly in events and processes. Glesne offers the following

LIVERPOOL JOHN MOORES UNIVERSITY
Aldham Robarts L.R.C.
TEL. 051 231 3701/3634

justification for interviewing as a data collection method in case studies: 'the opportunity to learn about what you cannot see and to explore alternative explanations of what you do see is the special strength of interviewing in qualitative inquiry. To . . . [this] add the serendipitous learnings that emerge from the unexpected turns in discourse that your questions evoke.'[5]

Organizational case studies

An organizational case study focuses on a specific information agency, tracing its development over time, in effect giving it the character of an historical study. Typically such a case study traces how the organization came into being, including treatment of its antecedents (the British Museum Reading Room as precursor to the British Library, for example), changes and developments over time, its current situation, and perhaps even future projections. For an organizational case study the researcher relies on a range of data sources, including written records (annual reports, meeting minutes, policy statements, personnel records and so on), interviews with past and present members of staff (especially those with a long association with the institution), and perhaps even observation of present operations.

The problem with such studies is a possible lack of adequate documentary data or historical records. Perhaps oddly, given the brief of libraries and archives to preserve information, many of them simply do not preserve their own institutional records consistently, which means that the historical continuity of evidence required for such studies simply does not exist. Therefore, the researcher must conduct a preliminary enquiry to ascertain the availability of sufficient historical data to enable the project to proceed. If such data are not available, then one has the option of moving on to a present-focused observational case study of the agency.

Historical case studies

Historical case studies are either organizational or personal in focus, the former clearly overlapping with organizational case studies. The latter, a 'life history' case study, involves a narrative collected about a single subject. The focus tends to be on a well-known individual or holder of a senior position in the profession (president of a records management association, for example) or in an organization (a long-serving university librarian, or an individual with a career including senior positions in a number of archives). The belief is that those who participated in the 'making' of history should be in a position to throw some light on this history from the advantage of either having been instrumental in it, or having been very close to the locus of power. Historians agree that through detailed knowledge of an individual's career it is possible to understand institutions better, or to discern trends in the development of a profession. Indeed, career is often the organizing principle of a life history case study, with the story following the subject's positions in the profession and major events in the subject's professional life. A life history case study of a prominent person would not only throw light on that person's life and achievements but also help illuminate the history of organizations, of professional bodies, scholarship, and other aspects related to the person's professional life.

Whether a life history case study of a living subject is feasible depends on a number of factors. First are qualities of the proposed subject: the person must be articulate and thoughtful, able to reflect meaningfully and accurately on past events. Second, the researcher must be able to relate well and informally to the individual; there is nothing less satisfactory than interviewing that is stilted, formal and superficial simply because the subject and interviewer are unable to develop a sense of trust and rapport. Third, the potential subject must have participated professionally in institutions that are significant to the purpose of the study and must have been either a force in the events of the time or have been an influence on those wielding power. Readers especially interested in historical research will wish to read Sydney Shep's Chapter 10 with particular attention.

Multi-site and comparative case studies

Generally a case study focuses on a single subject or single group of subjects, a single setting or a single depository of data. But it is also possible to have research in the case study tradition that comprises a multi-case or comparative study in the form of a single case study supplemented with selective data from other cases, or two or more cases of equal value and depth that are compared and contrasted.

Usually these multiple studies are undertaken for the sake of diversity in results or generalizability. Therefore, additional sites should be selected to reflect a range of subjects or settings applicable to the topic. Alternatively, if comparison or contrast is the intention, then additional sites should be chosen to highlight whatever is being compared or contrasted.

There are two particular approaches to, or methods of analysis in a comparative case study that are likely to have some value in the information area. These are the analytic induction approach, and the constant comparative approach. As in normal case study research, developing themes do guide and inform data collection throughout the project, but with either of these approaches analysis and theory building are not left until data collection is more or less complete. Rather, data collection and analysis occur in tandem, one informing the other throughout the research process.

Analytic induction

This is used when a specific problem or issue becomes the focal point of a project. Data are collected and analysed in order to create a descriptive model that covers all instances or cases of the problem, event or issue. Essentially the researcher begins by using preliminary data to create a descriptive model of the phenomenon, and then modifies this model as further data necessitate. In the early 1950s Robinson developed a simple model of analytic induction along the following lines, which is a useful summary of the technique:

1 The researcher develops an approximate definition/explanation of the phenomenon early in the project.
2 As data are collected, the researcher holds the definition/explanation up for examination against the evidence.
3 The definition/explanation is modified as new cases fail to fit the formulated definition/explanation.
4 The researcher redefines the phenomenon and reformulates the explanation until a 'universal' relationship has been established.[6]

Research Scenario 4.1 presents a summary of how analytic induction might proceed in a theory-building study of the success of school librarians. From this it will be seen that the pyramid described at the beginning of this discussion of case studies has been turned on its head. That is, the researcher no longer works up the pyramid from a broad base to a specific case. Instead, in analytic induction the researcher works *down* the case study pyramid, developing a theory from a single interview supplemented by data from additional interviews that broaden and refine the base on which induction is built. As the research base is widened, the theory develops into a more refined or sophisticated statement.

RESEARCH SCENARIO 4.1

A STUDY OF SCHOOL LIBRARIANS

A researcher wants to know why some school librarians seem to be more successful than others in serving the needs of schoolchildren. The study begins with an in-depth interview of a school librarian believed by other librarians to be successful. During an extensive open-ended interview the researcher draws the teacher out on aspects of her career, how school library services and community expectations have changed over the years, what makes a 'good' school library and so on. From this initial interview the researcher develops a general descriptive theory of school library 'success', and more particularly of what makes a 'good' school librarian. This theory includes a series of propositions about the qualities of teacher librarians, about stages in professional development, about school library environments, about pupil responsiveness to librarians and libraries.

A second school librarian, suggested by the first, is then interviewed, putting aside the descriptive theory already developed. After the second interview the theory is modified to fit the new case. This process continues, with the theory modified to fit the results of each new interview. In this way the researcher expands and revises the theory until the interviews no longer result in cases that do not fit the theory. This type of selection process is sometimes referred to as 'snowball sampling'.[7]

The end result, then, is a comprehensive theory about what makes for a successful school library and school librarian. Eventually the theory incorporates statements about school libraries and school librarians that emerge from the study, so the theory results in a typology of school librarians based on their careers, professional views and understanding of issues.

Constant comparative method

Developed most fully in the work of Glaser and Strauss, the constant comparative method is designed for developing theory from information collected from multiple data sources, especially where participant observation is used.[8] As in analytic induction, data analysis begins early in the research process and is more or less completed when all data have been collected, but in other respects this comparative method differs substantially from analytic induction. Glaser summarizes the constant comparative method as a series of logical stages, although he also admits that this is somewhat artificial, as the essence of the method is that the stages occur almost simultaneously and data analysis constantly circles back to encompass additional data collection and coding. Glaser's six stages are:

1 Begin collecting data.
2 Develop focus categories from key issues, recurring events or activities in the data.
3 Continue collecting data that provide multiple instances of focus categories, and develop multiple dimensions within the categories.
4 Describe in writing the categories being explored, accounting for all dimensions, and continue searching for new examples.
5 Discover basic processes and relationships by continually working with the data and the developing model.
6 As the analysis focuses more clearly on core categories, continue sampling, coding and writing.[9]

As these stages suggest, the constant comparative method is more attuned to theory development than is analytic induction, and it relies heavily on the creation of focus categories and properties relevant to these categories. It is particularly suited to the collection of data from multiple sites, with new sites constantly being chosen to broaden the emerging theory and new material in the theory leading to further data sites being chosen. In Research Scenario 4.2 we see how this constant comparative method might look in practice.

RESEARCH SCENARIO 4.2

INFORMAL RELATIONS AMONG CATALOGUING STAFF

A researcher is interested in how cataloguers cope with the repetitive nature of much of their work, and particularly how they use interpersonal relations to counteract the impersonal nature of this work. She plans to begin by observing the behaviour of cataloguing staff in the tea room of an academic library, and then move on from there as developments suggest. On the first few visits the researcher hears conversations of many types but is intrigued by those that are primarily of the 'who's-doing-what-to-whom' variety and also discussions about the personal attributes and habits of other library staff. The researcher terms these conversations 'social banter' and decides to focus her data collection on this aspect of cataloguer social relations. While concentrating on tea room conversations, the researcher also extends her data collecting to other sites: the area in which cataloguers work, lunchtime gatherings in restaurants, social outings, all the while developing categories of the diverse types of 'social banter'. As data continue to emerge from multiple observations in various settings, the researcher becomes interested in a number of related issues, such as who engages in social banter, the content of the banter and emerging categories, as well as behaviour that relates to the conversations.

As these issues become clearer, the researcher continues to examine the data, coding and reassessing them in order to determine connections among the types of talk and among the various interpersonal and content-related issues that have emerged. Categories and models of conversation and cataloguer behaviour are continually developed, expanded, revised and reviewed, and eventually a theory of cataloguers' social relations emerges from the data collected. In order to develop new dimensions of the model, the researcher moves to another setting, this time a public library, on the assumption that cataloguers in a different type of library in another place may engage in quite different kinds of social banter, thereby enriching the already developed categories and models. In each new site the researcher now limits data collecting to social banter, developing new dimensions of the theory of cataloguers' social relations. The project comes to a close when the researcher is satisfied that she has developed a complete theory of cataloguers' social relations based on analysis of their conversations and conversation-related behaviour.

Reliability and validity

While such procedures as analytic induction and the constant comparative method may seem abstruse, overall the several investigative methods and case study approaches described in this chapter should not be conceptually challenging or procedurally complex. Unfortunately, the same cannot be said of reliability and validity: unavoidable topics, covered in Chapter 2 but put off until now in this chapter. In our experience, these are concepts that students and practitioners often find difficult and confusing. At the same time they are key attributes of any successful project, and for this reason must be understood – whether you are the researcher, or simply reading the research of others. It is simply a matter of studying the concepts or attributes one-by-one and step-by-step, returning to them from time to time as one progresses through the book. These attributes *will* become clearer with experience and further study.

'Loosely speaking, "reliability" is the extent to which a measurement procedure yields the same answer however and whenever it is carried out; "validity" is the extent to which it gives the correct answer.'[10] Just to complicate matters, the relationship between reliability and validity is something akin to a schizophrenic two-headed Hydra. That is, there is a relationship, but it is not necessarily either consistent or clear: 'reliability and validity are by no means symmetrical. It is easy to obtain perfect reliability with no validity at all . . . [by using an imprecise, broken or wrong measurement device, for example]. Perfect validity, on the other hand, would assure perfect reliability, for every observation would yield the complete and exact truth.'[11] Still, a Hydra can be slain, and a champion slayer must be Elfreda Chatman, whose excellent study, *The Information World of Retired Women*, presents a simple but accurate description of these two attributes.[12] It is her discussion that forms the basis for the following presentation.

Before proceeding, however, it must be noted that reliability and validity are not universally worshipped in the qualitative research community. One of the most convincing iconoclasts in this regard is Harry Wolcott, who believes that neither concept should carry any weight outside quantitative circles.[13] His basic argument is that the language of quantitative research is not necessarily the language of all research, and that such concepts as generalizability, reliability and validity are simply inappropriate criteria by which to judge qualitative research, which is a different approach requiring different evaluative criteria. There is a great deal of truth in this, and Wolcott's views will be noted in the discussion where appropriate. In the final analysis, however, it is each researcher's responsibility to decide the extent to which reliability and validity in particular are desirable characteristics of any particular qualitative investigation.

Reliability

As noted above, Kirk and Miller define reliability as the extent to which a procedure yields the same answer time after time. Reliability is thus linked to *repeatability*. In quantitative studies an instrument is used as the measuring device, whereas in qualitative studies the researcher fills this role. As Chatman defines it,

> reliability pertains to the degree to which observations are reported as consistent with some phenomenon during the lifespan of the inquiry. Unlike quantitative measurement, which often applies an instrument (e.g., a thermometer) or a mathematical formula, in ethnographic research, it is the researcher who judges the findings as reliable or not.[14]

But this is perhaps too simple a definition, and one that disguises subtle nuances in the variations that occur in reliability. According to Kirk and Miller, it can be useful to distinguish three kinds of reliability, which they call quixotic reliability, diachronic reliability and synchronic reliability.[15]

Quixotic reliability

The first of these, quixotic reliability, 'refers to the circumstances in which a single method of observation yields an unvarying measurement. The problem with reliability of this sort is that it is trivial and misleading.'[16] For instance, if junior staff were asked 'how are you getting on in your job?' within earshot of their supervisors, they would most likely say that all was going well partly because this is what we expect people to say out of politeness and partly because saying anything else would have incurred the displeasure of the supervisors. Therefore, the reliability of this response makes it pretty useless in the context of determining anything meaningful about job satisfaction among junior staff.

Diachronic reliability

This second type of reliability 'refers to the stability of an observation through time. . . . Diachronic reliability is conventionally demonstrated by similarity of measurements, or findings, taken at different times.'[17] In the social sciences, however, this has minimal applicability, for it really relates to the measurement of phenomena that do not change over time. We all know that libraries and information agencies do not stand still, and that change is integral to any healthy organizational environment. Just consider the ways in which the internet has affected, and is daily affecting, everything from simple administrative tasks to information formats, and it becomes obvious that diachronic reliability has almost no place in information-based qualitative investigations.

Synchronic reliability

The third type of reliability identified by Kirk and Miller 'refers to the similarity of observations within the same time period. Unlike quixotic reliability, synchronic reliability rarely involves identical observations, but rather observations that are consistent with respect to the particular features of interest to the observer.'[18] This is a kind of internal reliability, then, that can be evaluated by comparing data gathered by different means, which is precisely what Chatman did in her study as described below under 'Ways to ensure reliability'. As Kirk and Miller add in their comments, there is a significant paradox in synchronic reliability for qualitative researchers. That is, when synchronic reliability fails, this forces the researcher to understand how multiple but different qualitative measurements of the same phenomenon can simultaneously be true – thereby contributing to theory building in an investigation.

Ways to ensure reliability

To achieve reliability, whether this be quixotic, diachronic or synchronic, most qualitative researchers employ a number of means in a single project. In Chatman's research on the information needs of retired women, for example, she sought to ensure reliability in her data by: consistent note taking, immersion in the context, exposure to multiple situations, and referring to other research experiences. Each of these is discussed in turn.

Consistent note taking is perhaps the main key to reliability, and Chatman admits that this can be both time-consuming and tedious. 'I recorded events immediately after leaving the field. If many things were going on that appeared relevant, I would exit into a bathroom to write notes, return to my car, or sit in a corner in an isolated part of Garden Towers [a retirement home] to jot things down.'[19] Despite this awkwardness and the often intrusive nature of note taking, faithfulness to the process helps ensure that observations and conversations central to the project are recorded. This in turn contributes to reliability.

The second technique, immersion in the context, means that the researcher participates in events that offer opportunities to observe phenomena at different times of day over an appropriate time span. Chatman, for instance, visited her subjects in the retirement home at various times of day on weekdays, weekends and holidays, arriving and leaving at different times in order to observe phenomena that occurred only at certain hours. It should be noted that there was not a predetermined schedule for this immersion in the retirement home context; rather the pattern of observation emerged as the project unfolded and as the researcher became aware of the distinctive pattern of activities in the home.

Third is exposure to multiple situations, which allows the researcher to participate more naturally in the lives of subjects, since observation is not artificially limited to a specific 'slice' of activity. This strategy helps the researcher achieve deeper insights into the phenomenon under investigation, since it broadens knowledge of the field and opens new avenues of awareness. For example, Chatman found that growing older was a common topic of discussion among the residents of Garden Towers. But in the dining room, where the older residents were seated first, the conversation was very different (more negative and resigned) than it was, for example, with more active women in the games room or on shopping expeditions. By sharing experiences in the dining room, on shopping expeditions and elsewhere, Chatman was able to develop a clearer and more reliable picture of women's views on aging.[20]

Fourth and finally, reliability is achieved when other research is drawn upon for assistance. This other research may be previous work in other projects by the same researcher, or earlier aspects of the current investigation, or complementary work by others. Chatman, for example, had conducted other qualitative investigations using observation and interviews before the project with retired women, and this previous experience would have sensitized her to be aware of subtle nuances in activities and conversations at Garden Towers. Equally, she was able to draw upon results of earlier observations and interviews at Garden Towers: 'I also incorporated into my interview guide several of the same questions that I had asked previous respondents . . . . This exercise allowed for further checks on the degree of personal bias entering the research process.'[21] This may be fine for the experienced researcher, but what about the newcomer? Here the literature review becomes of paramount importance, for in place of personal experience the new researcher relies on the experiences of others as reported in the literature. 'Examination of other research in which the same or similar phenomena have been explored increases one's confidence that the data being reported are reliable.'[22]

All of this discussion assumes that reliability is to be sought at all costs in qualitative investigations, when in fact it may not be relevant. As Wolcott bluntly puts it, 'reliability remains beyond the pale for research based on observation in natural settings.'[23] This is because in the qualitative approach we study something that happens once; at best we can talk about similarities between observations made at different times and in different places, but such similarity is not the same as accuracy. In the realm of reliability,

> *similarity* of responses is taken to be the same as *accuracy* of responses. The problem with equating them is that one might obtain consistent temperature findings consistently in error due to a faulty thermometer, obtain consistent responses to survey questions that make no sense to respondents or obtain consistent ratings among raters trained to look for the same thing in the same way, in each instance achieving a high degree of reliability on unreliable data. The strain for identifying consistency in findings thus yields to establishing consistency through procedures. Reliability is, therefore, an artifact.[24]

Validity

As reliability is linked to repeatability, so the concept of validity is linked to 'truth'. Is a research finding really the case? If one accepts that 'validity pertains to truth or the degree to which the researcher is given a true picture of the phenomenon being studied', then it is obvious that this is a crucial feature in any research investigation.[25] A finding may be neither reliable nor valid (hence we would put no trust in it); or reliable but not valid (such as in Wolcott's faulty thermometer example); or both reliable and valid (*pace* Wolcott, the hope of most researchers). However, it can never be not reliable but still valid. Validity builds upon a foundation of reliability.

As an example of the significance of validity, consider the following. In discussing management issues with public librarians in Hong Kong, one author found that few problems emerged from large group meetings involving both senior management and assistant librarians. When the assistant librarians met as a separate group without their superiors present, however, a number of problem areas emerged. These included a lack of communication with senior management, poor salaries, inadequate job descriptions and little encouragement to perform well. If we had relied only on data collected from large group meetings, the data might have been reliable, for the same results would have been achieved time after time (although we would tend to categorize this as quixotic reliability). However, validity would have been seriously compromised, for what emerged would not have been a true picture of the assistant librarians' perceived lot.

There are three basic components of validity, each of which has a bearing on generalizability – the ability to draw defensible general conclusions from the evidence one has obtained. These components of validity are face validity, criterion validity and construct validity.

Face validity

When observations in an investigation fit into an expected pattern or frame of reference and therefore make sense to the researcher, they are said to have face validity:

If a phenomenon failed to meet this initial stage of sense making, a researcher would be forced to suspend his or her everyday reality in order to create some form of meaning. In other words, in light of what one perceives to be normative behaviors for the population being studied, one question is whether certain behaviors are appropriate for a certain social milieu. Once this logical issue is resolved, then the researcher begins to explore what the phenomenon means.[26]

In her investigation at Garden Towers, for example, Chatman felt it reasonable to assume that the residents would spend considerable time sitting together and chatting. 'Once I established this "sitting around" as meaningful action, I could begin to examine it in light of the assumptions I was formulating regarding older people and information exchange.'[27] Behaviour falling outside the expected pattern is then treated as non-normative by the researcher, and either ignored or reported as outside the norm.

We need to remember that sometimes really important, significant research challenges our prior expectations – indeed, Schwartz has argued convincingly that truly significant research embodies the concept of 'effective surprise', when one's preconceptions are overturned.[28] Assumptions may need to be overturned. However, to the researcher the observations still make sense; here the challenge is to explain the paradox and convince the readers.

Criterion validity

This occurs 'when the research establishes the accuracy of findings by employing an additional method of inquiry.'[29] For example, in her research Chatman used field notes as the basic method of inquiry, but she also employed an interview guide: 'I have always used an interview guide shortly before I permanently leave a research site. I have found that this procedure addresses the concern raised in discussions of validity and it serves to verify observations recorded in my notes.'[30]

In a library, for instance, it might become apparent in a group setting that certain library staff who regularly converse animatedly invariably become more subdued when one of their colleagues, an attractive and highly competent divisional librarian, comes into the tea room. The researcher wonders whether this reaction is actually occurring and, if so, whether it is professional or personal. Subsequently, in the privacy of one-on-one interviews, several of these staff clearly state that they greatly resent the divisional librarian; she was hired from outside in preference to many of them who applied for her job, and they justify this not on the grounds of her competence (or their incompetence) but on the grounds of her physical attributes, the fact that sexism is alive and well among the (all male) senior management, and so on. Here the interviews confirm the observation of a phenomenon and also add substance to it. To some extent, then, criterion validity may be equated with what we elsewhere term 'triangulation'.

Construct validity

'This type of validity refers to the analysis stage of field work, in which a phenomenon has meaning in light of the conceptual framework guiding the study.'[31] A researcher begins by having a basic conceptual framework that permits the collection of data in a normative manner, as well as their categorization and reporting in a logical manner. One then examines phenomena in light of constructs based on the appropriate theory. 'By using the theory as the underpinnings of the study, a researcher can either support or refute constructs, suggest ways in which to modify the theory, or present ways in which to apply the theory in response to situations that have not been previously addressed.'[32] This is primarily a deductive process, and it does not encompass phenomena that might lie outside the initial theory around which a project is built. Therefore, theory building should continue during a project so that phenomena falling outside the initial conceptual framework may be incorporated – in this way the researcher achieves construct validity.

One additional – and important – way in which to establish validity is by the use of what Guba has termed 'member checks': the circulation of a draft report to members of the organization or group for review at the end of the case. 'The process of member checks is the single most important action inquirers can take, as it goes to the heart of the credibility criterion.'[33] This can help ensure that the interpretation which has been built upon it is indeed valid.

Again, however, we need to ask whether validity is an appropriate concept in qualitative research, its origins and importance in quantitative research being all too apparent. Wolcott makes a strong statement against considering validity within a qualitative context: 'to me, a discussion of validity signals a retreat to that preexisting vocabulary originally designed to lend precision to one arena of dialogue and too casually assumed to be adequate for another.'[34] In his view validity does not mean simply that a researcher has measured what the investigation sets out to measure, but in fact it has taken on a wider significance: 'today being associated more closely with truth value – the correspondence between research and the real world.'[35]

As noted in Chapter 2 on evaluation, another view is put by Guba. He equates validity, 'truth value', in quantitative studies with credibility in qualitative research.[36] As well as such 'member checks', noted above, other ways in which credibility can be enhanced include prolonged engagement and, again, triangulation. In fact, as summarized in Table 4.1, Guba goes further and proposes a whole series of alternative, qualitative equivalents for terms such as reliability and validity, claiming that their use in quantitative research is fundamentally inappropriate as this type of research 'has its own set of criteria for adequacy'.

There are fuller discussions of reliability and validity, but for the most part they provide highly complex explanations and intensely theoretical frameworks. What a researcher really needs to know is that reliability refers to the consistency of answers when phenomena are studied repeatedly, and that validity pertains to the truth, or credibility, of the picture that emerges from an investigation.

Table 4.1 Proposed qualitative equivalents to conventional research terminology

Conventional or quantitative term	Proposed qualitative term
Reliability	Dependability
Internal validity	Credibility
External validity	Transferability
Objectivity	Confirmability

Review of Chapter 4

This chapter has discussed the case study approach, which is the application of specific qualitative research methods in a specific setting. Four types of case studies were discussed: observational, interview, organizational and life history. Multi-site and comparative case studies are also used in qualitative investigations, often employing procedures known as analytic induction and the constant comparative method. These may be somewhat advanced for the neophyte investigator.

Finally, in any investigation, case study or otherwise, it is essential that the results are reliable and valid. Although these two attributes are problematic, they can be achieved by careful attention to possible sources of bias, by the use of triangulation and other means of control.

Where to now?

After you review the focus questions that appeared at the start of this chapter, turn again to Chapter 14, and see if you can answer the following additional questions:

- Is this really a case study and, if so, what type does it appear to be?
- How did the researcher achieve reliability and validity in the investigation?

You might also like to identify another research report said to be a case study – perhaps one from the bibliography at the end of this volume – and assess it against the same criteria.

Chapter 5 discusses fieldwork in information research, and outlines preliminary work that must be undertaken before a satisfactory research project can proceed.

Further reading

From an information research perspective there are three useful overviews of the case study method: R. Fidel, 'The Case Study Method: A Case Study', *Library & Information Science Research*, **6**, 1984, pp. 273–88, which is reprinted under the same title in *Qualitative Research in Information Management,* eds. J. D. Glazier and R. R. Powell (Englewood, CO: Libraries Unlimited, 1992), pp. 37–49; L. Stenhouse, 'Using Case Study in Library Research', *Social Science Information Studies*, **1**, 1981, pp. 221–30; and P. Clayton, 'No Easy Option: Case Study Research in Libraries', *Australian Academic & Research Libraries*, **26** (2), 1995, pp. 69–75. A standard textbook, focusing on the social sciences more generally, is R. K. Yin, *Case Study Research: Design and Methods,* 3rd edn (Thousand Oaks, CA: Sage Publications, 2003).

Readers will scarcely need reminding that there is a wealth of information available online. One worthwhile introduction to case study research undertaken in an information setting is provided by W. Tellis, published in *The Qualitative Report,* **3** (2), 1997, and available online in full text form at www.nova.edu/ssss/QR/QR3-2/ tellis1.html.

Useful supplementation of our discussion on reliability and validity may be found in J. Kirk and M. L. Miller, *Reliability and Validity in Qualitative Research,* Qualitative Research Methods, 1 (Newbury Park, CA: Sage Publications, 1986). See especially pp. 21–32 on 'the problem of validity' and pp. 41–52 on 'the problem of reliability'.

Notes

1 This is based on a definition found in H. S. Becker, *Sociological Work: Method and Substance* (Chicago: Aldine, 1970), p. 75.

2 O. Werner and G. M. Schoepfle, *Systematic Fieldwork.* 2 vols. (Newbury Park, CA: Sage Publications, 1987).

3 L. M. Smith, 'Broadening the Base of Qualitative Case Study Methods in Education', In *Conducting Qualitative Research,* ed. R. G. Burgess. Studies in Qualitative Methodology, 1 (Greenwich, CT: JAI Press, 1988), pp. 25–57.

4 P. Dewdney, The Effects of Training Librarians in Interview Skills: A Field Experiment. PhD dissertation, University of Western Ontario, 1986. This research is recommended as an exemplary model of qualitative research and may be consulted in a readily available summary version: P. Dewdney, 'Recording the Reference Interview: A Field Experiment'. In *Qualitative Research in Information Management,* eds. J. D. Glazier and R. R. Powell (Englewood, CO: Libraries Unlimited, 1992), pp. 122–50.

5 C. Glesne, *Becoming Qualitative Researchers: An Introduction,* 2nd edn (New York: Longman, 1999), p. 69.

6 W. S. Robinson, 'The Logical Structure of Analytic Induction', *American Sociological Review,* **16,** 1951, pp. 812–18.

7 A. Bryman, *Social Research Methods* (2nd edn (New York: OUP, 2004), p. 99; K. Williamson [and others], *Research Methods for Students and Professionals: Information Management and Systems* (Wagga Wagga, NSW: Centre for Information Studies, Charles Sturt University, 2000), p. 213.

8 See B. G. Glaser and A. L. Strauss, *The Discovery of Grounded Theory: Strategies for Qualitative Research* (Chicago: Aldine, 1967); A. L. Strauss, *Qualitative Analysis for Social Scientists* (Cambridge: Cambridge University Press, 1987).

9 B. G. Glaser, *Theoretical Sensitivity: Advances in the Methodology of Grounded Theory* (Mill Valley, CA: Sociology Press, 1978).

10 J. Kirk and M. L. Miller, *Reliability and Validity in Qualitative Research.* Qualitative Research Methods, 1 (Newbury Park, CA: Sage Publications, 1986), p. 19.

11 Ibid., p. 20.

12 E. A. Chatman, *The Information World of Retired Women*, New Directions in Information Management, 29 (Westport, CT: Greenwood Press, 1992).

13 See, for example, two challenging works by H. F. Wolcott: 'On Seeking – and Rejecting – Validity in Qualitative Research'. In *Qualitative Inquiry in Education: The Continuing Debate*, eds. E. W. Eisner and A. Peshkin (New York: Teachers College Press, 1990), pp. 121–52; and *The Art of Fieldwork* (Walnut Creek, CA: AltaMira Press, 1995).

14 Chatman, op. cit., p. 8.

15 Kirk and Miller, op. cit., p. 41.

16 Ibid.

17 Ibid., p. 42

18 Ibid.

19 Chatman, op. cit., pp. 8–9.

20 Ibid., pp. 10–11.

21 Ibid., pp. 11–12.

22 Ibid., pp. 12.

23 Wolcott, *The Art of Fieldwork*, op. cit., p. 167.

24 Ibid., pp. 167–8.

25 Chatman, loc. cit.

26 Ibid.

27 Ibid.

28 C. A. Schwartz, 'Research Significance: Behavioural Patterns and Outcome Characteristics', *Library Quarterly*, **62** (2), 1992, pp. 123–49.

29 Chatman, op. cit., p. 13.

30 Ibid.

31 Ibid., p. 14.

32 Ibid., p. 15.

33 E. G. Guba, 'Criteria for Establishing the Trustworthiness of Naturalistic Enquiries', *Educational Communication and Technology Journal*, **29** (2), 1981, pp. 75–91. R. K. Yin, *Case Study Research: Design and Methods*, rev. ed. (Newbury Park, CA: Sage Publications, 1989) also recommends member checks, pp.143–6.

34 Wolcott, op. cit., pp. 168-169.

35 Ibid., p. 169.

36 Guba, op. cit.

5 Laying the foundations for fieldwork

FOCUS QUESTIONS

- What is fieldwork, and how does it fit into the overall framework of qualitative research and the case study approach?
- What is the researcher's role, and to what extent do experience-near and experience-distant concepts help define it?
- How do I lay the foundations for fieldwork?
- How should I go about choosing a research topic?
- How should I formulate and test research questions?
- What is the purpose of a literature review?
- What is the role of theory in preparing to conduct fieldwork?

This chapter describes the preparation for fieldwork in information agencies. To help you prepare, each step is discussed in turn. First, however, we introduce the concept of fieldwork, discuss the role of the researcher, the value of 'experience-near' and 'experience-distant' concepts, and help lay the foundations for fieldwork.

Overview of fieldwork in information organizations
Definition of fieldwork

In Chapter 1 we noted that qualitative research embodies five characteristics (context, description, process, participant perspective and induction). All of these characteristics, except perhaps induction, can be fulfilled by only one method of data collection – fieldwork. That is, researchers collect data within the natural setting of the data, and the key data collection instruments are the researchers themselves. This use of the natural setting has led to the fieldwork stage in qualitative research, and indeed to the whole qualitative process, being termed 'naturalistic enquiry'.[1]

> Fieldwork is the interface between researcher and data in the case study approach characteristic of qualitative research; it involves collecting data 'in the field', being out among the subjects of one's research, becoming immersed in their milieu and seeing events and activities as they see them.

Because the qualitative researcher wants to know what subjects think and how they act in their natural setting, the only way to do this thoroughly is by being alongside them to the extent that this is feasible.

The role of the researcher

In a way, then, the researcher 'inserts' his or her presence into the natural setting of the subjects. At the start of a project this can be most disconcerting to all involved. But a competent and sensitive researcher soon learns how to become just part of the everyday fabric and thus less noticeable. When this happens, the initial awkwardness and stiffness disappear, both researcher and subjects become more comfortable with one another, and the setting returns to something very close to 'normal'.

This is not unlike the situation when a new staff member commences work. At first the 'old hands' might try to take this person under their wings, perhaps show off their inside knowledge a bit, and pass on some of the institutional mythology. After a week or two, though, the new staff member is accepted as one of the team and largely left alone to get on with the job. And so it is with the fieldworker: at first everything is rather strange to both observer and observed, but in a very short time almost no attention is paid to the researcher, who is no longer a 'stranger' but just part of the setting.

Now, this does not mean that the researcher literally becomes part of the subjects' world. This is what Geertz refers to as 'the myth of the chameleon field-worker perfectly self-attuned to his exotic surroundings – a walking miracle of empathy, tact, patience, and cosmopolitanism.'[2] Rather, there is always a certain detachment and aloofness, always a reflective empathy rather than total identification. The researcher remains detached in order to observe and record what transpires, and stays far enough outside events in order to record descriptive data. One may become enough 'like' the subjects to learn from them, but not so like the subjects that objectivity disappears – a difficult balancing act, to be sure, but one that must be achieved if data are to be collected in any meaningful way. Through the entire process the researcher is a data-collecting instrument, and like any instrument, tries not to be swayed by emotions, beliefs and personal views. The extent to which one tries, though, depends on where the researcher sits on the participation continuum described below.

Experience-near and experience-distant concepts

This 'in-but-not-of' issue has exercised theoreticians and practitioners of qualitative research, especially ethnographers, for decades, and is not to be dismissed lightly by the qualitative researcher in an information setting. There have been many attempts to address the problem, summarized by Geertz as 'inside' versus 'outside' or 'first person' versus 'third person' descriptions, or 'cognitive' versus 'behavioural' theories. Another pair of terms often used to describe this phenomenon is 'emic' and 'etic' – the former from 'phonemic',

LIVERPOOL JOHN MOORES UNIVERSITY
LEARNING SERVICES

which refers to the internal functions of sounds in language; the latter from 'phonetic', which refers to the external acoustic properties of sounds in language.[3] But for Geertz the simplest distinction is one developed by Heinz Kohut and referred to as 'experience-near' and 'experience-distant'. We believe this can be adapted for qualitative research in information work.

> An experience-near concept is roughly one which an individual – a patient, a subject . . . an informant – might himself naturally and effortlessly use to define what he or his fellows see, feel, think, imagine . . . and which he would readily understand when similarly applied by others. An experience-distant concept is one which various types of specialists – an analyst, an experimenter, an ethnographer . . . employ to put forward their scientific, philosophical, or practical aims.[4]

The choice is not so much black and white as between shades of grey. The experienced fieldworker tries to tread a path that is neither bound totally by the horizons of those being investigated nor so theory-driven as to meander off, oblivious to the subtle nuances of their world. 'To grasp concepts which, for another people, are experience-near, and to do so well enough to place them in illuminating connection with those experience-distant concepts that theorists have fashioned to capture the general features of social life, is clearly a task at least as delicate . . . as putting oneself into someone else's skin.'[5]

For the fieldworker in an information area, who is probably a professional as well, the experience-near/experience-distant model is far less difficult than for the anthropologist studying tribal customs in East Africa or the sociologist investigating street gangs in Liverpool. The anthropologist and sociologist are both dealing with communities in which the disparity between experience-near and experience-distant approaches are likely to be significant. The information researcher, on the other hand, will bring to the research setting a number of experience-distant concepts with which the subjects are likely to be tacitly familiar from their own training or workplace experience. Furthermore, the experience-near concepts of the research subjects are unlikely to be totally alien to the researcher who shares a common profession with the subjects. That is, the fieldworker in an information setting, as a professional who has worked in the area, will already be a member of the same professional group as the subjects, or will know a great deal about the type of milieu in which the investigation occurs.

Group membership can greatly enhance a researcher's understanding. 'Group membership influences an individual's values, knowledge system, and communication patterns. Within each group there exists a commonality of knowledge and culture, unique to that group, which provides continuity and growth potential.'[6] From this common knowledge base the researcher is able to understand a great deal of the language and many of the 'signals' to be found in a research setting, and this can only assist the fieldworker both in quickly becoming part of that setting and in understanding much of what is seen and heard without undue puzzlement.

This overview of fieldwork might lead to the assumption that it is appropriate only for participant observation. True, fieldwork is the *sine qua non* of the researcher as observer, but this should not be taken as excluding other forms of qualitative research. What we are really describing here is a generic approach, a sensitivity to experience-near concepts of others, that informs qualitative research of all types. In interviewing, for example, the researcher seeks to establish a rapport and sensitivity with those being interviewed so that they will feel free to expound on topics openly and personally, and in the depth that formal interviewing techniques do not foster. For the researcher using content analysis of documents in historical studies the fieldwork approach is equally relevant, although in a somewhat less personal sense. Specifically, the researcher wants to develop a 'relationship' with the documents that will enhance understanding of their context and content, especially the content that is experience-near. In other words, it is the *attitude* of fieldwork that holds the key to any type of qualitative methodology.

Stage 1: laying the foundations

In the pyramid model of research, discussed in Chapter 3, Stage 1 involves what we have termed preliminary preparation. It includes the following steps: considering the focus and choosing a topic, describing a problem and formulating research questions, reviewing relevant literature, and establishing a theoretical framework. In this stage you start to build your research pyramid by laying firm foundations (see 'Preliminary preparation', Figure 3.3, Chapter 3, p. 38). Alternatively, using our other metaphor you begin to move down the recursive model (see the top four boxes in Figure 3.2, again in Chapter 3, p. 37). This preliminary preparation is every bit as important as the succeeding stages, for it establishes the parameters and guiding principles of the entire investigation. Each step in this first stage is now dealt with in sequence.

Step 1: considering the focus and choosing a topic

In Chapter 3 the section 'First questions' asked 'What should be the focus?' as the most basic question at the outset of a qualitative investigation. This is the question that is asked as the first step in the preliminary preparation stage of any research project. Key factors in selecting a focus or topic are:

- Is it practical?
- Can I ensure access to the data?
- Is the proposed site neutral?
- Is the topic intrinsically valuable?
- Can I be flexible in my approach to the topic?

Is it practical?

Begin by looking at your own abilities, skills, knowledge and experience. Try to choose a topic that from the outset seems consistent with at least some of these. If you are an absolute novice, select a topic with which you feel comfortable, that is closer to 'where you're at' personally than other possible topics. In addition, practicality demands that one consider the time available and possible research funds: pick a topic that is neither so large nor so complex that it cannot be completed within these temporal and financial restrictions. In our experience, novice researchers very frequently consider projects that are too ambitious: our regular advice is, 'Cut it down!'

Can I ensure access to the data?

Practicality leads naturally to the second consideration, the accessibility of data sources. An ideal topic will have the necessary data concentrated rather than scattered widely, either geographically or in time. Especially if you are new to qualitative research, it is a great help if the data sources are close at hand, as this both saves travel time and encourages you to return to the data more frequently. It is worth remembering that a key component in qualitative research is the researcher's direct involvement – the more remote the data sources, the more difficult this involvement.

Is the proposed site neutral?

Most texts on qualitative research exhort novices to use neutral sites for data collection, sites in which they are not personally involved as employees or colleagues, or in which their interest is not predetermined by existing relationships. Although well intended, such advice may at times be misguided, or at least misinterpreted. Of course, valid research cannot be undertaken when the researcher is determined to 'prove' that something is or is not the case. On the other hand, a key characteristic of qualitative research is the direct involvement and 'commitment' of the researcher, so it seems counterproductive to counsel new researchers against intimate involvement. Rather the advice should be to use a site in which one's powers of observation will not be clouded by personal preconceptions. Remember that in qualitative research one comes into a situation with an open mind and allows the collected data to drive the investigation forward.

Where you are already intimately familiar with the setting or data sources, there may be significant in-built biases of which you are unaware. But a trade-off here is that you already have ready entry to the environment and do not need to develop rapport with the subjects – surely a bonus well worth considering. The issue then becomes one of how well you can use your existing relationships to facilitate access, while at the same time not allowing these relationships to colour perceptions during the investigation. If you can put personal preconceptions aside, and collect data *as if* from an unknown site, then the site can be viewed as neutral.

The more experienced the researcher, of course, the less this is an issue, for one develops an ability to use familiarity as a facilitator rather than a bias-prone burden.

Is the topic intrinsically valuable?

Considering the intrinsic value of a topic is more crucial today than in the past, for in recent decades information science has caught the research disease. There are thousands of postgraduate dissertations and theses and countless papers by underemployed academics on almost every topic imaginable. Think, for example, of the myriad references in the literature to research on reference enquiries or use of OPACs. Faced with this flood of research activity, our professional community has developed something of a Noah mentality, looking for unique species to take on board. Is the issue of some ultimate significance? Will it have an enduring impact on professional practice? The closer one can come to answering these questions in the affirmative, the more likely the topic is to have intrinsic value.

This is not to say that every investigation must contribute to the betterment of humanity, but you must ask how the topic will be received by others in your professional community. If it will be 'Ho hum, not another boring piece of fieldwork that means nothing' as distinct from 'Well, this looks interesting', then perhaps you should rethink the topic – after all, we all want others to find some value in what we do. Also, the frisson of feeling that one is breaking new ground helps immeasurably in maintaining high adrenalin levels during the long hard slog of data collection and analysis.

Can I be flexible in my approach to the topic?

Finally, you must be flexible, both in considering these criteria and in the actual conduct of your study. Being practical means that you are open to the need to change plans as unexpected obstacles arise. If access to data is limited, you must either find new data sources or new means of enhancing access. If the neutrality of a site is compromised in an unforeseen way, then the location may need to be changed. If a topic proves to lack any value or significance, then it must be changed. Above all else, during the conduct of a qualitative study you must be open to suggestion and allow the subjects to suggest directions. It is fatal for the researcher in this paradigm to follow a set research pattern, although a newcomer will certainly be tempted by the comfort of a set game plan. Be open to suggestion, and allow reality and practicality to inform the development of your project.

Within all these considerations it is most important to choose a topic that is neither too broad nor too narrow. For example, the project 'The role of electronic networking in university life' is probably too general for most researchers; but 'Why postgraduate library science students in my research methods class use *Library Literature* online' may be too specific (and also probably of little consequence). However, a project that investigates the dynamics of a networked reader education group might be just about right for a reasonable investigation resulting at least in a research paper and perhaps in a master's thesis (see Research Scenario 5.1 below).

Remember the recursive nature of the research model. In reality the choice of topic tends to evolve as a project is actually conducted, so the problem statement helps define the topic, and the literature review often suggests further refinements. In addition, the actual fieldwork should suggest new directions, revised focal points, and unexpected avenues of investigation. This is entirely as it should be in the qualitative approach, though it should never be so radical that the topic changes completely.

Step 2: describing the problem and formulating research questions

When a topic has been chosen, considered, revised and given what seems to be an appropriate focus, it is time to move on to the second step of the foundations. This is actually a step in two parts: the issue being investigated is framed as a problem statement, or perhaps a series of problem statements, and the problem is then formulated as one or more research questions.

Describing the problem

The problem statement helps to clarify the topic. It should also suggest approaches to be used in the investigation and perhaps lead to initial theory formulation. Rather than stating relationships between variables as happens in quantitative research, the qualitative researcher tries to phrase a problem statement to indicate the kind of understanding that the project seeks to achieve. A classic problem statement in the qualitative mould is: 'The primary goal of this study was to enhance the understanding of the networked learning community that emerged in an internet-based graduate-level course.'[7] That is, the problem in this project was to understand a networked learning community.

Blaise Cronin suggests seven guiding criteria that might be used to identify problems suitable for research.[8] Some of these are perhaps more appropriate to the quantitative framework, and some have too applied a focus for many of the most interesting, theoretical topics. Nevertheless, they are presented here as a summary of problem selection, with the suggestion that the more questions that can be answered positively, the more likely you are to have a researchable problem.

- *Actionability.* Can appropriate recommendations be implemented in the organiz- ation?
- *Definition.* Can the problem be formulated clearly and explained to others?
- *Congruence.* Does the problem relate to the mission and objectives of the orga- nization?
- *Centrality.* Does the problem account for a significant consumption of resources?
- *Externality.* Does the problem have a significant impact on users?
- *Utility.* Will the results have value in use?

- *Communicability.* Can the results be communicated clearly and effectively to the target audience?

Most often answers to some of these problem selection questions emerge when the problem statement is phrased more specifically as a series of research questions. Rice-Lively does this very nicely, her problem-related questions being:

- Will a class conducted in a mostly electronic environment form a unique culture, complete with rules for communication and behaviour?
- Do the traditional educational roles of the students and the instructor change in the virtual classroom? If so, how are these new roles different?
- To what extent can ethnographic research techniques, using the traditional data-gathering methodologies of observation, interviews, and recording of field notes, be applied in an electronic community?[9]

Here the general problem statement of understanding a networked learning community has resulted in specific questions to do with class (or student) culture, student–teacher roles and ethnographic research techniques. This is in fact a most interesting set of questions, showing how a qualitative problem statement can lead not only to case-specific questions (a class culture), but also to more general issues (educational roles in the virtual classroom) and to matters of research theory and practice (research techniques in an electronic environment).

Formulating the research questions

Moving from research problem statement to research questions may look simple, but one suspects that Rice-Lively agonized considerably over both her problem statement and its development into a set of research questions. Marshall and Rossman recognize this difficulty when they say that 'the research questions should be general enough to permit exploration but focused enough to delimit the study – not an easy task.'[10] They go on to suggest that the other preliminary stages preceding actual fieldwork interact with the problem statement stage as part of a developmental process. That is, stating the research problem and research questions is influenced in part by what emerges in the subsequent literature review and initial theory formulation. In fact, question formulation can continue right through the entire project, concluding only with final data analysis: 'often the primary research goal is to discover those very questions that are most probing and insightful.'[11]

We need to understand not only the purpose of problem statements and research questions but also to recognize the interactive role that other stages at the foundations level have on this process, for in many ways it is the research questions that drive the research forward – as, indeed, they are designed to do. It might assist to view the research questions as the core of an interactive triangle (see Figure 5.1), in which problem statement, literature review and theory formulation all have an impact on the research questions, and vice versa.

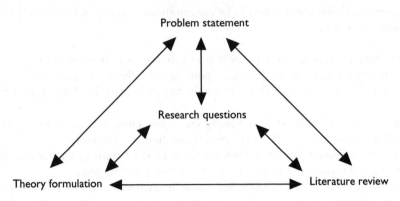

Figure 5.1 The research question triangle

The research questions arising from the problem statement may have one of a variety of focal points. Following the classification of Marshall and Rossman, we term these foci theoretical, population-specific, and location-specific.[12]

A theoretical question can be investigated in a range of unspecified sites and among a number of different populations; for example, 'Does mentoring affect the development of managers?' could be investigated among archivists or school-teachers or manufacturers with equally valid results. A research question may focus on a specific population or group of individuals, but not be limited to a specific location: 'How do county librarians manage relations with members of the library board?' is limited to county librarians, but could be investigated in any county in England, Wales or indeed anywhere else in the world with a county library service. Finally, a research question may focus on a specific location; thus (with apologies to Tom Sharpe) 'Why is the reader education programme at Groxbourne College in South Salop successful?' could not be investigated anywhere other than at this very minor public school. Of course, in practice elements of each focus may be combined. The research question could be to investigate the effectiveness of mentoring by county librarians in two named counties, for example.

Once you have stated the research problem to be investigated, and refined this into one or more research questions with a theoretical, population-specific or location-specific focus, the way is open for a detailed literature review. This in turn will exercise some influence on your research questions, with a flow-on effect to the problem statement and, at this preliminary stage, perhaps even to the topic itself.

Step 3: reviewing the relevant literature

Telling an information professional how to conduct a literature review would be akin to showing a used car salesman how to wind back an odometer, so this brief section on the third step in the preliminary planning process merely indicates the importance of literature reviews and suggests further reading for those who might feel inadequately prepared in the area.

Reading around in the literature

There simply is no substitute for 'reading around' in the relevant literature before beginning a qualitative research project. Reading literature that is related to the proposed topic of a qualitative study has several benefits.

- First, if others have done research on similar or related topics, this can help confirm that an appropriate topic has been chosen – or that the topic has been overworked and should be changed. Alternatively, if nothing even remotely similar has been done, this may mean that the field is wide open and awaiting attention, or perhaps too difficult and to be avoided.
- Second, the literature review can aid in focusing the topic, as other studies show what is known and unknown about a topic – a chosen topic should aim to fill the gap, or at least put a new complexion on existing research.
- Third, the review should assist in developing a research design and choosing an appropriate methodology. If others have succeeded in using certain designs and methodologies to investigate a similar problem, then this can confirm what one intends to do. Alternatively, Martin has suggested that sometimes choosing an unconventional method can provide significant results.[13] Certainly, reports of failed designs and methodologies – unfortunately, all too rare – should indicate what to avoid.

All of this means that the researcher will be influenced by what others have done, but in our view this contributes to the experience-distant theory and assumptions that guide any good research. There is usually no point in simply replicating what someone else has done previously, unless you believe you can add to (or refute) what is already known. The point of research, after all, is to learn something new, to apply techniques in a new way, or to apply methods in a new setting.

Structuring a literature review

Much useful guidance exists on conducting literature reviews and on analysing published research literature, but none of it focuses specifically on qualitative research in library science. Perhaps the fullest discussion of literature reviews is presented by Cooper in *Integrating Research: A Guide for Literature Reviews*.[14] The qualitative researcher looking for relevant studies on library-related matters must consult the two primary indexing services: *Library and Information Science Abstracts (LISA)* and the American counterpart which includes abstracts, *Library Literature* (both available in hard copy and electronically). In addition some useful citations may be found in *ERIC* and *Information Science Abstracts*, as well as some of the smaller country-specific guides, such as *Australian Library and Information Science Abstracts* (ALISA).

Using combinations of chosen terms and time limitations, you will find that searches of these databases regularly refer to a handful of journals, nearly all American, as most likely sources of qualitative research studies. Depending on your subject interests, these journals will repay regular scanning: *College & Research Libraries*, *Journal of Academic Librarianship*, *Library & Information Science Research* and *Reference & User Services Quarterly* (formerly *RQ*). Perhaps not surprisingly in view of the predominance of the quantitative paradigm in information science research, such respected journals as *Library Resources and Technical Services* and the *Journal of the American Society for Information Science and Technology* contain little of value to the qualitative researcher. In their place some journals not directly related to the field are worth considering, many of which straddle the disciplines of information technology, information science and library science, such as *Internet Research*, *The Electronic Library*, *Library Hi Tech* and *Online Information Review*. Do not forget *Dissertation Abstracts International*, which lists doctoral-level research at institutions worldwide including information science research of all types, but with the inevitable emphasis on North America.

In addition to searching the literature through abstracting and indexing services, you should scan the footnotes in retrieved papers to find other related publications; such citation analysis often points to older materials missed in a search of current databases. Finally, it is important to remember that a literature review is really never completed until the final draft of the research report has been written, as one always comes across an unexpected reference late in the project – although if a thorough search has been conducted at the outset, such a reference should not be to a seminal paper.

Once found, what is found needs to be assessed. How useful is it? Can it be relied upon? Evaluation of qualitative research was, of course, considered in Chapter 2.

Step 4: establishing a theoretical framework

The fourth and final step at the foundations stage involves the establishment of a theoretical framework for the investigation. As we have seen in Chapter 1, a principal function of qualitative research is the development of theory from the intensive study of cases. In particular the qualitative researcher uses theory to help interpret and understand observed events or interactions, and through this interpretation in turn adds to the theory.[15]

This does not mean, however, that theory generation happens only at the conclusion of a research undertaking. Indeed, theory plays an important role in the initial stages of research as well, often flowing from ideas developed during a literature review. Here interpretation is used for predictive and explanatory purposes, especially by quantitative researchers but also, to some extent, by their qualitative colleagues. Glaser and Strauss, for example, readily accept the role of theory to help predict and explain, but for them such theory is a function of induction based on observation and data analysis.[16]

Development of concepts

From such theory based on induction, hypotheses and concepts are developed. These can be used by subsequent researchers to help establish a framework for their own work. Especially for the neophyte this is an important preliminary function of predictive and explanatory theory (as distinct from interpretation). Again, the purist may say that this already gives the researcher a bias and a mindset determined by others, but in our view the sensitive researcher will use theory sparingly and in full awareness that this is just a starting point. Also, of course, even the most experienced researchers, having a wealth of fieldwork to their credit, almost without thinking bring such predictive and explanatory theory to their subsequent work. This is part of what we call experience-distant observation, after all.

Types of theories

Qualitative researchers use theory at various stages and in various ways during their investigations. In this respect they differ somewhat from quantitative researchers, who tend to use theory primarily in the early stages to generate research questions or testable hypotheses. This use of theory is most clearly explained by Turner, who presents a three-fold classification: empirical generalization, causal (or theoretical) models, and middle-range theories.[17]

- *Empirical generalizations* are often based on literature reviews. The knowledge from studying related research is used to stimulate questions for further or new research. This approach is used frequently by qualitative researchers in the initial stages of theory building.
- *Causal models* tend to focus on the input–output paradigm in which independent variables – different circumstances – are used to explain dependent variables – different results. They are thus common in quantitative research. Causal models are often less useful for qualitative purposes, although sometimes they help inform the initial direction of a qualitative project. For example, one may choose to study a particular aspect of a causal model through qualitative means.
- *Middle-range theories* are related to variables that exist in multiple cases and 'try to explain a whole class of phenomena'.[18] These fairly broad theories are useful both in the initial questioning that occurs in qualitative research and in the later analytical stages, so they are really a bridge between fairly basic empirical generalizations and the altogether 'higher' interpretive use of theory proposed by Glaser and Strauss.

To summarize what occurs in the four steps in laying the foundations, the qualitative researcher chooses a topic taking into account a number of factors, and within this topic a particular issue or problem is identified. Having stated this problem in a manner that is conducive to investigation, the researcher then conducts a literature review. This review enhances the procedure in a number of ways, not least being the initial establishment of a theoretical framework to guide the investigation.

From topic to problem to review to theory the researcher is seeking to do one thing – to undertake sound preliminary preparation that will lay the foundation for the next substantial stage in the research. Some of this preliminary preparation is described in Research Scenario 5.1, in which the researcher becomes interested in a topic based on personal experience and gradually shapes and amends the ideas through a process of study and literature review. The researcher's reading leads not only to refinement of the problem into a series of research questions, but also to the development of a preliminary theoretical framework for the research.

RESEARCH SCENARIO 5.1

GROUP DYNAMICS IN AN INFORMATION LITERACY CLASS[19]

A training librarian regularly uses computer-aided instruction (CAI) in information literacy programmes for users who wish to learn how to consult electronic information sources and communicate with colleagues via electronic networks. As part of this work, the trainer becomes interested in teacher–student relationships where much of the instruction is done electronically. The trainer then decides to become a researcher in order to investigate this problem, which is stated as a question: Do the traditional educational roles of students and library instructors change in the electronic classroom? If so, how are these new roles different? Given the trainer's regular contact with appropriate groups through her workplace, she decides that the simplest procedure is to conduct a case study of an information literacy class in her own library. Because the project thus involves a case study of group dynamics, the researcher knows from the start that qualitative research methods are the best option.

Following this preliminary assessment, the trainer-as-researcher conducts a basic literature review and finds nothing in *LISA* or *Library Literature* on the topic. The search is extended to educational databases, from which she retrieves a number of references to research on group dynamics when CAI is used in secondary schools. Reading some of this research sensitizes the trainer to other issues, especially the group dynamics operating among students in these networked learning environments. The problem thus broadens to include not only group dynamics between students and teachers but also between students and students, and a second research question thus becomes: Will a class conducted in a mostly electronic environment form a unique culture with regard to communication protocols and behaviour?

The researcher then continues the literature review in order to see what methods other projects have used when investigating group dynamics, CAI or electronic networks. In fact most of the research has been quantitative, which the researcher knows is not appropriate for the case study approach to be used in this project. The researcher wonders why the emphasis has been quantitative, and whether qualitative research techniques are actually appropriate for studying an 'electronic community'. This then becomes the third part of the problem, with the relevant question being: To what extent can qualitative research techniques, using the data-gathering methodologies of observation, interviews, and recording of field notes, be applied when studying an electronic community? To address this adequately, the researcher needs to learn a great deal more about qualitative research methods so reads works by Strauss and Corbin (*Basics of Qualitative Research: Grounded Theory Procedure and Techniques,* 1990) and Spradley (*Participant Observation,* 1980), among others. Strauss and Corbin convince the researcher that, in relation to the first two research questions, a principal aim of the project should be discovery of a grounded theory for networked learning groups. Spradley presents an ethnographic research cycle that the researcher feels would be useful for initial data collection procedures and data analysis. From this point the researcher goes on to prepare for the fieldwork stage of the project.

Review of Chapter 5

This chapter has described preparation for conducting fieldwork in information contexts by focusing on the first four steps of the process that lay the foundations for any qualitative investigation. Fieldwork is the process by which case studies are conducted, during which the researcher treads a path between experience-near and experience-distant concepts. Some of these concepts begin to emerge during the early steps of project development, especially as the researcher selects a topic, describes the problem to be investigated and then asks a series of problem-specific research questions. The literature review should also suggest useful concepts to guide the research, and also present some initial theoretical underpinnings for the investigation. Establishment of a theoretical framework helps to give logic and order not only to the problem under investigation but also to the subsequent stage of broad (but still preparatory) exploration to be discussed in Chapter 6.

In each of these four steps numerous guidelines have been suggested. Thus topic selection should be guided by four factors of an essentially practical nature; the formulation of research questions should be guided by the interrelationships between problem statement, literature review and theory; the literature review should be carefully structured to reflect the exact issues of the topic and should include careful evaluation of information retrieved; and early theory development should relate to emerging concepts within the topic, and be guided in part by the literature retrieved.

Where to now?

Chapter 5 has, in short, covered a considerable amount of territory, so it is advisable to reflect on what we have discussed thus far, perhaps by reviewing the focus questions. Stage 2 (discussed in the next chapter) builds on an understanding of Stage 1, and anything that seems unclear at this point should be revised before moving to the next stage. To assist in this, rather than re-reading the knowledge management case study (Chapter 14) yet again, you might like to turn to another excellent example of qualitative research. This is the article by E. A. Chatman, 'Life in a Small World'.[20] Read it carefully, and consider the following questions:

- What is her general topic? Can you confirm that she followed any of our suggested criteria for topic selection?
- Can you identify the research problem in her project, and the related research questions?
- Is there any indication that a literature review was conducted?
- What seems to be the underlying theoretical framework that might have guided the investigation initially? Does Chatman say that the theory evolved during the course of the project?

Further reading

In many ways, the best further reading on the topics covered in this chapter are examples of fully thought-through, carefully executed and thoroughly documented research – such as Chatman's, noted above, or the final chapter in this volume. Despite its discipline-specific focus, T. H. Schram, *Conceptualizing Qualitative Inquiry: Mindwork for Fieldwork in Education and the Social Sciences* (Upper Saddle River, NJ: Merrill, 2003) will be of interest to first-time researchers as it works through the process of planning a field-based qualitative study using a 'model' student researcher. An older education title, D. R. Hittleman and A. J. Simon, *Interpreting Educational Research: An Introduction for Consumers of Research*, 2nd edn (Upper Saddle River, NJ: Merrill, 1997), will also repay study.

Notes

1 See, for example, C. A. Mellon, ed., *Naturalistic Inquiry for Library Science: Methods and Applications for Research, Evaluation and Teaching* (Westport, CT: Greenwood Press, 1990).
2 C. Geertz, 'From the Native's Point of View: On the Nature of Anthropological Understanding'. In *Interpretive Social Science: A Reader*, eds. P. Rabinow and W. M. Sullivan (Berkeley, CA: University of California Press, 1979), p. 225. This entire paper by Geertz is a wonderfully descriptive and insightful discussion, in an anthropological context, of how fieldworkers are able to get close to their subjects; it is highly recommended for anyone undertaking qualitative research.
3 Ibid., p. 226.
4 Ibid., pp. 226–7.
5 Ibid., p. 227.
6 R. Grover and J. D. Glazier, 'Structured Participant Observation'. In *Qualitative Research in Information Management,* eds. J. D. Glazier and R. R. Powell (Englewood, CO: Libraries Unlimited, 1992), p. 106.
7 M. L. Rice-Lively, 'Wired Warp and Woof: An Ethnographic Study of a Networking Class', *Internet Research*, **4** (4), 1994, p. 20.
8 B. Cronin, 'When Is a Problem a Research Problem?' In *Applying Research to Practice: How to Use Data Collection and Research to Improve Library Management Decision Making*, ed. L. S. Estabrook (Urbana-Champaign: University of Illinois, Graduate School of Library and Information Science, 1992), pp. 128–9.

9   Rice-Lively, op. cit., p. 21.

10 C. Marshall and G. B. Rossman, *Designing Qualitative Research*, 2nd edn (Thousand Oaks, CA: Sage Publications, 1995), p. 26.

11 Ibid., p. 27.

12 Ibid., pp. 27-8.

13 J. Martin, 'Breaking Up the Mono-method Monopolies in Organizational Analysis'. In *The Theory and Philosophy of Organizations: Critical Issues and New Perspectives*, eds. J. Hassard and D. Pym (London: Routledge, 1990), pp. 30–43.

14 H. M. Cooper, *Integrating Research: A Guide for Literature Reviews*, 2nd ed., Applied Social Research Methods, 2 (Newbury Park, CA: Sage Publications, 1989).

15 C. Geertz employs the memorable term, 'thick description', for such interpretation, indicating that this goes far beyond simple description to look at meaning and motive. See C. Geertz, *The Interpretation of Cultures* (New York: Basic Books, 1973).

16 Glaser and Strauss call this 'grounded theory' – that is, theory that is grounded in the reality of observed data. B. G. Glaser and A. L. Strauss, *The Discovery of Grounded Theory: Strategies for Qualitative Research* (Chicago: Aldine, 1967).

17 J. Turner, 'In Defense of Positivism.' *Sociological Theory*, 3, 1985, pp. 24–31. Note, however, the title of his paper – no acknowledgement here of the interpretivist approach of qualitative research.

18 Ibid., p. 27.

19 This scenario is based very loosely on Rice-Lively's internet research project; see Rice-Lively, op. cit.

20 E. A. Chatman, 'Life in a Small World: Applicability of Gratification Theory to Information-Seeking Behavior', *Journal of the American Society for Information Science*, 42 (6), 1991, pp. 438–49.

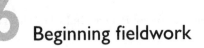

6 Beginning fieldwork

FOCUS QUESTIONS
- What criteria should be considered when selecting sites for an investigation?
- What criteria should be considered when selecting subjects for observation or interview?
- How do you gain access to a selected location?
- What is the purpose of a pilot study and preliminary data collection in the process of formulating a research plan?
- What is a broad research plan intended to achieve?

Stage 2: broad exploration

Having described the four steps of the foundation stage of fieldwork in information agencies, we are now ready to begin Stage 2. This involves broad exploration of sites and testing of methodologies. The first step in this stage is Step 5 (Steps 1 to 4 having been covered in Chapter 5). This step involves selecting locations and subjects, and within this the procedure for gaining access to libraries and participants. These are key procedures upon which many a project founders, so are given particularly detailed treatment. The next step, Step 6, deals with the blueprint phase of formulating a research plan. This is less problematic, although as pilot studies and preliminary data collection do have an impact on all remaining steps in qualitative investigation they must be conducted with care. Each of these steps is described in enough detail to enable you to follow it through in your own investigation.

In the pyramid model the broad exploratory stage of fieldwork builds upon the earlier, foundation stage of preliminary preparation (see Figure 3.3, Chapter 3, p. 38). In the recursive model (see Figure 3.2, again in Chapter 3, p. 37) it consists of the two steps that follow the four preparatory steps: selecting the locations and subjects, and formulating a research plan.

It is during the course of completing the two steps in this stage that researchers actually 'get their hands dirty' for the first time. That is, they make preliminary forays into the field in a search for suitable locations and subjects, investigate the possibilities and test data-collecting procedures. Then a preliminary research plan is drawn up to guide the researcher during the exploratory fieldwork of Stage 2. In Step 5 we answer the second basic question noted in Chapter 3 (see 'First questions', p. 39): *what* phenomena should be studied? Step 6 addresses the third question: *how* should the phenomena be studied?

Step 5: selecting locations and subjects

The selection of locations and subjects actually involves three interrelated activities: a search for suitable locations and subjects, the preliminary selection of possible locations and subjects, and then the testing of the selected locations and subjects to ensure their suitability (see Figure 6.1). That is, the researcher searches, selects and tests before making a final determination as to which location or subjects will be used. This applies whether one is using observation, interview or any other investigative methodology. Note, however, that the testing actually occurs as part of the pilot study in Step 6 (see below), when you first venture into the field.

Search   ⟶   Select   ⟶   Test

Figure 6.1 The location and subject selection process

Like the recursive model of qualitative research, this is not a straightforward linear process. Those selected may prove inappropriate for a variety of reasons, in which case the search must begin anew; or the testing of a selected location may divulge undesirable characteristics, in which instance another site must be selected. During this process it is crucial that you come to grips with matters of generalizability and sampling, as both determine where the investigation is conducted and who the subjects are.

Generalizability

Most important is the matter of generalizability, the ability to draw defensible general conclusions from the evidence one has obtained. Should a case be studied because it is typical, or because it is unique (or at least out of the ordinary)? If you choose what appears to be a typical organization, or a typical group within an organization, or typical subjects within a group, the intention is to focus on a setting (location, group or subjects) that is not demonstrably different from other settings of the same type. By choosing a setting that is similar to other settings, either those known to you or reported in the research literature, you hope to have the potential to reach some general conclusions.

However, the search for generalizability and similarity means that you are using predetermined categories or assumptions at the outset of your study. In other words, you are prejudging your cases, asserting that they *are* typical in some way. The alternative view is that these judgements should arise out of the research itself, and not be allowed to determine the research design. Some writers go further and dismiss generalizability entirely. That is, while generalizability may be highly desirable, some would argue that it is simply outside the scope of qualitative investigations, which look at individual units (libraries, archives and so on) rather than frequencies, distributions or averages across a number of units.

Our view is that the particular circumstances will largely determine what is appropriate for any particular study. One of us undertook a major project in which two pairs of libraries were sought: one of each pair I thought likely to be innovative, the other conservative. I hoped to learn from the contrasts between the two. This did not work. First of all, the head of one of the libraries decided not to grant me access after all, despite having initially agreed to this. (We discuss problems of access later in this chapter.) Second, closer enquiry into my remaining libraries established that labels such as 'innovative' or 'conservative' were far too simplistic. The better approach, then, seems simply to choose a case that is accessible and interesting, allowing others to determine whether it is possible to generalize from this case. In whatever way you choose your case study sites, though, you must allow yourself to remain open to what they tell you. Any preconceptions you may bring to them may well have to be discarded.

When a study has been properly narrowed to a specific population in a specific place, it is sometimes possible to observe all members of the population, interview everyone in the group, and analyse all the relevant documents. But when this is not the case, it is essential that sampling be done in such a way that all types represented in the population are included. If this does not happen, then the research will fail to consider the full range of perspectives or views within the population.

The quality of data produced during the initial sampling may determine further sampling. For example, if a subject proves to be particularly helpful or knowledgeable, this person becomes a key informant on whom the researcher relies more than others. When a subject, site or document has this quality, it deserves more attention because of the data provided. Qualitative researchers view this as quite acceptable, maintaining that the fieldworker should allocate time to subjects in proportion to the value of data the subjects provide. As noted, at the end of the study it is often desirable to have such key informants review the accuracy and balance of the report produced.

In fact the literature on qualitative research is somewhat coy about how one searches for and chooses either sites or participants, and the published reports of completed research are even more elusive. In searching for sites, the researcher begins with what is known, and gradually extends the search as required. Before searching, of course, it is important to have a list of desirable characteristics (see Marshall and Rossman's list below), and to select sites that meet all of the requirements. With any luck, there will be more locations and subjects than are needed, and one can then reject those that appear less suitable.

Selecting sites

It is important to recognize that site selection involves the choice of locations in which people interact – that is, the interaction of people is our focus, not the site or location per se. But we must also be aware that locations embody meaning and create an atmosphere that affects how people interact; therefore, during the research process we must learn to decode places and read them as we would a text, for by doing this we can begin to understand how and why people interact with their locations. Place and location are thus sometimes referred to as 'lived visual data' in which 'questions of motion in time and space, arenas of visibility and invisibility and the patterning of zones, objects and activities are central'.[1] Emmison and Smith, in their chapter titled 'Lived Visual Data: The Built Environment and Its Uses', go on to discuss the movement of people in time and space, or how subjects interact with their built environments, which we need to accept as a key issue in selecting and studying sites. The location, in other words, can be a major variable in any study, and not merely a passive backdrop.

Of course, sometimes the choice of location is ready-made. In Rice-Lively's study of a networking class, for example, 'the selection of this networked learning community for study was an easy one. At the time of the research it was the only such community on the campus of this university.'[2] When there is only one instance of a phenomenon being studied, the researcher is saved the agony of choosing where to base the investigation. Similarly, a site-specific question (for instance, Why is the reader education programme successful at St Kevin's School in Grub Street and not at Groxbourne College in South Salop?) is automatically limited to the sites named in the research problem. A population-specific question (How do county archivists manage relations with members of the county archives subcommittee?), on the other hand, opens up more choices, since the population is specified but not the site. Finally, a theoretical question (Does mentoring affect the development of managers in the public service?) is neither site- nor population-specific, making the choice even more difficult.

How, then, do you choose a county, a public service department or a group of managers? You begin by searching for locations that meet the most basic criterion – that is, they include examples of what the study is investigating. For instance, if I am researching county archivists and their relations with archives subcommittees, I need sites that have both county archivists (a post may be vacant) and archives subcommittees. Second, you need to use locations that are readily accessible physically or geographically. Thus from my base in, say, East Sussex it would be foolish to study a site in Humberside. Let us assume, then, from my initial search for locations it emerges that Kent, East Sussex, West Sussex and Hampshire meet my initial criteria of (1) having county archivists and archives subcommittees, and (2) of being within reasonable travelling distance by car.

When you have searched for and found a number of potentially acceptable locations, the second step is to choose the desired number of sites from this group. That is, you seek an ideal location from all the possible locations, which according to Marshall and Rossman is one where:

- access (in terms of being allowed entry) is possible
- there is a high probability that the appropriate mix of features (processes, people, programmes, interactions, structures, and so on) is present
- you will be able to build interactive relationships with study participants
- data quality and credibility of the study are likely to be ensured.[3]

These are in descending order of importance – if you cannot gain entry, then the other criteria are irrelevant. (Given the importance of access, this is treated in detail in a separate section below.) If you *can* gain entry, then it becomes possible to determine the presence or otherwise of that 'rich mix' essential for effective research. This judgement is made during Step 6 (Pilot Study and Preliminary Data Collection), when you test the location. If the desired mix is missing, then the you select another location from the pool of possibilities.

With regard to Marshall and Rossman's two remaining criteria, it should be noted that they speak of the likelihood of building trust in the location, and of being reasonably assured about data quality. While testing in Step 6 will assist in determining these features, in our view they can be assessed definitively only as the research progresses. There has been more than one instance of a project having to change location because the researcher was unable to build the necessary relationship with his subjects, or because it emerged in the early stages that data quality was being compromised by manipulative subjects.

It is possible that these last two criteria might be more easily determined if the investigation is conducted in the researcher's 'backyard', because there, one already will know whether there is mutual trust between participants and researcher. Some writers on qualitative research, however, look less favourably on investigations being conducted in the researcher's workplace. In their view 'backyard research can be extremely valuable, but it needs to be entered with heightened consciousness of potential difficulties'.[4]

In fact, this advice is often not appropriate for many qualitative studies in the information area, for much of it is workplace-based and in response to observed workplace problems in need of solutions. Rice-Lively's project is but one example of this. Naturally, securing entry to the workplace is not a problem if the researcher is already working there. The researcher also has the advantage of knowing the situation intimately, and thus knows at the outset whether the mix is appropriately rich and whether data quality can be assured.

It is Marshall and Rossman's third point, the ability to build trusting relationships, that may be problematic in a location where the researcher is known.

> Previous experiences with settings or peoples can set up expectations for certain types of interactions that will constrain effective data collection . . . . When studying in your own backyard, you often already have a role – as principal or teacher or case worker or friend. When you add on the researcher role, both you and your others may experience confusion at times over who you are or should be playing.[5]

Indeed it may, but is this any more problematic than going as a stranger to a location, and having to build a relationship 'from scratch' with totally unknown people? The answer to this will, of course, depend on the history and abilities of individual researchers. In our view both known and unknown locations pose difficulties, and neither should be discounted out of hand. For research that has arisen in response to a workplace problem, of course, there may be no option but to situate the project in the workplace.

Selecting subjects

Thus far we have focused on selecting locations for data collection, but of course within a location the researcher must also select subjects for study, unless all subjects in a location or engaged in a particular activity are to be studied. Following ideas developed by Johnson (see Figure 6.2), we believe that subjects are best selected according to two sets of criteria.[6] First are criteria concerning 'theoretical qualifications', or criteria known in advance (for example, position in a library). Second are criteria concerning 'innate abilities' of subjects, or criteria used as a screening device (for example, the willingness to divulge information).

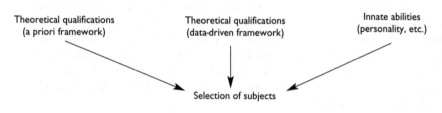

Figure 6.2 Criteria affecting subject selection

'Theoretical qualifications' include such criteria as status, role, position, expertise, knowledge, group and subgroup membership. There are two ways in which appropriate theoretical criteria may be established:

- First, you may have detailed a priori knowledge of categories, classifications or structures relevant to the situation being investigated. One would expect an experienced librarian-researcher, for instance, to have a reasonable working knowledge of library organization and professional staff structures which would be used to establish preliminary categories for selecting participants. But note the use of 'preliminary', for it is rarely possible to establish all likely categories before immersion in a setting. If you are genuinely open to influence from the setting and participants, then there must always be the possibility of additional categories suggesting themselves as the investigation progresses.
- Second, the 'theoretical qualifications' are data-driven, arising out of the context being investigated and tending to be more informal than those determined on the basis of a priori theoretical knowledge. For example, a

researcher may determine from a priori theoretical knowledge that the structure from which staff are to be selected involves associate librarians, divisional librarians, section librarians and assistant librarians. Once the project begins, however, and staff are being selected as subjects, it may emerge that in the collection development and technical services divisions there exists an informal sub-group of assistant librarians involved in selection and acquisition of materials. In such instances the researcher takes this data-driven factor into account, and includes subjects from the informal sub-group as well as from the formal structure.

The third set of criteria, that concerning innate abilities, '. . . become more a matter of personality, personal chemistry, interpersonal compatibility, the ability to establish a trusting relationship, and so on'.[7] These innate abilities come into play after you have selected possible subjects, based on 'theoretical qualifications' that are both a priori and data-driven. From individuals with the appropriate theoretical qualifications you choose participants who seem most compatible and approachable for the purposes of the project, or who are simply available, in relation to your own personal requirements.

There is in most environments an increasingly important phenomenon that now underlies these various sets of criteria, and that is the reality of multiculturalism or cultural diversity. When selecting informants, it is essential first to identify the extent of cultural diversity in any setting before selecting informants, as this diversity must be reflected in the sample. Metoyer clearly considers the various issues in defining and identifying culturally diverse populations, drawing on her own research on information-seeking behaviour in multicultural communities.[8]

It is the third set of criteria (innate abilities) that contributes most significantly to the choice of both key informants and serendipitous informants in projects. A key informant is one to whom the researcher relates particularly well, and with whom strong rapport develops. Some researchers feel uncomfortable when such a relationship begins to develop, for fear that this may bias the results. This would be the case if the investigator relied solely on a key informant – much like the (probably not) apocryphal journalist who based his war-time dispatches solely on information from a regular patron of the hotel bar.

However, no respectable qualitative researcher would rely solely on a key informant. Instead, such a subject is used to gain deeper insights which you then test by means of subsequent observation. A key informant can also assist you to gain access to other subjects who might otherwise be unavailable. You should also try to select a range of key informants 'from the pool of theoretically representative informants. By doing so, the ethnographer will have a more complete understanding of the potential biases associated with reliance on one or only a few informants.'[9] Much the same can be said of serendipitous informants, who are accidentally encountered rather than selected from predetermined categories. When such informants prove valuable, they should not be rejected but should be placed into theoretical categories *ex post facto* so that their information can be considered in the appropriate context.

Gaining access

Whether access to locations or to subjects, this is a major issue in the selection process, as suggested above. Unfortunately, as Burgess observes in a school context, 'access has, until relatively recently, not been regarded as a problem by many researchers and has received little attention in basic methodology texts . . . . In some studies access has been taken for granted or ignored completely.'[10] Much the same is still true in an information science context – not only is the issue largely ignored in the few writings on qualitative methodologies in the information area, but it is also not addressed in most of the research papers that report on qualitative investigations in this field.

In qualitative research there is a distinction to be made between covert and overt investigation, the former occurring without knowledge of the participants. There is probably no instance of research in a library or archival setting being totally covert, as someone must grant permission for the researcher to be in the library or archives in the first place. This cannot be stated too strongly, especially for the benefit of first-time researchers: it would be quite unethical for a researcher to conduct a study in a library or archives without first seeking permission from the director or the parent institution. Therefore, we will assume that all research is overt to the extent that it has been approved by someone in authority, that it is undertaken with permission and therefore full knowledge of, if not the participants, at least those responsible for the overall operation of the organization. (This does not mean that it will necessarily be overt to all participant – for example, library users whom one may wish to observe unobtrusively.) It should also be pointed out that covert research, which often seems so attractive because of the lack of obvious red tape, can have serious drawbacks. In Burgess' words,

> If a study is covert the researcher only has access to those situations which are observed. In these circumstances, it is not possible to conduct interviews, collect life-histories or documentary evidence that is produced by the group. In short, covert research places limitations on the conduct of an investigation while bypassing the negotiation of access with a gatekeeper.[11]

Gaining access or entry is important whether you are observing participants, interviewing people or consulting documents. As an information study requires access to services or materials, permission must be granted. For interviewing, there is the added complexity that each subject must agree to be interviewed, so you may need to request access many times over. Also, when consulting documents, whether records of the organization or archival materials or manuscripts, there may be special requirements for gaining access. For example, an institution may be willing to grant access to collections only if it feels that the topic can be serviced from its materials, or that the content of the materials will not be compromised in some way by allowing access.

Very often gaining entry is a simple process either because of the institutional ethos or because of researcher characteristics. For example, in some libraries (those of universities and research institutes, for example) research activity and the presence of researchers is perceived as quite normal, so the chief librarian at least understands what a researcher is asking for when permission is sought to use the library as a research site. Like university libraries, archives are used to the presence of researchers, even if usually using their collections rather than investigating the institution. Similarly, a school librarian will be used to dealing with students and will have a broad understanding of educational requirements, so it should not seem unusual for a research student to seek permission for access as part of a study requirement.

Public libraries on the whole do not offer these advantages and there may be some question as to who actually grants permission, whether it is the librarian or someone at a higher level in the appropriate authority. Also, for a special library attached to a government department or private enterprise, permission may be rather tricky, first because the libraries tend to be smaller operations in which a researcher may be more intrusive, and second because the library's activities and information may be viewed as institutionally or commercially sensitive. Records management studies also present potential problems as this tends to be an under-researched area, often with under-qualified and apprehensive staff, and here again sensitivities will need to be appreciated.

If organizational type or context affect access, so does researcher background. In some instances you may already have good contacts that will ease access – for instance, I may know and be on friendly terms with a chief librarian through other professional activities or from having worked with that person in another library, or I may be a previous employee of an organization to which I am now seeking access. In fact existing contacts in a setting often have more to do with the selection of library sites than many researchers would like to admit. In other instances one may not know individuals in a particular organization but may have general knowledge of the type of setting that helps gain access. For example, past work experience in an archives might help a researcher understand the institutional culture, and to know how best to seek permission for access from the archivist. Looking at our own research activities, access has always been most straightforward when relying on contacts (though one of us has also been denied access simply because of these contacts!), or when sought from academic or research libraries.

The qualitative researcher is usually at an advantage because most of the procedures are less intrusive than those used by quantitative researchers. You will be observing, or perhaps interviewing individuals privately, or (more rarely) interviewing groups. You will not be administering large questionnaires, setting up collecting stations or locating 'bean counters' at strategic locations with lots of explanatory signs. The qualitative researcher is much more likely to 'slip in' and 'slip out', which means that a relatively low profile is maintained; and this often disposes a chief librarian to grant permission more readily than otherwise might be the case.

The strategy for gaining access involves moving on several fronts almost simultaneously. 'Study your quarry' is how one colleague put it – get to know what the person in charge (the gatekeeper who controls access to locations or individuals) is like, wants to hear, and attempt, within the bounds of honesty, to satisfy these wants. You will probably need to start at the top, with the director (always the notional gatekeeper at least). Before doing this, however, it helps to use contacts within an organization to ascertain how easy or difficult it is likely to be, and where you are likely to meet resistance. A director may object, but not the immediate supervisor of the section. In this case you may need to use the supervisor as a go-between, to try convincing the higher powers that the project is valid.

Contacts from within the organization can also provide a good deal of formal and informal information on how the system operates, who the key people are, whom you should cultivate to ensure full access, what might be done to anticipate resistance, and so on. A good director will consult managers and senior staff further down the hierarchy, so it is as well to have them on your side from the start. Hence it is sensible to put out feelers at the level at which the project will be conducted, and with the person most directly responsible for granting access – the archivist if institutional archives are to be consulted, the head of reader services if reference procedures are being observed.

Securing permission from the chief librarian or other appropriate gatekeeper is only part of the process. You also need to gain the goodwill of those who will be most directly involved. A bad way to start is just to appear, or for these staff to receive a memo about the research out of the blue from senior management. Only in the most tyrannous organization will staff have no opinion and wish to pass you on directly to the chief – this is probably a good signal to avoid this organization, unless it exemplifies the type of organization that you are studying! If there appears to be strong but not implacable resistance, you need to assess whether time should be spent trying to win over the decision-maker in this instance, or whether another site should be selected where resistance is likely to be less.

In other words, securing permission to study a particular organization and specific sections within it, or to use specific subjects within the library, may well not be a once-for-all process. There may be a number of gatekeepers, from the director down to individual section heads, and even individual subjects being observed or interviewed. For each of these you must be prepared to negotiate entry and request permission. As Burgess reminds us,

> We cannot talk of a gatekeeper and a point of access. Instead, we need to think in terms of gatekeepers who can grant permission for the researcher to study different facets of the organization. There are, therefore, multiple points of entry that require a continuous process of negotiation and renegotiation throughout the research. Research access is not merely granted or withheld at one particular point in time but is ongoing with the research.[12]

In our study of county archivists, for example, it may be necessary to seek permission both from the County Archivist and the Director of Information Services to whom the archivist answers; then there is the matter of negotiating access with the Chairman of the Archives Subcommittee. Further into the project it may become necessary to negotiate access with each member of the subcommittee if it is deemed appropriate to interview them individually. Then it might become apparent that other people in County Hall, or journalists on the local paper, or selected archivists around the county, have something to contribute. Access must be negotiated with each of these individuals as the investigation progresses.

It is quite possible, therefore, that securing access may in fact be a complex, arduous and time-consuming task, so you need to take this into account when selecting sites. There may be a formal application procedure to be followed, with requests considered at regular intervals. Permission may also be denied as a matter of course. (We know of one Australian university, with a library school, at which senior library management deny access 'as a matter of principle' to researchers interested in studying aspects of the university library. This same library also routinely refuses to complete quantitative research questionnaires, so at least researchers across the spectrum are treated with equal contempt.)

Before requesting entry to a location you should think through the reasons for wanting access and anticipate questions that may be asked. It might be worth incorporating such information into a formal statement made available when asking for right of access, or it may be used as a prompt when informally discussing access with relevant gatekeepers. Typically, three key questions are asked of researchers by gatekeepers, and such questions should be addressed clearly and simply.

- What does the research really involve?
- Why do you want to study this particular institution?
- What benefits will there be (or, what will be done with the results)? [13]

What does the research really involve?

You will be expected to say what you are going to do, but not necessarily in any great detail. Those who grant permission will want concise, jargon-free information. Give enough but not too much information – remember that the study evolves as you progress, so it is not wise either to make false statements or to lock yourself into a procedure that may not be appropriate. State briefly the topic or problem being studied, the method being used to study it, and the time involved.

A typical statement might be (1) that you want to develop an understanding of how clients behave at a service desk in order to see whether the service can be more responsive to their needs, (2) that you wish to conduct unobtrusive observations of client interactions and perhaps interview a sample of service staff and clients, and (3) that the investigation will involve four visits over four weeks, and a number of interviews to be negotiated at a later date. Stress the fact that you will be learning from people in the setting and that you will not be an imposition, interfering with daily routines and service activities in any significant way. It is also worth stating that the process will develop as the study progresses, and that you will request further permission if the procedure changes significantly.

Why do you want to study this particular institution?

This question tends to be asked out of pride or worry. That is, the director may feel that his institution has been chosen as an exemplar of something, or because you believe it is particularly bad at something and intend to expose it. If an institution has a particularly good reputation in the field of your investigation, then say so – you want to study this situation to determine how they have done it so well. Few managers can resist this ego massage. If, on the other hand, you wish to study an institution because it has a negative reputation, it is best to focus on other attributes when seeking entry.

It is essential that you remove any cause for suspicion. In particular, make it clear that you are not investigating a particular organization *as that particular organization* – rather, you are interested in a specific topic, problem or issue and are using this institution as a means of access to data, not as an end in itself. Therefore, this organization has been chosen as a site because it is convenient, it has a good mix of what you are looking at, it has a good reputation, etc.

What benefits will there be to this institution?

Often this question masks a hidden agenda, which is to determine what you intend to do with the results. If an organization gives access, what will it gain in return? It is best to indicate the short-term goal, that a report or paper will be written, and that you will share this with the organization (either a copy of the published paper, or a summary of a longer research report). Be sure to highlight the fact that the name of the institution will remain confidential and that you will provide only the background detail needed for understanding the research. If you hope to do something more with the results, discuss this later, when you have shown the organization that you are not a threat.

Other than sharing the results of the research in a printed report or article, there are other inducements that the researcher might offer, although this applies more to experienced investigators than to research students. The researcher might offer to report the full results in a formal staff presentation, or to advise management on how to deal with any problem issues that might have been uncovered, or perhaps to lead a staff seminar or continuing education workshop on a more general topic related to the specific investigation.

Throughout the process of gaining entry remember that there are many problems to be overcome. Burgess summarizes these as follows:

- access is not a straightforward procedure;
- access influences the kind of investigation which can be done;
- access occurs throughout the research process.[14]

In Research Scenario 6.1 access is shown not to be straightforward, for here the researcher almost had to change his stripes from place to place; and in each setting this access is negotiated anew according to different entry requirements. One might reflect, too, on the type of investigation that might have been done had the investigator been just a librarian. Specifically, might he have gained more inside knowledge in this guise?

RESEARCH SCENARIO 6.1
GAINING ENTRY BY FITTING THE SURROUNDINGS

This scenario is based on personal experience of research among librarians in theological colleges. The investigation involved self-perceptions of librarians as to their 'worth' in the overall theological college culture, and involved data collection by interview. At the time of the research I was also a priest, although not working in that capacity. The colleges represented most Christian traditions, from Roman Catholic to conservative Protestant. Each Christian tradition has specific and strongly held views on the nature of priesthood, role of the clergy, and gender issues – all of which proved unexpectedly significant for the researcher. Most of the male librarians were also clergy, but the majority of librarians were women (none ordained).

Based on long-standing personal involvement with the professional association to which most of these librarians belonged, I knew that access to locations and subject receptiveness would depend on how I presented myself, and that this self-presentation would vary significantly from place to place.

In most instances I did not begin by indicating my own affiliation but waited to see whether this status would be advantageous. For example, in some of the more conservative Protestant circles it was clear that access might well be denied; I was just another outsider who should be kept at bay. But when I alluded to my 'ministerial' status ('priest' sounding too popish), access tended to be granted most graciously. Then it became necessary for me to dress the part, wearing a dark suit and tie in some places, a clerical collar in others.

As observation progressed, I became more concerned to find a key informant who could provide me with inside information on how theological colleges function. I had assumed that one librarian in particular, who also happened to be a reasonably close personal friend, might be such an informant, but after several attempts at initiating conversations about 'behind-the-scenes' college operations, it was obvious that he was not going to oblige. I therefore began looking elsewhere. Another librarian, widely recognized as a very senior member of the profession and with an outward demeanour indicating that he took this seniority seriously, was not initially in the running for key informant. On more than one occasion, however, he made such statements as 'what the others [other librarians] fail to understand is . . .' and 'you and I both know . . .'. It was not until my notes were being reviewed that it struck me – this librarian was taking me into his confidence by indicating that we were equals. Once I recognized this, I played up to his bias, even to the point of allowing him to believe that I favoured 'his' football team (when in fact I did not and never will!). As a consequence, he became the most valuable informant in the investigation. None of this I viewed as dishonest or unethical; it was simply a matter of fitting myself to the situation in order to gain the most detailed information from my subjects.

Because access is not a simple, straightforward procedure, different approaches must be made to different individuals at different levels in different organizations (as Research Scenario 6.1 demonstrates). That is, how entry is negotiated in one place may not be the way it should be negotiated elsewhere. Different gatekeepers must be approached in different ways, and they respond differently to inducements. Also, just because the director agrees to allow access does not mean that you will be welcomed with open arms by all members of the staff – you must earn the trust of your subjects for access to be meaningful.

How you gain access influences what can be done. If the director allows access and then tells staff that they must be prepared to co-operate, then the researcher is likely to be viewed as an ally of senior management and so may not be told certain things. Likewise, if a researcher is introduced to a reader education class by the head of reference services, this automatically creates a barrier that makes it difficult for the researcher to collect certain kinds of data that might reflect on the reference staff. And obviously the researcher cannot engage in unobtrusive observation if people have been told about the research in advance.

It is worth remembering that researchers need to be flexible in seeking entry, to be thick-skinned and prepared for rejection, and to be prepared to say diplomatically what the gatekeepers expect to hear (so long as this does not involve telling an untruth). Also, view gatekeepers as allies rather than adversaries. They are there in part to protect the institution, its users and its resources; they have a responsibility to determine whether what you wish to do is acceptable, whether it fits the broad mission of the institution and that it does not interfere with service delivery. You, the researcher, have a task to discover information that may be beneficial to the institution, or at least to the profession of which the gatekeeper is a member. To that extent gatekeeper and researcher should be working together.

Step 6: formulating a research plan

Formulation of a research plan to guide the 'real' fieldwork involves a three-point process: development of a broad plan, the undertaking of a pilot study and preliminary data collection, and revision of the broad plan (see Figure 6.3). The initial broad research plan guides the pilot study and preliminary data collection, which in turn contributes test data used to revise and fine-tune the broad research plan. In this three-point process you undertake some of the final activities as a trial before embarking on the actual data-collecting phase of an investigation. The end

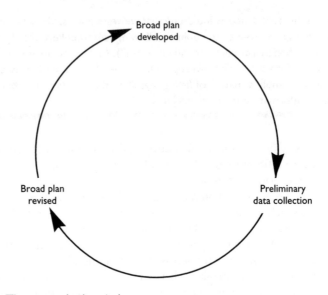

Figure 6.3 The research plan circle

result of Step 6 should be a clear understanding of how the chosen locations or subjects will be studied, and a blueprint for the actual fieldwork to follow.

Developing a broad research plan

The elements of any research plan must include the particular methods to be adopted and the time frame in which the study will be undertaken. The methods in turn will influence appropriate types of record-keeping, discussed in subsequent chapters but also usefully trialled during the pilot study.

Choice of data collection technique

Choosing an appropriate data collection technique or set of techniques is the most important activity when developing a broad research plan, and may also be the most difficult. It is here that the recursive nature of qualitative research becomes most apparent, for you now have to return to that early step in Stage 1, research problem and research question formulation, in order to match these research questions with the most useful data-gathering techniques.

According to Marshall and Rossman (see Table 6.1), research problems and research questions can be divided into four types: exploratory, explanatory, descriptive and predictive. Each of these types in turn is most suitable for investigation by two or more data collection techniques. Exploratory questions, for example, are most suitably investigated by means of participant observation and in-depth interviewing. Perhaps this point needs emphasizing: often novice researchers are

Table 6.1 Linking data collection techniques to problems and questions[15]

Research problems	Research questions	Data collection techniques
Exploratory		
To investigate little-understood phenomena, to identify important variables	What is happening in this programme? What are the salient themes, patterns, categories in participants' meaning structures? How are these patterns linked with one another?	Participant observation In-depth interviewing
Explanatory		
To explain the forces causing the phenomenon in question, to identify plausible causal networks shaping the phenomenon	What events, beliefs, attitudes, policies are shaping this phenomenon? How do these forces interact to result in the phenomenon?	Participant observation In-depth interviewing Survey questionnaire Document analysis
Descriptive		
To document the phenomenon of interest	What are the salient behaviours, events, beliefs, attitudes, structures, processes occurring in this phenomenon?	Participant observation In-depth interviewing Document analysis Unobtrusive measures Survey questionnaire
Predictive		
To predict the overall outcomes of the phenomenon, to forecast the events and behaviours resulting from the phenomenon	What will occur as a result of this phenomenon? Who will be affected? In what ways?	Survey questionnaire Kinesics/proxemics Content analysis

tempted to use a particular *technique* (interviewing, perhaps) for its own sake, because they feel comfortable with it. This is like choosing a home because you like the view, without thinking through how many bedrooms you might need. The method *must* be chosen to suit the type of investigation being undertaken, not vice versa.

Once you know the particular strengths and weaknesses of each technique (discussed in Chapters 7 to 10), and your own strengths and weaknesses, it becomes relatively simple to select some techniques to be used in a particular investigation. Given the importance of triangulation, it is wise to select more than one method so that each can be tested in the preliminary data collection phase.

Note that Table 6.1 does not include all the possible types of investigation you might consider using. It omits both the group processes we consider in Chapter 9, for example, as well as historical research, discussed in Chapter 10. Depending on the circumstances, historical research could be of special value in both explanatory and descriptive projects – and as for prediction, the well-known maxim that 'those who cannot remember the past are doomed to repeat it' comes to mind.

We do not imagine Marshall and Rossman intended theirs to be a comprehensive guide. It is, however, of evident value to be able to categorize your research problem into one of their four types, draw out the relevant research questions from it and then allow these to suggest appropriate ways of tackling your problem. Alternatively, having made some tentative decisions about what you might do, you might wish to return to Table 6.1 to check that you have thought your project through fully, and that the data collection techniques you intend to use seem appropriate.

Another factor that may be relevant is resources: will the study involve you in direct expenditure – for travel and accommodation, perhaps, or for equipment such as an adequate tape recorder? If so, can you obtain some kind of financial assistance, or will you be paying for these yourself? If the latter, in some cases (where the research is closely associated with your paid employment) you may be able to claim at least part of your expenses against your income tax, provided you have kept adequate records. Sometimes, however, lack of resources will inevitably dictate what methods or sites may be feasible for your study.

Time frame

An important consideration when developing the broad research plan is its timing: time to be spent in planning and on the pilot study; time to be spent on fieldwork; and time to be devoted to writing up the study. Therefore, it is worth including a timetable in the research plan. 'Doing so helps to assess the needs of the possible research aspects and to anticipate the requirements of each: arrangements to be made, letters to be written, people to be phoned, and places to be visited . . . . The timetable serves as a reality check on the feasibility . . . of your choice of research methods, sites and participants.'[16]

Some activities can proceed simultaneously. The literature review, for example, is likely to be continuing throughout a project. Other activities must fit sequentially one after the other. A procedure often adopted in larger or more complex research projects is to graph the stages, perhaps using a Gantt chart. This can show deadlines, dependencies (when one stage has to precede another) and, often, that too much has been scheduled into too short a period. In addition, you will probably have varying amounts of time you can devote to the project yourself, so scheduling must be designed with this in mind as well. A sample research timetable, presented as a simple Gantt chart, is included as Figure 6.4. Note that there is a very useful Web tool for creating Gantt charts; this is a simple device that is quickly learned.[17]

Research Timetable

Item	Key activities	1 to 3	4	5	6	7	8	9	10	11	12	13	14	15	16	17	18	Post-research Activity
1	Meet and discuss project with project adviser	█		█		█			█		█		█		█			█
2	Literature search and identification of problem	█																
3	Prepare and refine statement of research problem	█																
4	Gain agreement from organization		█															
5	Obtain a list of staff members' names		█															
6	Trial focus group discussion				█													
7	Undertake focus group discussions					█												
8	Prepare interview questions and interview strategy	█			█													
9	Test interview questions and interview strategy	█			█	█												
10	Conduct interviews						█	█										
11	Code, record and analyse collected data							█	█	█								
12	Write draft report chapters		█	█	█	█	█	█										
13	Distribute draft report to peers for review/comment													█				
14	Submit draft sections/report to project adviser				█			█			█							
15	Submit final report															█		
16	Post-research administration and liaison; thank-yous																	█

This figure is based on the work of Bruce Murn

Figure 6.4 Example of a Gantt chart used to plan a research project

Institutional factors also affect scheduling. As any researcher knows, the time at which a site or individual is visited frequently affects the quality and level of data collected. An academic library, for instance, has a very different aura during the long vacation than in the middle of a term, and a school librarian is quite unlikely to want to devote time to an in-depth interview at the beginning of a new school year. Such factors must be considered when time sampling. On the other hand, if you want to look at the impact of stress on the performance of a busy service area, it would make little sense to observe it during the long vacation.

Do not assume that other people will necessarily be happy, or even able, to fit in with your proposed research schedule. Those higher up have more autonomy to set schedules. 'In general it appears that individuals who hold higher places in the institutional hierarchy have greater autonomy to declare when they are free. Yet they often are busy individuals who reschedule appointments as a matter of course. Those lower in the hierarchy often have little autonomy to set a time to talk.'[18] Yet, precisely because those at the top of the hierarchy are more busy, it is often necessary to set appointments well in advance. Even then, these may be changed or cancelled at the last minute – it can be very frustrating to travel at one's own expense to another city to meet an appointment, only to have it cancelled after you have arrived.

Even experienced researchers regularly underestimate the overall amount of time they will need. Particularly in qualitative studies this issue can be more problematic than one might assume. Most researchers in this mode collect far more data than they can use, because the temptation as subjects, activities and sites change is to continue collecting data and exploring new vistas that seem interesting. Tempting as this may be, you must have a clear concluding time in mind, and not proceed beyond this to the point of data overload.

Finally, allow sufficient time for the final writing-up of the research. While much of the work can be done in days off, in the evenings or at the weekend, it is usually a good idea to block in a solid period of several weeks for this final stage, in order to work at it virtually uninterrupted. This is particularly important if the research is to be presented as a dissertation or thesis: both the length and complexity of the typical thesis can too easily overwhelm the part-time postgraduate.

Conducting a pilot study

Using the draft research plan just developed, ideally you will then undertake two related activities: a pilot study in a neutral location that will not be used in the actual fieldwork, and preliminary data collection in the actual location(s) from which data are to be collected. The pilot study allows you to test several variables and iron out any initial problems before preparing the broad plan that will direct the remainder of the project. 'The idea is not to get data per se, but to learn about your research process, interview schedule, observation techniques, and yourself.'[19] The variables being 'tested' thus include the chosen data-collecting method, the time frame of the investigation, and the researcher as a research instrument.

> To figure out what techniques to use, once again contemplate carefully what you want to learn. Different questions have different implications for data collection. In considering options, choose techniques that are likely to (1) elicit data needed to gain understanding of the phenomenon in question, (2) contribute different perspectives on the issue, and (3) make effective use of the time available for data collection.[20]

The pilot participants should know they are part of a pilot, and that they should not only take part in your methodology (interviews or whatever technique you have chosen), but also reflect on what they are requested to do. Are the questions clear? Are they appropriate? Are there other questions that should be asked?

Use the pilot study to test the language and content of questions, and the length and approach of interviews. Use the pilot to test observation techniques: what is the response of those being observed? What might make them feel more comfortable? Can you take field notes as you observe, or should this be done later? Is writing up observations at home in the evening satisfactory? Also, use the pilot to test yourself. How do you present yourself? How should you dress and behave? How do you relate to others? How do you establish rapport? 'Learning an institution's rules and expectations, its major actors, and its taboos can direct you to personal behavior that will help you to gain access and keep it.'[21]

Collecting preliminary data

Gathering preliminary data at one or more of your 'real' case study sites enables you to test whether it or they are likely to be suitable sites for the investigation. It will be useful to bear in mind the factors identified above by Marshall and Rossman. Do they have an appropriate mix of structures, subjects and processes? Is there a likelihood of building trusting relations with subjects? Do you gain some assurance of data quality and project credibility? It is only by an initial testing of the waters that you can determine whether these conditions will be met by the selected locations and subjects. If they are not, then you will have to select additional locations or subjects – another example of the recursive nature of the qualitative research process.

Preliminary data collection also allows you to test whether the promised access, which should have been granted earlier as part of the selection process, actually materializes. That is, during the preliminary investigation are you able to gain entry, and how easily? As noted above, in one of our experiences this did not happen. If entry is not as easy as you think it should be, are there additional gatekeepers to be consulted? Are there unforeseen barriers or suspicions to be overcome, and if so, how?

Revising the broad plan

By now, both your work on the pilot project and your preliminary investigations at one or more of your actual case study sites are almost certain to have exposed some deficiencies in your plan of attack. This is *not* a major setback; it is perfectly normal and, indeed, to be expected. The reason you have undertaken these steps first is precisely to ensure that you have an opportunity to revise your broad plan.

In some rare cases, if the results of the pilot study suggest that a complete change of approach is needed, then a further pilot of the new methodology or approach may be necessary. In most cases, however, all that will be required is some minor adjustment to ensure that the work itself will go smoothly. One of the most important additional benefits of undertaking these initial steps is that you, the researcher, gain confidence that you can indeed carry out your project. Because a qualitative methodology relies so heavily on the abilities and experience of the researcher, a reasonable amount of self-confidence is always necessary.

Overall, this should be a very exciting stage of your project: for the first time, after much thought and planning, you are at last starting on the real research. At this stage, too, you are likely to realize how valuable the initial preparation has been – and, probably, how much more you will need to do before starting in earnest.

Review of Chapter 6

This chapter has dealt with what we term the broad exploratory phase of qualitative research, in which you actually begin your fieldwork by taking two major steps. The first of these involves the selection of locations and subjects in a process of searching, selecting and testing (although testing actually straddles the artificial boundary between this step and the next). Criteria for selecting both places and people are offered to help you decide on locations and subjects. A rather lengthy treatment of the access issue indicates the pivotal role this plays in qualitative investigation, and numerous guidelines are offered on how to negotiate entry successfully.

The chapter then discusses Step 6, which involves both planning and acting – planning in the sense of providing a blueprint we call the broad research plan, and activity in the field through pilot studies and preliminary data collection, both of which allow the research to gauge whether the appropriate methods, locations and subjects have been selected. In both steps detailed 'how-to' guidelines have been presented, but no amount of writing can substitute for actual experience. Therefore, with the ideas from this chapter in mind, it is advisable to start planning your own project and to think about how this planning can be supplemented by preliminary fieldwork. The following activities are intended to direct your thinking to the practical aspects of how to begin your own fieldwork.

Where to now?

After reviewing the focus questions at the start of this chapter, we suggest that you again turn to the knowledge management case study in the final chapter of this book, and ask yourself the questions listed below.

- Why was this particular organization chosen?
- How did the researcher negotiate access to this organization? Were there any conditions or limitations placed upon her access?
- Is there any evidence that a pilot study or preliminary data collection were undertaken?
- Based on the evidence in the published report, can you create a draft project outline for this study?

Further reading

Useful additional reading for the topics covered by this chapter are R. G. Burgess, *In the Field: An Introduction to Field Research*, Contemporary Social Research, 8

(London: Routledge, 1991); C. Glesne, *Becoming Qualitative Researchers: An Introduction*, 2nd edn (New York: Longman, 1998); and J. C. Johnson, *Selecting Ethnographic Informants*, Qualitative Research Methods, 22 (Newbury Park, CA: Sage, 1990). In addition several parts of C. Marshall and G. B. Rossman, *Designing Qualitative Research*, 3rd edn (Thousand Oaks, CA: Sage, 1999) are informative on the subject of fieldwork in general. For those who prefer a more anecdotal approach to understanding the pain and pleasure of fieldwork, a most entertaining volume is C. D. Smith and W. Kornblum, eds., *In the Field: Readings on the Field Research Experience* (Greenwood, CT: Praeger, 1996).

Notes

1 M. Emmison and P. Smith, *Researching the Visual: Images, Objects, Contexts and Interactions in Social and Cultural Inquiry* (Thousand Oaks, CA: Sage, 2000), p. 152.

2 M. L. Rice-Lively, 'Wired Warp and Woof: An Ethnographic Study of a Networking Class', *Internet Research*, **4** (4), 1994, p. 22.

3 C. Marshall and G. B. Rossman, *Designing Qualitative Research*, 2nd edn (Thousand Oaks, CA: Sage, 1995), p. 51.

4 C. Glesne, *Becoming Qualitative Researchers: An Introduction*, 2nd edn (New York: Longman, 1999), p. 28.

5 Ibid., p. 26.

6 For a full discussion of sampling categories see J. C. Johnson, *Selecting Ethnographic Informants*, Qualitative Research Methods, 22 (Newbury Park, CA: Sage, 1990), pp. 21–39. The discussion in this section draws heavily from Johnson's categories, which are particularly applicable in library-based qualitative research.

7 Ibid., p. 38.

8 C. Metoyer, 'Issues in Conducting Research in Culturally Diverse Communities', *Library & Information Science Research*, **22** (3), 2000, pp. 235–42.

9 Johnson, loc cit.

10 R. G. Burgess, *In the Field: An Introduction to Field Research*, Contemporary Social Research, 8 (London: Unwin Hyman, 1984), p. 38.

11 Ibid., p. 48.

12 Ibid., p. 49.

13 Glesne, op. cit., p. 35 refer to this activity as developing a 'lay summary' that addresses nine points: (1) who you are, (2) what you are doing and why, (3) what you will do with the results, (4) how the study site and participants were selected, (5) any possible benefits as well as risks to the participants, (6) the promise of confidentiality and anonymity to participants and site, (7) how often you would like to observe or hope to meet for interviews, (8) how long you expect each session to last, (9) requests to record observations and words by whatever means. While none but the most difficult manager would require such detail, this list is a useful reminder of what researchers should have considered for themselves before seeking entry to a location.

14 Burgess, op. cit., p. 45.

15 Based on a set of criteria posited by Marshall and Rossman, op. cit., p. 41.

16 Glesne, op. cit., p. 35.
17 See http://associate.com/gantt/.
18 Glesne, op. cit., p. 34.
19 Ibid., p. 38.
20 Ibid., p. 31.
21 Ibid., p. 38.

7 Observation

FOCUS QUESTIONS

• What are the main characteristics of unstructured observation as a qualitative research method?
• What are the various observation 'positions' on the participation continuum?
• What factors should be considered when selecting an appropriate observation position?
• How does one begin observation?
• How does one go about the actual observation process, and what does one observe?

Stage 3: focused activity

Once you have completed all the preliminary preparation (Stage 1) and broad exploration (Stage 2) for a qualitative study, it is time to begin the fieldwork. In our schema this is Stage 3: focused activity. In this chapter, after noting this stage and its several steps, we turn to the first data-collecting method, observation. Chapters 8, 9 and 10 then deal with the other data collection methods to be discussed, interviewing, group processes and historical study, before we move on to the final steps in this stage of the research project.

In the pyramid model (see Chapter 3, Figure 3.3, p. 38) the focused activity stage of fieldwork represents the pinnacle in which you finally collect data, amend the research plan if required, narrow your data-collecting activities, analyse data collected during fieldwork and report findings. The first three of these activities are discussed in this and the following three chapters. In the recursive model (see Chapter 3, Figure 3.2, p. 37) data collection is the third last in the series of activity 'boxes'.

Two types of observation

This discussion builds on the introduction to observation in Chapter 3 (pages 40–41), which might be worth re-reading before continuing with the present chapter. Two broad types of observation are described in the general research methods literature: structured and unstructured observation. *Structured observation* samples a predetermined event or activity, using a prearranged instrument or form into whose categories the observer records whether specific activities take place, when and how often. This might be numbers of enquirers who approach an information counter. A well designed data collection form will also make provision for some unanticipated activity to be recorded. This is essentially a quantitative research method, and so not considered further in this volume.[1]

Of interest in the present context is *unstructured observation*. Here the observer records any behaviour or event that is relevant to the research questions being investigated. This process is much more open-ended and, as with much qualitative research, is of particular benefit in exploratory research or when a situation is incompletely understood.

Why choose observation?

Every research method has its own inbuilt advantages and disadvantages. In qualitative just as in quantitative research the best approach is to make a considered choice of method or methods, bearing in mind not only these advantages and disadvantages but also the nature of the problem you have identified and the research questions you are asking. This was covered in greater detail in Chapter 6, in particular in the section 'Choice of data collection technique' and in the discussion of Table 6.1 (see pp. 94–96).

Advantages of observation

Having said that, what are the advantages and disadvantages of unstructured observation as a qualitative research technique? Within the context of information organizations there are probably seven *advantages* that make unstructured observation particularly attractive to qualitative researchers:

- It permits a variety of researcher perspectives or degrees of involvement with the situation or activity being observed.
- It has a present orientation, recording what occurs as it occurs.
- It has a 'reality verifying' character, whereby what people say they do can be compared with what they actually do. (All three of these characteristics are covered in more detail in the following section.)
- It allows behaviour to be observed in its natural setting. There is an obvious problem with the 'simulation' type of research, where behaviour is unlikely to be typical.
- It permits the study of people who may be unable to give their own reports of their activities. For example, very young children or the frail aged in nursing homes may be difficult to study using any other technique.
- It permits the study of people who may be unwilling to give their own reports of their activities. If you wanted (or needed) to study the behaviour of users improperly removing items from a repository, for example, no other method could be substituted.

- It enables data to be analysed in stages or phases as understanding of its meaning is gained. This is an advantage of most qualitative research methods.

Disadvantages of observation

With these advantages go a complementary set of *disadvantages* or limitations. Again within information organizations, there are six disadvantages that researchers should consider before adopting this technique for an investigation:

- People who are aware of being observed tend to change their behaviour. For this reason it is important for the observer to blend into the environment, to be taken for granted. Ways of achieving this are discussed later in the chapter; however, unless observation is truly covert, to some extent the observer will always be likely to have some effect on behaviour.
- This in turn raises questions of ethics, including not just the need for the researcher to gain permission to study a site, but also the rights of those being observed to privacy, to give informed consent to their taking part in a research project and, since their identities are usually known, to have any concerns about the confidentiality of the data collected properly addressed.
- It is not always possible to anticipate a spontaneous event and so be ready to observe it. This might be termed the 'watched pot' syndrome: it seems inevitable that, however many hours you spend on site, any disaster or sudden crisis will arise during your absence.
- Not all types of event lend themselves to observation. Some, such as personal growth and development, are too drawn out; others are too brief; still others are too personal or intimate; and some, of course, such as the unconscious decision processes users make during online searching, are not necessarily visible at all.
- Observation can be very time consuming, even when appropriate events and situations are chosen.
- Finally, the subjectivity of the observer must always be taken into account. This is especially the case if, as usually the case with information research, the researcher is also a professional with expertise and experience in the area under observation. (This too is considered in more detail later in this chapter.)

Careful, considered use of unstructured observation as a technique can help make best advantage of its strengths as a data collection technique and minimize, so far as possible, most of these inherent limitations.

Characteristics of observation in information settings

In the information professions, unstructured observation as a qualitative research method has a number of important characteristics. These include its variety of possible researcher perspectives, its present orientation, and its reality-verifying character. This section discusses each of these in turn.

Variety of researcher perspectives

As the overview of observation in Chapter 1 indicated, as a data collection technique observation can be unobtrusive, structured or participant. In fact, it does not consist of a set of discrete choices made by the researcher but appears rather as a range of flexible positions in a continuum of participatory involvement, moving from unobtrusive observer, through observer-as-participant and then participant-as-observer to complete participant (see Figure 7.1).[2]

As an unobtrusive observer the researcher functions, to the extent that this is possible, as a cipher, a simple recorder of events. In this capacity the researcher has little or no interaction with the people or events being observed. For example, a researcher may simply sit at a table in the reference section and watch how users and reference librarians interact, making detailed notes on the interactions. The researcher does not participate in any way in the interactions being observed, and none of the participants is made aware of the researcher's presence.

Observer-as-participant and participant-as-observer are perhaps subtle variations on a theme, with one role merging imperceptibly into the other. The observer-as-participant is essentially an observer but does interact to some degree with the research subjects, especially at later stages in the project. For example, one may observe unobtrusively the interactions of users and reference librarians, but then later interact with participants in order to verify or clarify observations. Thus Elfreda Chatman, in a study of retired women, regularly sat with her subjects in the retirement home, took part in their games and meals, and towards the end of the project interviewed a number of the participants.[3] She did not, however, become involved in the care of her subjects as a member of the home's staff.

The participant-as-observer, by contrast, interacts more extensively with the subjects. In this role the researcher takes part in events with them in order to achieve a closeness that would not otherwise be possible. Here the researcher does become involved as a participant in the lives of the subjects, advising, assisting and otherwise intervening in day-to-day events. In the knowledge management case study included in this volume as Chapter 14, for example, the researcher might have been employed as a temporary staff member in the organization. It is important in this sector of the continuum to recognize that 'a paradox develops as you become more of a participant and less of an observer. The more you function as a member of the everyday world of the researched, the more you risk losing the eye of the uninvolved outsider; yet, the more you participate, the greater your opportunity to learn.'[4]

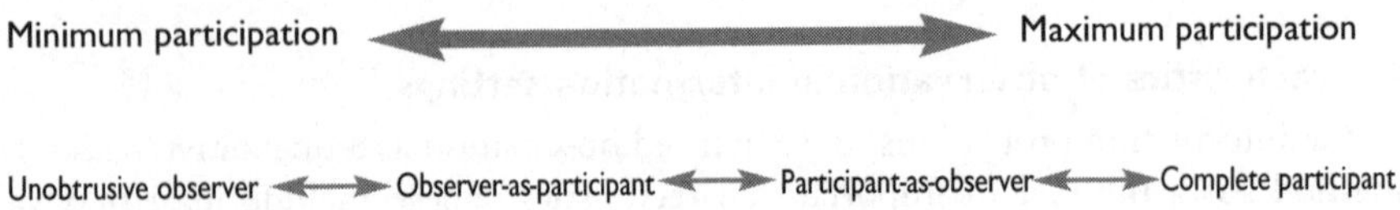

Minimum participation ◄――――――――――――――► Maximum participation

Unobtrusive observer ◄――► Observer-as-participant ◄――► Participant-as-observer ◄――► Complete participant

Figure 7.1 The participation continuum in observation

Finally, as a complete participant the researcher becomes an integral and fully active member of the community being studied. Thus Chatman might have entered the retirement home as a resident. The researcher in this situation is actually seeking to fill two distinct roles, as participant and as researcher, and this can lead to significant role conflict both within the researcher and the setting. Labaree has discussed some of what he calls the 'hidden dilemmas' of being a complete participant and at the same time conducting a research project.[5]

The researcher is able to select the role or position on the participation continuum which is most suited:

- to the questions being investigated
- to the environment in which observation occurs
- to the subjects being observed.

This variety of possible researcher perspectives gives observation more flexibility than most other data-collecting methods, and for this reason alone it is a powerful technique in the qualitative armoury. In most situations it is likely that the two middle roles – observer-as-participant and participant-as-observer – have most to commend them, for they allow considerable flexibility, whereas the roles at either extreme lock one into a specific mode, and in both cases that mode has severe limitations. In Chatman's view, unobtrusive observation 'means that the researcher is not privy to motivational factors or to subtle influences affecting behavior', whereas total participation 'means that the researcher has given up an important measure of objectivity in which to report data free of bias'.[6]

How does a researcher know which role to adopt in a particular investigation, or at a specific time in a project? This is a key question for most researchers – even those with considerable experience, who tend to fall back on known methods time after time rather than opting for less familiar techniques that might be more appropriate in a given situation. The only way to answer it is to consider the relevant contextual variables:

- the stage of the investigation
- the research questions being investigated
- the context of the investigation
- theoretical perspectives
- personal capabilities.

In the following paragraphs we consider each of these in turn.

In most projects involving observation the researcher begins as an unobtrusive observer, trying to understand how to fit in and become accepted by the subjects. Later in the same project the researcher may become more participatory as a means of drawing closer to the subjects in order to gain their confidence. Greater participation can also enable additional information to be gathered, perhaps to establish *why* participants are behaving in particular ways.

The research questions also help determine the type of observation employed. For example, a research question involving 'body language' of library staff in the circulation or ILL sections will almost certainly require unobtrusive observation, whereas questions related to job satisfaction of records management staff will probably require a certain amount of participation in the workplace.

Similarly, contextual constraints help determine the observer's role. For example, if one is studying reader education programmes in a school library, this situation may not permit observer-as-participant involvement because of the age factor that sets a researcher apart from pupils. On the other hand, in a university library the observer-as-participant role may be entirely appropriate if you are a younger person able to fit comfortably in the guise of a university student. What kind of rapport is necessary to achieve your ends, and what kind of rapport is possible? The answers to these questions may be mutually exclusive, requiring early adjustment either to the issue being investigated or the method of investigation.

With regard to theory, if a researcher is uncomfortable with a more scientific approach, then unobtrusive observation will not be very attractive whereas more interactive participatory techniques will be. This tends to be reflected in the initial theories adopted to give shape to an investigation.

An interesting example of participant observation is provided by the study of behaviour in internet chat rooms and online discussion lists. Here, it is well known that some of those online will be 'lurking': reading but not contributing to the discussion. If a researcher observed group behaviour online without contributing to the discussion, he or she is clearly an unobtrusive observer. However, the researcher could choose to move on to a role more akin to observer-as-participant or even participant-as-observer – but most would still start in the role of an unobtrusive observer. Such observation might be done anywhere, at any time, by anybody. An online study such as this also has the benefit that, by its nature, the fieldwork data come conveniently to hand already in electronic form.[7]

In the final analysis, where a researcher sits on the observation–participation continuum depends to a high degree on personal values and personality traits, especially the researcher's 'normal' behaviour. If, for example, a project requires a researcher to be less gregarious than normal, this role probably can be sustained only for a short time without frustration intruding on the quality of observation. On the other hand, a researcher who lacks confidence or who feels uneasy dealing with people in new, challenging situations will naturally tend towards techniques that are less participatory. An all-online study of the type mentioned in the previous paragraph could be ideal for such a researcher.

Research Scenario 7.1 provides an illustration of a study that used only relatively unobtrusive observation.

OBSERVATION IN A BRANCH LIBRARY

This scenario is based on the experience of one of the authors, at the time associate librarian in a university library. The university librarian was considering whether to close a small branch library, close to the main library and used principally by architecture and design students. I was asked to establish the usage patterns of this branch library. Five research questions were asked:

- How heavily is the branch library used?
- Does usage vary during the times the library is open?
- Who uses it?
- How is it used?
- What staffing is required to support this use?

The traditional statistics (loans, numbers of photocopies, and so on) kept by the branch library staff were considered inappropriate for a study such as this. ('Inappropriate' meant that the university librarian was not sure whether they could be believed.) Accordingly, I decided to carry out the study by using unobtrusive observation. Reasons for choosing this approach included that it would avoid pre-judging which activities might be significant; that, as the observer, I would gain an impression of the importance of services and activities, not just their frequency of occurrence; that by not interacting with users I would be less likely to alter their normal use of the library; and that the study could be completed over a limited period of time.

I was aware of the disadvantages of this approach before I started. These were that, because I was not concealed, my presence might still cause some changes to behaviour patterns, and that because of the limited time frame of the study, the observed patterns of behaviour might be atypical. Both of these concerns could only be addressed in part. I attempted to minimize my impact on the normal use of the library by sitting at a desk at the back, by taking other work with me in which I could be seen to be engaged, and by deliberately *not* asking students or staff what they were doing, or looking over their shoulders. However, the library was small and there was no place in which I could 'hide', as it were. Branch library staff were naturally asked who I was, and what I was doing – and enquirers were told I was interested only in overall patterns of use, not in what they as individuals were doing.

I structured my pattern of observation in an attempt to overcome the second potential problem, the limited time frame for this study, by:

- spreading out observation periods over a number of weeks in order to avoid choosing an atypical week (and so that users were more likely to become accustomed to my presence)
- observing at different times of the day, and on different days of the week; every period of the week in which the library was open was sampled at least once
- avoiding times at which usage might be expected to be abnormal (public holidays, non-teaching periods)

- discussing the observed usage with the branch library staff, and where they believed observed usage was atypical noting this in the final report; a draft copy of this was given to them before submission, in order to take account of these and other comments they might have.

I found that usually there were between six and 12 students in the library during normal office hours, with a minimum of two and a maximum of 22. Outside normal office hours and at the weekend, however, the library was very quiet, with only a couple of students working there or visiting. Accordingly, I recommended that evening and weekend opening hours be reconsidered.

Usage was mostly by students, with staff appearing to visit only in order to carry out a specific task or transaction, and then leave. On a couple of occasions a staff member stayed to work with a student in the library. However, it was not always possible for me to distinguish staff from mature age students without interrogating them, which I was reluctant to do.

Three separate but related patterns of use were observed, which I categorized as directly resource related, study related, and 'other' use. This categorization was developed and tested during the period I was in the library carrying out my observations, so arose directly from them. 'Resource related' use was of the materials provided by the library; 'study related' involved such activities as private study, use of scissors, stationery, group discussion and general social contact; 'other' activities included the borrowing and return of equipment such as slide projectors, and occupied relatively little time.

These patterns of use suggested that the library served at least as much as a study facility or laboratory for the faculty as it did as a library, and consequently the branch library staff were involved largely in clerical support activities, such as attending to the photocopier.

At the conclusion of this study, I suggested several options, which included reducing the branch library's hours of opening and staffing it professionally only part-time. However, for financial reasons the university librarian decided to close the library completely. Its staff and collections were transferred to the nearby main library. Several years later, this time as an academic member of the university's staff, the university librarian asked me to undertake a survey of undergraduate student needs. A new generation of undergraduates in that faculty, unprompted, said that their greatest need was for a resource collection/study facility/laboratory in their own faculty building, serving almost exactly the same role that the branch library once had.

In the study just described, note the use of what Sproull has termed 'time sampling'.[8] This was the use of spread-out periods of observation to ensure, so far as possible, that typical usage of the library was observed. Sproull recommends a similar approach to 'event sampling' if a series of recurring phenomena are to be observed.

In Research Scenario 7.1 the researcher stayed in the role of an unobtrusive observer throughout rather than gradually participating in the context of the branch library. This was partly because this was a study conducted within a quite short period of time, and partly because of the political sensitivities associated with it. The limited research questions asked were able to be answered without extending this approach.

Still, it is unrealistic to view the observer as a static object, for in reality the observer and the observer's perceptions change as observation progresses. If this does not occur, then one should question the validity of observer status and what is being observed. Observation, after all, is a way of becoming involved in a place, with subjects and events. As involvement increases, the observer begins to notice things that had been missed before, and begins to comprehend events and issues from the perspective of the subjects being observed. This certainly happened during the branch library study described above.

When this happens, the researcher often feels compelled to understand phenomena more deeply, to look for relationships between events or subjects that may lie well below the surface. To achieve this understanding, the researcher should be willing to adopt methods or techniques that might have seemed alien or risky at the outset of a project. This is for the observer

> a time of transformation, when a research persona emerges with a life of its own. This persona is one that fits your research field. It is not that you become some unrecognizable other person, but that, as you respond to the needs of being present somewhere in the role of researcher, you learn that you cannot just be the person you are in other settings playing more familiar roles. You are more or less yourself, moved to unexpected behavior in order to facilitate research opportunities and constrained from ordinary behavior that would interfere with your progress.[9]

No matter which role a researcher takes at any given time, there are always anxieties associated with one's presence in a new setting. At first the primary sensation is one of feeling unwanted and superfluous, of being hesitant and afraid to make mistakes. All of this should pass as you learn the norms of behaviour and begin to see how you can fit into the scenario. When the process seems threatening to self-esteem and too challenging, and it sometimes will, it helps to remember that you are there for a purpose and to achieve a specific end. The fact that you are gathering useful data should compensate for the initial uneasiness. Remember that you are only temporarily stepping into another environment; at the end you will be returning to your own ground, able to resume your normal personality and mode of behaviour.

Present orientation

A second characteristic, the present focus or 'here-and-now' orientation, means that you are able to record what is happening at the present time in a natural setting. That is, you observe activities or events in their context and record them at the time they take place. Such data are thus unclouded by memory or time, which should give them greater purity. For example, interviewing service desk staff at the end of a particularly busy shift may be particularly fraught with difficulties: not only are people tired, but they also may be unable to remember precisely what occurred and when because of pressures at the time. Quantitative statistics kept by reference staff are notoriously suspect, for that very reason.[10] Observation overcomes this problem by permitting you to note precisely what occurred as it happened. This 'here-and-now' orientation in turn complements the third characteristic, which we term reality-verifying.

Reality-verifying

The reality-verifying characteristic means that the researcher is able to compare what subjects may say they do or believe – their 'espoused' beliefs – with what they actually do or manifest as belief when observed in practice. Is it a matter of 'do as I say' or 'do as I do'? If there is any doubt about the accuracy of staff self-perceptions (as there was about the statistics collected by the staff in the branch library study) data from an objective observer may be more credible.

'One problem researchers encounter is that participant reports of activities and beliefs may not match their observed behavior. Participant observation is a check, enabling the researcher to verify that individuals are doing what they (and the researcher) believe they are doing.'[11] Thus if data are collected by means of interviews, for instance, observation allows the researcher to elaborate on these data by either confirming or questioning their accuracy by means of observing actual behaviour or an event in its natural setting.

Reality verification, in other words, contributes to triangulation and to construct validity. This, together with its variety of possible researcher perspectives and present orientation, is one of the real strengths of the technique of observation. It is now time to describe how the process of observation itself is carried out.

The observation process in information settings

When a competent researcher engages in observation, three questions are constantly being asked:

- What is going on?
- Am I seeing only what I hope or expect to see?
- Why am I doing this?

First, you must constantly analyse what is being observed in order to tease out the meaning in these observations. This gives direction to the study, as well as meaning, at the time phenomena are observed. Second, you want to be certain that your personal views or bias are not clouding what is being observed, or perhaps filtering out whatever does not fit your preconceived theoretical framework. This second question actually exists in creative tension with the third question, which you need to ask as a means of keeping the research on track. That is, the broad goals and objectives of the research, the main research questions, must be kept in mind so that the research continues moving forward – but never to the exclusion of unexpected but still important observations that, if powerful enough, *will* change the direction and focus of a project.

With these questions in mind, and having gained access to the chosen site, you are at last ready to begin fieldwork. Uncertainty, confusion, nervousness, perhaps even a hint of fear, often characterize the start of observation in the field. After all, this is when you are bound to make most mistakes, will have least rapport with subjects, and are most likely to be misunderstood. Whether one is inexperienced or quite an old hand at the game, there is always a certain amount of anxiety at the beginning of data collection, much as an actor feels 'first night' nerves no matter how many opening nights have been experienced.

It helps to know that all researchers go through the same painful experience at the beginning of every project, and to have a few hints on how to minimize feelings of anxiety and incompetence. The basic and overriding rule is 'softly, softly'; but we can expand this into five procedures and characteristics that you might usefully cultivate at the outset:

- ease yourself into the context
- place yourself carefully
- be approachable and friendly
- be receptive
- dress and behave appropriately.

Ease yourself into the context

It helps to start with what is easy. That is, locate subjects with whom you feel some rapport and use them as a safe starting point, a springboard to more challenging situations. By dealing with friendly, easy-going individuals at the outset, you are able to foster self-confidence while also learning the lie of the land. As these individuals come to accept your presence as non-threatening, try to give them an idea of what you are doing and how you are doing it, so that they can explain the process to others. Usually those familiar with you will be quizzed by their colleagues, in much the same way as we ask co-workers about their impressions of a new staff member.

It often helps that an initial contact, say the person from whom permission was sought or a colleague known from another context, will offer to make initial introductions and to show you around. Unless there are very good reasons for doing otherwise (for instance, you wish to remain anonymous, or you feel that this person may not be acceptable to the other subjects), it is advisable to use this contact as your entrée to a site, as it can save considerable time.

At the very beginning it is probably best not to make too many notes in the field but simply to get a feel for the place and its inhabitants (making notes at the end of the day). Spend relatively few hours at a time on site until the subjects begin to accept your presence as 'normal'.

Place yourself carefully

Part of easing yourself into the context involves gaining a sense of place, and of learning where you can go that is neutral and non-threatening to the subjects. Neutrality is important if you are to gain confidence of the people being observed. For example, observing subjects from a supervisor's desk conveys a very strong message – you are identified with the supervisor's authority, for good or ill. Therefore, it is important to learn which places are not identified with a particular individual or authority figure. These should be used as your sites early in the project as a means of getting to know subjects where they are most likely to behave in a natural manner.

Having gained confidence of subjects by relating to them in neutral settings (a tea room, for example), you are then more likely to be accepted as an observer in the work area. However, this raises another aspect of placing oneself carefully. That is, never assume that permission granted by the chief librarian to conduct research gives you carte blanche to intrude wherever you like. Always ask permission of those whose work space you will be invading: if you are observing archives users, for example, ask the service desk staff or others whose area is the primary focus. On the whole, covert observation, if taken to mean that no one knows what is occurring, is not acceptable in an information agency.

Be approachable and friendly

This point should not require discussion, but in fact many researchers forget to consider their personal presentation at the beginning of a study and thereby create unnecessary barriers to observation. As a researcher you do not exist on some higher or external plane, but are actually part of the workplace. Arrogance, or nervousness masquerading as arrogance, will be repaid in kind, and it will become much more difficult to gain the confidence of your subjects. Our advice is to behave naturally, to be reasonably approachable and as friendly as you would be in your own workplace. This does not mean behaving like an Irish Setter, but simply showing common courtesy and respect.

Most important, when asked, be willing to tell people why you are there and what you hope to achieve, and do this with some enthusiasm and without any pretension. Berg has some advice on this:

> Researchers should remember that when they explain their presence in the field to locals, it is not a good idea to elaborate on technical aspects of the study. Generally, inhabitants are only interested in hearing a cursory answer to the questions, What are you doing here? and Who are you? A brief response typically will suffice. It is important,

however, to answer any questions these inhabitants may ask about the project as clearly and truthfully as possible.[12]

It is useful to know how to open conversations with your subjects, and how to discuss matters in a general and uncontroversial manner. You are an information professional dealing with information personnel or users so there should be many common points of interest; these should be used as conversational gambits. But in these conversations it is important that you remain neutral and avoid the use of prying questions.

Be receptive

The corollary to being approachable is being receptive to others and to what they say. Again, early in the piece this may not be as simple as it sounds. After all, you will probably be in a strange organization, trying to find your own way. Listening to others, especially if they are criticizing you or what you are seeking to achieve, can be quite offputting. In fact, it is important not to take criticism personally.

Part of being receptive means that you are open to what you see. As a professional observing in a professional setting, the tendency is to bring preconceived ideas to the site, having 'been there, done that' yourself. Instead, remember why you are there – to learn about that unique site and those specific subjects.

Every researcher experiences some alienating behaviour during the opening days of a project. After all, some people will be suspicious or will not understand why you are there, and one way of expressing this is to be critical. 'It seems pointless for you to study this here, because research is just a waste of time, and we really don't have either space or time ourselves to accommodate you' is the kind of blanket criticism that most researchers hear. Use this criticism constructively, and try to show by example that you will be relatively unobtrusive, that you will not impinge unnecessarily on your subjects' professional activity.

Dress and behave appropriately

In the final analysis none of the preceding pointers on how to begin an observation-based data collection project will succeed if you stand out as 'different' because of your dress or behaviour. You are not entering a particular context in order to make a personal statement, after all, but as a means of learning from others without affecting the message being conveyed. This means that you should dress to suit the situation, to fit in, and follow the lead of those with whom you wish to identify.

In most libraries, archives and information agencies the dress codes are unstated, but nevertheless very real. They often reflect one's status within the system. Among men, for example, a more junior staff member might dress somewhat casually in open-necked shirt and jumper; the section head might add a tie, and the division manager a jacket. Further up the hierarchy a suit rather than a jacket might be the norm, with the 'chief executive' favouring dark pinstripes because this is the 'uniform' of those with whom he associates. (As male authors, we must allow our women readers to make the appropriate sartorial adjustments to these comments!)

If, in order to fit into the appropriate category, this means that you must wear smart, relatively formal clothes when you normally wear jeans and a threadbare jumper, then take time to adjust to the new way of dressing so that it does not feel uncomfortable and interfere with your observations. This is an important point. Many researchers in organizations tend to dress too casually. If in doubt, err on the side of formality – you can always take off your coat and roll up your sleeves.

It is too late to realize that you are dressed inappropriately when you arrive on the morning of your first fieldwork visit. Often, you will have needed to visit your host organization in order to arrange access. If not, visit your site as a user, and note what people are wearing, where offices and service desks are, and generally orient yourself in advance.

As with dress, it makes good sense not to behave in too boisterous or too passive a fashion (even if either is your normal behaviour). This tends not to instil confidence in you as either a researcher or a confidante – and remember that you may well want subjects to confide in you. Without coming across as 'Twit of the Year', the researcher should behave in a manner that is discreet, restrained and trustworthy. In practice, this means that you try to fit in with the normative behaviour of the situation being studied, and of those with whom you seek to identify. (Incidentally, 'normative' is a word often come across in a research context. By it we mean the assumed standard of correctness: what people say or believe they *should* do – whatever they may do in practice, which might be 'normal'.)

You want to be accepted as one of the group. This will help you collect your data without calling attention to the fact that you are collecting data. Notes should for the most part be written when you are on your own. Also, you should resist divulging what you have learned to others who may report back to your subjects. Keep the content of your notes as confidential information. The only exception will be when you are directly asked to show your data: here, it may be churlish to refuse. Show some of your data and explain them briefly, without talking about any conclusions you may have reached. After all, as your observation continues your tentative conclusions may well change significantly.

Problems and difficulties you may experience should be discussed only with people outside the site of your research. Even when subjects clearly are incorrect in their views or are feeding you information that you know to be inaccurate, it does not pay to disagree with them as this will create a barrier. Furthermore, you may learn something unsavoury – for example, that a administrative staff member is doing private work during office hours, or that a senior member of staff is misusing, even misappropriating, organizational resources. One of us was once told by several staff of someone using sexual favours to gain advancement. Leaving ethical issues aside for the moment, you should avoid allowing knowledge of such behaviour to colour your views of information provided by these individuals. If this cannot be avoided, try to seek other subjects against whom you are not biased.

Making observations in information settings

At the beginning of immersion in a site, the researcher should try to make note of everything that happens. That is, pay little attention to the research questions, and instead make notes that will help define and refine the problem, remembering that what you see during observation contributes to the shape and direction of the research. The setting, participants, conversations and events are all equally important at this stage, and you should make detailed notes on all of them. The setting (in which participants exist and conversations and events occur) should be described in as much detail as possible, including notes on elements that might seem inconsequential: the furniture, lighting, arrangement of shelving, floor covering, amount of space, noise levels, and so on. In many cases, the use of a camera equipped with a flash will enable some of these physical details to be documented photographically – some of the newer digital cameras are especially small and unobtrusive.

It is, in fact, much easier to make these observations at this stage of the research than it will be later. Now you see the situation with the eyes of a newcomer; later it will all appear as you expect, precisely because it has become familiar.

The intention in such careful description of place is to open up possibilities for insight that would not exist if one were less observant. The participants (who exist within settings and who are the actors in events) should be described in terms of all variables that might prove useful – age, gender, appearance, demeanour, interactions with others, and so on. Also, conversations should be noted, with special attention to content, tone, intention, gestures, nature of message (both verbal and nonverbal). Finally, events (which occur in settings and are the vehicles for participant action) should be described, as these carry the messages of participants. Try to view the event as a whole, and then break it down into its component parts, as this will help understand precisely what is happening:

- *Setting.* Where is the event taking place? What does the setting look like? Will a diagram or sketch help describe it? What does the setting *feel* like?
- *Participants.* Who is taking part? What do they look like? Do some appear to have different roles from others?
- *Conversations.* What types of conversations seem to be taking place? Can you record sample or typical conversations word for word? What non-verbal messages are being exchanged?
- *Events.* What are the events taking place? Can they be categorized in some way?

As you ease yourself into your setting, you will start to take many of these matters for granted. This is the time to review your initial research questions: do they still seem the right questions to ask? Are there other questions which seem worth considering? Do your observations so far suggest tentative answers to some questions, which subsequent observation may be able to test? This is precisely the non-linear, iterative or recursive approach which is typical of qualitative research (see the discussion of this in Chapter 3, and the discussion of Figure 3.2, p. 37). At this stage, too, you will almost certainly wish to interview some participants as well as merely observe their actions.

Making observations is thus a complex task, as you are looking at multiple factors (setting, participants, events, self), which together and individually carry data-rich messages. As you are observing and absorbing, it is essential to be fully aware of what is being seen and heard, and to be aware of your reactions and thoughts to these stimuli. At the outset it is best to focus on behaviour rather than on the individuals manifesting the behaviour, as it is the behaviour that carries the messages in events. Pay less attention to physical appearance initially. As you become familiar with the setting, participants and events, certain aspects will begin coming to the fore, suggesting themselves as features for special attention. Do not try to rush this, as rushing tends to force issues rather than letting them emerge naturally. Finally, as with most things, experience and familiarity will help bring self-confidence and, with careful application, mastery.

Dealing with subjective reactions

One of the benefits of observing settings, participants and events is the enhancement of what we have called experience-near phenomena. Such nearness, of course, runs the risk of causing you to react to them, especially with feelings of sympathy or outrage. For example, you may feel sympathetic towards a client who clearly is confused in a library and receives short shrift from the staff when asking for assistance, or may feel outrage upon learning that a senior archivist is using 'stand-over' tactics to control junior staff.

There are two points to be made about the self and personal reactions. First, your own reactions to events or feelings about what you observe, especially if they are different from the reactions of your subjects, can clearly introduce bias into the observation process. This must be recognized from the outset, and a competent researcher will be on guard for the appearance of bias. We all know when our own feelings come into play; in a research setting we cannot become involved by intervening, losing our temper or behaving in a disruptive manner. Rather, the best approach is to make notes of your feelings. Part of note taking should be a safety value for your own emotions. Once written down, the feelings can be dealt with more objectively, and can also lead to new observations as other emotion-laden observations are made. If you are reading through your own notes much later, or perhaps working on a group project, these observations of your emotions will also help you or your colleagues take into account any possible bias in analysing your data.

Second, personal feelings or reactions, especially if they are shared by the subjects, can have a positive impact on research. In particular, your own, non-objective reactions to an event or phenomenon can be used to establish rapport with subjects who appear to have similar reactions. 'I know how you feel about...' or 'That was a pretty disturbing scene...' and similar comments can break down barriers that otherwise might be a significant hindrance to close relations between you and a subject. Likewise, our own feelings can enrich our understanding of a subject's perceptions.

Renato Rosaldo presents a more detailed discourse on subjectivity and personal feelings in research, and how they can be used to advantage. This work is recommended for anyone who feels that this is likely to be a significant issue in a particular research project.[13] You must, of course, make certain that the notes you take clearly differentiate your reactions from the events which they also record. One convention for doing this is to enclose your reactions in brackets. Any discussion of the degree to which an observer becomes emotionally involved in the situation under observation leads naturally to the next major consideration: how should issues of reliability and validity be addressed?

Reliability and validity

The second question, noted above, that should be asked during the observation process was, 'Am I seeing only what I hope or expect to see?' The preconceptions we bring with us to a study site, and the knowledge and expertise we have as professionals in the area, can blind us to what is actually going on. Any variation between what is actually happening and what we think we see can introduce both inconsistency and lack of credibility or, using the technical terms introduced in Chapter 3, problems with both reliability and validity.

Just as one of the ways in which the reliability and validity of qualitative research in general can be improved is by using a plurality of methods, triangulation, so can the reliability and validity of an observational study be improved by the use of a variety of observers. As we all know, different people will see different things, even when observing the same reality. In some social science circles this is known as the 'Rashomon effect', after the Kurosawa film of the same name. In it, the accounts of an event from different observers amounted to completely different stories; one might reasonably conclude that these accounts were not particularly reliable.

If you can employ different observers, do so. The different perspectives gained from different observers with different backgrounds, experiences and approaches can be invaluable; so too, the ability of the team to discuss their observation experiences together afterwards. However, you will need to make sure that there is some degree of commonality in approach. This is not to say that everyone should be asked to look for exactly the same things; indeed they should not, or else why employ a team at all? However, it is clearly desirable that all members have had adequate research method preparation, are interested in the same or similar research questions, and adopt compatible note-taking methods.

There is another way of gaining some of the benefit of having different observers of a situation. If the field notes that record it are sufficiently full and descriptive, then another reader or readers can examine these and see if their conclusions match those of the original observer or, at least, whether the observer's conclusions seem reasonable and are justified by the notes taken.

Finally, we expect that in practice few will be likely to use observation as a technique on its own. Most observation studies involve at least some interviewing, and even the almost purely observational study reported above as Research Scenario 7.1 (p. 109) also drew upon both the quantitative statistics collected by the branch library staff, and their comments on the draft report. Both added elements of triangulation.

Note taking

How should you record all these observations? Taking field notes is considered in some detail in Chapter 11. There are, however, some points we need to make in this chapter. The first of these is that you should allow yourself to be guided in large part by what you find. After all, why adopt a qualitative methodology if you then attempt to see a situation primarily in terms of the preconceptions you brought with you? This means that your note taking as well as your personal observation should reflect the setting, participants, conversations and events that you see around you. If you start to see a pattern that may be significant, create a category of some kind to record this so that you provide an opportunity for later reflection about it.

Next, we would wish to stress the importance of taking notes either as events unfold, or at least on the same day – and preferably at both times. Berg's advice was to complete field notes 'immediately following every excursion into the field, as well as following every chance meeting with inhabitants outside the boundaries of the study setting (for example, at the supermarket, in a doctor's office, at a traffic light, and so on)'.[14] He recommended recording key words and facts while in the field, making notes about the sequence of events, not attempting to observe for too long a period at once, writing up your full notes immediately after exiting from the field, and getting your notes written before talking about your findings with any colleagues, lest the conversation cloud or 'embellish' subsequent recollection.

Always ensure that your notes include the date, time of day and location where the observations were made. How are the notes to be made? A small notebook is least obtrusive; a tape recorder can ensure everything is caught – at least, if participants talk sufficiently loudly and clearly adjacent to it; and a computer (ideally a lap-top used on location) most flexible. The pros and cons of tape recording are considered more fully in the next chapter, on interviewing; it will rarely be appropriate in a purely observational study. As mentioned above, though, however they are recorded, verbatim quotations can add immeasurably to the life and credibility of a research report.

As noted, a camera can be valuable to record the physical appearance of a study site. Another alternative sometimes seen in information research is the use of video recording. While individual transactions may not necessarily be discernible, patterns of activity can become very apparent. Time-lapse photography, for example, has been employed to show peak periods, queue length and waiting time at a library circulation desk.[15] In an observational study where every effort has to be made to address the issue of subjectivity, the apparent objectivity of photography may also be welcome – 'apparent' because, as we all know, photographs and video recordings too can mislead.

Finally, consider the security of your notes. If they are in a small notebook, its accidental loss could be devastating. Perhaps pages should be removed and filed securely once completed, or alternatively photocopied and the copies securely filed. If you use a computer, ensure you have backup disks, ideally stored in another location. However you record your field notes, how are you going to ensure that others cannot read them without your consent, and that of the participants? It is simply not acceptable to leave such confidential and potentially embarrassing material in an unlocked desk drawer on site.

Review of Chapter 7

This chapter started by placing fieldwork, and observation as one particular technique used in fieldwork, in the context of the overall research project. This is the point at which you finally start to collect data, amend the research plan if required, and narrow your data-collecting activities.

Unstructured observation is a technique that uses a variety of researcher perspectives in a continuum ranging from unobtrusive observer through observer-as-participant and participant-as-observer to complete participant. Choice of an appropriate position on this continuum will depend on the stage of the investigation, the research questions being investigated, the context of the investigation, the theoretical perspectives involved and your own personal capabilities.

Valuable aspects of observation as a research method include its present orientation and reality-verifying character. In the process of observation you ease yourself into the context, placing yourself carefully, being approachable and friendly, receptive, and dressing and behaving appropriately. In making observations you should focus only gradually upon the research questions in order to open up possibilities for insight. By recording your own subjective reactions to the events you are observing, you can hope to distance yourself from them, one important way in which you can address questions of reliability and validity, along with the use of research colleagues. Finally, note taking should be undertaken as close in time as possible to the events being recorded.

Where to now?

Once again, we suggest that you review the focus questions at the start of this chapter. Then, as in Chapters 4 and 5, we suggest that you might find analysis of a published research report valuable. We recommend you either obtain a copy of an article by Tami Echavarria and her colleagues, which was published in *College & Research Libraries*,[16] or perhaps the more recent article by Merchant and Hepworth, recommended below as further reading. For either of these items consider the following five questions:

- What position on the participation continuum did the investigators adopt? Why did they adopt this position, and would they have had any other alternative?
- How did they ease themselves into this study?
- Did they have any subjective reactions to this study? Did they appear to take any steps to counteract these?
- Would you have chosen the same approach, and why, or why not?
- Do the conclusions from this study appear to be supported?

By now it should be apparent that, towards the complete participant end of the participation continuum, the boundaries between observation and interviewing begin to get very blurred. This is only to be expected, and in the following chapter we turn to interviewing as a research technique often used to complement observation.

Further reading

Several items provide a useful starting point for further reading on observation as a research technique, two of which address it from a methodological perspective. Most recent is J. Rowley, in 'Researching People and Organizations.' *Library Management*, **25** (4/5), 2004, pp. 208–14, an article which also discusses case studies and action research. In 'Information Literacy of Teachers and Pupils in Secondary Schools', L. Merchant and M. Hepworth report on a study of the information literacy of teachers and pupils in two UK schools, which involved observation of ten teachers and 40 pupils in the classroom, complemented by observation of pupils' behaviour in the school library and computing facilities: *Journal of Librarianship and Information Science*, **34** (2), June 2002, pp. 81–9.

V. J. Janesick's curiously titled *'Stretching' Exercises for Qualitative Researchers*, 2nd edn (Thousand Oaks, CA: Sage, 2003) uses the dancing class as a metaphor:

> Stretching implies that you are moving from a static point to an active one. It means you are going beyond the point at which you now stand. Just as the dancer must stretch to begin what eventually becomes the dance, the qualitative researcher may stretch to become better at observation and interview skills.[17]

Accordingly, Janesick includes a number of observation (and interview) exercises to help the new researcher actually see what is in front of him or her.

Still useful is J. D. Glazier's 'Structured Observation: How it Works', *College & Research Libraries News*, **46**, March 1985, pp. 105–8, which reports on a project designed to test structured observation as a research methodology, and determine information use patterns of a specific target group. Alternatively, an example of observation in use is provided by J. E. Lashbrook in 'Using a Qualitative Research Methodology to Investigate Library Media Skills Instruction', *School Library Media Quarterly*, **14**, 1986, pp. 204–9. This describes a study that included participant observation as well as collection of life stories from informants and use of structured interviews.

Notes

1 Brief details of its use appear in standard texts such as N. L. Sproull, *Handbook of Research Methods: A Guide for Practitioners and Students in the Social Sciences*, 2nd edn (Metuchen, NJ: Scarecrow, 1995), pp. 247–50. See also our own forthcoming work, *The Information Professional's Guide to Qualitative Research: a Practical Handbook* (working title) (London: Facet, 2006).

2 L. Westbrook, 'Qualitative Research Methods: A Review of Major Stages, Data Analysis Techniques and Quality Controls', *Library & Information Science Research*, **16**, 1994, p. 243. Westbrook credits Raymond Gold with having devised these categories; see R. L. Gold, 'Roles in Sociological Field Observation'. In *Issues in Participant Observation: A Text and Reader,* eds. G. J. McCall and J. L. Simmons, Addison-Wesley Texts in Behavioral Science (Reading, MA: Addison-Wesley, 1969), pp. 30–9.

3 E. A. Chatman, 'Life in a Small World: Applicability of Gratification Theory to Information-seeking Behavior', *Journal of the American Society for Information Science*, **42** (6), 1991, pp. 438–49.

4 C. Glesne, *Becoming Qualitative Researchers: An Introduction*, 2nd edn (New York: Longman, 1999), p. 44.

5 R. V. Labaree, 'The Risk of "Going Observationalist": Negotiating the Hidden Dilemmas of Being an Insider Participant Observer'. *Qualitative Research*, **2** (1), 2002, pp. 97–122.

6 E. A. Chatman, *The Information World of Retired Women*. New Directions in Information Management, 29 (Westport, CT: Greenwood, 1992), p. 3.

7 L. Kendall, 'Recontextualizing "Cyberspace": Methodological Considerations for Online Research'. In S. Jones, ed., *Doing Internet Research: Critical Issues and Methods for Examining the Net* (Thousand Oaks, CA: Sage, 1999), pp. 57–74.

8 Sproull, op. cit., p. 170.

9 Glesne, op. cit., p. 60.

10 J. M. Maxstadt, 'A New Approach to Reference Statistics', *College & Research Libraries News*, February 1985, pp. 85–8.

11 M. LeCompte, J. Preissle and R. Tesch, *Ethnography and Qualitative Design in Educational Research* (New York: Academic, 1993), p. 197.

12 B. L. Berg, *Qualitative Research Methods for the Social Sciences*, 2nd edn (Boston: Allyn and Bacon, 1995), p. 105.

13 R. Rosaldo, *Culture and Truth: The Remaking of Social Analysis* (Boston: Beacon, 1989).

14 Berg, op. cit., p. 107.

15 C. E. Kenchington, 'On-Line Circulation System at James Cook University of North Queensland'. In *Outpost: Australian Librarianship '73: Proceedings of the 17th Biennial Conference of the Library Association of Australia* (Perth: Library Association of Australia, 1974), p. 469.

16 T. Echavarria, et al., 'Encouraging Research Through Electronic Mentoring: A Case Study.' *College & Research Libraries*, **56** (4), July 1995, pp. 352–61.

17 V. J. Janesick, *'Stretching' Exercises for Qualitative Researchers* (Thousand Oaks, CA: Sage, 1998), pp. 1–2.

8 Interviewing

FOCUS QUESTIONS

- What are the principal advantages and disadvantages of interviewing as a qualitative research method?
- What preparation must be made before commencing a series of intensive interviews?
- What factors should be considered when deciding whether to tape record interviews and, if taped, whether to have the tapes transcribed?

Why interview?

The most obvious way of finding information is to ask someone who may be able to help. All of us routinely use this technique in an informal way in daily life. Interviews also have a large number of potential advantages for a qualitative researcher; these are alluded to in the brief introduction to interviewing in Chapter 3. Specifically, in an information setting five of these advantages are especially significant:

- immediacy
- mutual exploration
- investigation of causation
- personal contact
- speed.

The first advantage of interviewing is that it allows you to receive an immediate response to a question, unlike other forms of data collection (for example postal surveys), which may result in significant delays in the data collection process. In addition, interviewing allows both parties to explore the meaning of questions posed and answers proffered, and to resolve any ambiguities. Open-ended questions, in particular, may lead to unexpected insights. The third advantage is that interviewing can enable a researcher to explore causation, that is, to enquire into *why* individuals or organizations behave in the way that they do – something that most quantitative research cannot really answer.

Interviewing gives a friendlier and more personal emphasis to the data collection process. As a result, individuals reluctant to take part in a quantitative research study may agree to be interviewed. Personal contact may also be of special importance if the questions refer to any matters that are confidential, unflattering, embarrassing or sensitive in any way. In addition, not having to write such sensitive details down may be significant. Fifth, interviews facilitate the collection of a large quantity of rich data in a relatively short space of time, as most of us can talk much more quickly than we can write.

A final point is less likely to have much impact in the information settings with which most of us are familiar; that is, interviewing may also be appropriate if respondents are unable to read or write for some reason (such as young children, the illiterate or the infirm aged). This may well have been the case in some of Chatman's research in more 'unconventional' information settings, such as homes for the elderly or among partially illiterate maintenance staff, or indeed the more recent study by Durrance and her colleagues of the information needs of immigrants.[1] In more traditional settings illiteracy is less likely to occur.

For all that, these potential advantages may come at a price. In particular interviews may be:

- costly
- uncritical
- too personal
- especially open to bias.

With regard to cost, one-to-one interviews can consume a frightening amount of researcher time, both in their execution and in their recording if written transcripts are needed. Second, lack of selectivity means that sorting out the important points from a large quantity of data can be difficult, and may raise questions about selective reporting. 'Verbal data, by virtue of its quantity and varying degrees of structure, are particularly susceptible to errors in interpretation.'[2] Third, because interviews are face-to-face events, anonymity is lost. This may be of particular concern if potentially sensitive or embarrassing data is sought, and can, of course, lead to interviewees being tempted to lie or omit to mention some relevant facts. In other circumstances, both interviewee and interviewer may find the experience emotionally draining. Finally, the ever-present danger of bias may be overwhelming. The approach, personality and even appearance of the interviewer always has a significant effect on the quality and direction of an interview – and even on whether agreement is reached for an interview to be held at all.

All of these potential problems suggest that, as with any research method, the interview is best seen as only one of a number of approaches to data collection. As previously noted, this technique of triangulation is one of the best ways of addressing weaknesses in any single research method.

Types of interview

There are two basic types of interview: structured and unstructured. *Structured or survey interviews* are those where 'the questions and the answer categories have been predetermined' by the interviewer.[3] While this type of interview is occasionally used as an adjunct to qualitative research, its primary value is in an interview survey – that is, for a survey whose data is gathered by tightly controlled interviews rather than by a questionnaire. Written questions are read out using as close to the same wording every time, and answers are coded into predetermined categories, sometimes using response cards to assist respondents choose appropriate answers. This is principally a quantitative methodology, and so is not considered further here. No doubt because of their value in market research, much has been written about the design and execution of such surveys.[4]

Unstructured interviews are often referred to as in-depth or intensive interviews. (The terms 'in-depth' and 'intensive' are used interchangeably in the literature, and in this chapter.) Here, neither the exact wording of the questions nor the answers have been predetermined, although it is usual to have a set of questions or interview guide prepared as a starting point. Instead, through an interactive conversation the research issue or range of issues are explored in as much length as necessary or available.

Following Patton, unstructured interviews may themselves be divided into a range of sub-types.[5] In a standardized open-ended interview, the exact wording and sequence of questions is, in fact, decided in advance. Because respondents answer the same questions in the same order, all issues are covered and responses can be compared between interviews. However, obviously some flexibility is lost, and the interviews may become somewhat formal. Using an interview guide, a second approach, the topics are specified in advance but the wording of them is spontaneous; this enables the interview to be more natural and conversational. It is easier for the interviewer to respond to points made by the interviewee, and to gather quite detailed, comprehensive data. Nevertheless, it is possible some issues may be inadvertently overlooked, and different respondents are inevitably asked slightly different questions, limiting the usefulness of comparisons between interviews. Finally, in an informal conversational interview, the questions emerge from the discussion itself and the researcher is led by the discussion to a much greater extent. This is an exploratory interview, and the organization and synthesis of data from such interviews is not straightforward. This last category is less suited for an inexperienced interviewer.

Characteristics of interviewing in information settings

As is so often the case with qualitative research, interviewing seems so natural that the reader may wonder why we have decided to devote a chapter to it. Surely this is something we have all learned to do since childhood? While this may be true, we have not necessarily learned to gather specific data from strangers with minimal intrusion of personality issues, and keeping an accurate record of all that is said.

In preparation for interviewing you will need to consider who should be interviewed, what questions need to be asked, and when and where the interviews should take place. Reliability and validity will also need to be considered. Each of these is now discussed in turn. Following Research Scenario 8.1, we will then consider how interviews might be recorded and, if tape recorded, whether the time and expense of transcription will be warranted.

Who should be interviewed?

How should you go about choosing who should be interviewed? In quantitative research, *random selection* of respondents is normally used. Statistically, 'random' sampling means that every member of a population has an exactly equal chance of being selected. The advantage of random sampling is that meaningful statistical analysis can be carried out on the findings, because a representative sample of the population is most likely to be obtained.

The same technique can be applied in qualitative research, again in order to obtain a representative sample even though no statistical analysis is intended. You could, perhaps, get a staff list for an organization you are about to study and number every name listed. Then, by using a table of random numbers (found in the back of most quantitative research methods texts), you could randomly select potential interviewees.

While this approach is theoretically possible, it is not common. If you can only interview a relatively small number of people, you might not happen to select some in important sub-groups (for example, in a library you might wish to include both reader services and technical services staff). Most qualitative researchers prefer to select a *purposive sample*. This is one chosen by the researcher to include representatives from within the population being studied who have a range of characteristics relevant to the research project. To return to the library example, as well as both reader services and technical services staff, you may wish to include professional, para-professional and support staff; or junior and senior staff; long-serving and recently appointed staff; both men and women, and so on. If the research question is related to perceived chances of promotion within the organization, all of these groups may have different perspectives which it would be useful to incorporate.

This approach to choosing representatives from particular groups is known as *stratification*. In geology a stratum is a layer of sedimentary rock; by analogy, layers within society are referred to as strata. Choosing the layers or groups of people relevant to a particular research project is, then, stratification. If you are undertaking research in an organizational setting, there is good reason to interview a full range of staff stratified within the organization in order to ensure a representative range of views is heard. This range could include managers, those involved in the areas studied, and onlookers within as well as outside the organization. Various researchers have noted that the perspectives of managers and staff can at times vary considerably.[6] Similar concerns were noted by Zaltman and Duncan:

One potential pitfall in interviewing is that the [interviewer] may not talk to a representative number of people. For example, in studying an organization, a good rule of thumb would be to talk to at least two people occupying the same organizational role . . . . Time permitting, it would also be useful to interview people at each level in the organization, since people at different levels might have very different perceptions of the organization.[7]

This is related to the principle of triangulation again. Here, instead of using different research methods to gain a variety of perspectives on a problem, you interview a number of different people in different organizational positions, again to gather a variety of perspectives on the research problem. The credibility of the data you gather is enhanced if it can be confirmed from several sources, just as it can be if gathered using several different research methods.[8] Conversely, if different individuals see the same events or issues from different perspectives, this can only enhance your understanding of them. This was the reason Zuboff adopted triangulation in a series of longitudinal case studies.

While my goal was to understand the living meaning of a collective situation, much of my data gathering focused on individuals and what they felt and did. As a result, it was extremely important to apply the principle of triangulation, which calls for a continual juxtaposition and comparison of data culled from distinct sources that purport to describe the same phenomenon.[9]

Finally, note that there is an important difference between purposive sampling and convenience sampling. *Convenience sampling* is, as the name implies, a sample chosen because it is convenient, easy or quick for the researcher. Such a sample might consist of a researcher's friends, or those staff at a site which is easy for the researcher to visit, or those who happened to be available when the researcher called. While such a sample may be appropriate enough for pilot testing of interview questions, it should not be used for the research proper because of the evident potential for bias. The staff who happened to be available when the researcher called, for example, might be only those not involved in an important meeting.

What questions should be asked?

What questions should be asked will, of course, depend very much on the research topic being investigated. In our experience, many new researchers come up with over-long and sometimes unclear or very general draft lists of interview questions. There are two ways of refining these. First of all, ask yourself the following: 'Does every one of these questions relate directly to something I need to know?' If it does not, eliminate it or tighten its expression. In addition, it should not be necessary to ask at interview for background information which should have been obtained in advance. Then ask, 'Have I asked about everything I need to know?' If not, add that point. A list of questions one of us used in a case study appears in Research Scenario 8.1.

Having gone through this revision process, preferably with a supervisor, research adviser or colleague, the next step is to carry out a couple of pilot interviews. Choose interviewees in another, similar organization, if possible. If this cannot be done, then look for interviewees whose data will not be needed in your final report. Look for pilot interviewees who approximate those you hope to interview. Use the pilot interviews not only to test your draft questions, but also your proposed recording arrangements (see below). One of the greatest benefits of carrying out pilot interviews, however, is to your own self-confidence. After a successful pilot interview, you will be able to go into your first 'real' interview knowing that you are fully prepared, and ready to start your research.

After commencing your first round of interviews, it will be worth revising your questions in the light of your growing familiarity with the topic and the likely responses. In fact, if you are undertaking longitudinal cases of the kind described in Research Scenario 8.1, each stage of the project will require new questions. The obvious opening question when reinterviewing an informant is, 'Well, what's happened since I talked to you last time?' You will probably find that in almost every case your earlier interviews raised points specific not only to each case, but often to each interviewee. It is thus good practice to re-read your draft case study report prior to each subsequent interview, noting points to raise with specific interviewees as well as any more general issues not fully understood.

Reliability and validity

The interviewer is a principal determinant of the value of any interview, as Brenner reminds us.

> It is one of the characteristics of intensive interviewing that the interviewer should follow rules in his/her relationship with the informant. For example, he/she must try to obtain accounts on all the topics listed in the interview guide; his/her questioning must always be nondirective; that is, must never suggest a 'right' answer or direction of answering; he/she must take care that the accounts obtained are adequate (as complete as possible, linguistically comprehensible, free of internal inconsistencies, for example); he/she must also enact a facilitator role by being nonjudgmental and supportive, among other things.[10]

This can be as difficult as it sounds, perhaps especially because, as an information professional yourself, you are likely to have strongly held views on some of the issues raised. As noted by Brenner, these views must not be allowed to influence the interview. Your role is to listen and to learn, not to preach, praise or condemn. Inappropriate or evaluative comments can dissuade any interviewee from volunteering anecdotes or 'insider' comments – and it may be just such potentially unflattering anecdotes or comments that can help you get 'inside' the culture of an organization. By both being and coming over as sympathetic, supportive and understanding you are likely to be more successful.

Accordingly, you should attempt to use what are sometimes termed 'non-directive probes' to elicit additional information. Such probes typically take the form of open-ended questions, typical examples including the following:

- 'Is there anything else?'
- 'In what way?'
- 'Why do you think this happened?'

All of these are 'value neutral', since they do not imply any evaluation of what you are being told; and this may encourage the respondent to be more forthcoming.

In our interviewing, we have found it useful to practise what has been termed 'reflective listening'. In this, you reflect or repeat back to an interviewee your own understanding of what has been said, in order to check that you have understood it correctly and to address any ambiguities. Equally important, it also provides assurance that you have indeed been listening carefully. Finally, rephrasing the thoughts yourself serves as an aid to your own subsequent recollection of what has been learned. However, in reflecting back what you have heard take care not to express, inadvertently or otherwise, your personal views on it.

Despite all the care you take to ensure reliability and validity in interviewing, it is always desirable to be cautious about the results. As Brenner suggests, 'intensive interviewing, as *any* [research] method (in particular the survey interview and the laboratory experiment), in all likelihood will fall short of the ideal of accurate data collection; and it will usually be impossible to know just how far.[11]

Research Scenario 8.1 provides an illustration of a study which used intensive interviewing.

RESEARCH SCENARIO 8.1

INTERVIEWING ABOUT INNOVATION

This scenario is based on the experience of one of the authors, who carried out a series of longitudinal case studies to follow through the implementation of a series of innovations in academic and research libraries.[12] To help ensure validity, data were gathered by a number of methods: interview, observation, and documentary study. Data were gathered from as many different levels and groups within the organizations studied as possible, so addressing a question posed by Reynolds and Whitlatch: 'Does the same innovation take on various hues when viewed from different employee points of view?'[13] Data gathering was also as widely spread in time as possible.

The interviews undertaken could be described as 'intensive', in the sense used by Brenner.[14] Brenner suggested three ways of addressing questions of reliability and validity in intensive interviewing: checking accounts against 'verification data', such as documents and observations; guarding against undesirable influences in the interview process; and attempting to assess interviewees' cognitive states during interviews. No clear guidance on undertaking this last was provided, and it was not attempted.

However, I did employ the other two strategies. Whenever possible, independent evidence was sought to verify statements. In every case where a major discrepancy was found, this was noted. Most interviews were held in quiet offices or deserted tearooms or similarly appropriate places free of distractions. However, a couple of staff running single-person libraries had to be interviewed on the job, in circumstances recalling all too clearly Brenner's term 'strong bystander interference' – here, users and telephones.[15]

Interviews were not tightly structured but used a set of prepared points as a guide, principally to ensure that no important factor was omitted. One group of these is quoted here; the italic numbers in brackets refer to the hypotheses which had been developed. This was used as a check to ensure both that every aspect of the hypotheses – every sub-hypothesis – was included, and also that every question did relate to an hypothesis.

- What are the advantages of this innovation? (*1*)
- How does the innovation fit in with organizational objectives? (*1*)
- Is there anyone who might feel threatened by it? (*1*)
- Who's going to benefit from it? (*1*)
- How urgent would you say it was to implement this innovation? (*2*)
- How has the implementation of this project been managed? (*3, 4, 5*)
- Could you tell me about some particular problem you encountered with this project? How was it resolved? (*3, 4*)
- How will it fit in with the way the library does things? Have you talked about its impact? (*4*)

In this study, most interviews were tape recorded. Although it was known that tape recording could serve as a constraint upon candour and openness and result in the accumulation of large quantities of data of limited relevance, in practice my impression was that in most cases the presence of the tape recorder had only a minimal impact, although some exceptions to this are noted below. The tape recordings proved most valuable as an *aide-mémoire* in a study undertaken by a single person. Tapes were not transcribed *in toto*, though taping did allow some particularly pertinent comments to be transcribed verbatim. Review of tape recorded interviews was done towards the conclusion of the study. In addition to the taped interviews, informal discussions were held before and/or after these interviews, in staff common rooms, over meals, and in a professional or social context. Fidel has also used 'casual conversations' as an additional source of data.[16]

Individual interviewees were consulted prior to taping, and it was suggested some 'off-the-record' comments need not be taped. Some interviewees did request this: 'You can turn the tape off now!' Others made remarks such as 'Better not put this on the record!' or 'You know, there's a lot that I shouldn't record in any way at all!', but did not ask for the machine to be turned off. Still other interviewees visibly relaxed when the tape ran out or the recorder was turned off after the 'formal' interview, and then volunteered comments withheld earlier. Noticing this, I often did not insert a new tape. One interviewee only relaxed when I arranged a group of papers on top of the recorder in an attempt to hide it from sight.

This experience is consistent with that of Pettigrew, who in his study of ICI found that only one of 134 interviewees refused to be recorded.[17] In my study, I was at times surprised at some of the personal, unflattering or otherwise revealing details volunteered to me. In general, it was not necessary or appropriate to quote these remarks in the published reports on the study. However, they did serve to strengthen my conviction that a majority of interviewees were indeed telling their story as they saw it, and by no means attempting to portray themselves or their organizations in the best possible light. No doubt the personal rapport established as part of a successful interview partly accounted for such candour. Skrtic, in reporting on an educational case study, concluded that 'had we come onto these sites with questionnaires to be analysed statistically, we would not have been greeted as favorably or been made privy to so much information as we were'.[18]

Each tape was numbered and dated, so that appropriate reference could be made to particular verbatim transcripts. The tape citation system adopted used a Roman number for the tape, followed by A or B to indicate tape side (C120 compact cassette tapes were used), followed by a counter reading from the tape recorder. For example, a quotation from tape 1, side A, at counter reading 348 was cited in the study as IA348. A record was kept of the interviewee's name, pseudonym used and organizational position, and of the date, length of interview and recording duration and citation. A similar system for organization of tapes was described by Stenhouse.[19] Yin regarded such record-keeping as an important element of maintaining a 'chain of evidence'.[20]

At the conclusion of each case, copies of a final draft were given to at least two staff members in the organization to review. Guba referred to this method: 'The process of member checks is the single most important action inquirers can take, as it goes to the heart of the credibility criterion.'[21] For each of the cases, one of these reviewers was an 'informant', an interviewee whom I had interviewed on several occasions and whose insights had helped guide the investigation. The informant was asked to check that specific details of the case, as written up, were accurate. The second reviewer could be described as an 'observer' with the organization: a staff member not involved with the innovation being studied, but able to provide an 'inside' perspective on it. As someone not too close to the innovation to see it in proportion, the observer was asked to check that the report 'made sense', appeared to be a fair, unbiased assessment of the case, and that the organization was recognizably 'their library'. To judge from the comments of these reviewers, the care taken with the interviews (and other aspects of each case) was well justified.

The interview process

Despite the apparently natural and spontaneous character of interviewing, careful preparation will help ensure success. There are a number of items that should be taken into account in preparing for a series of intensive interviews. The most important of these, selection of those to be interviewed and the questions which will be asked, have already been noted. Some of the other issues which need to be considered are setting up interview appointments, the venues which will be used, and structuring and controlling the interviews.

Setting up the interviews

Assuming you have already negotiated access to the organization (see Chapter 6), once you have decided who you wish to interview you will need to set up appointments, at least with more senior staff. Allow sufficient time, both to allow appointments to be made in advance, and to cater for the likelihood that appointments once made have to be postponed.

You will probably be asked how long you need for each interview. Here your experience with the pilot interviews will stand you in good stead. For an initial interview, less than half an hour is unlikely to be sufficient, and with senior staff ask for an hour if possible. In general, you will probably find that interviews with senior staff tend to take longer because they are able to comment on a wider range of relevant issues, but often these staff have less time to give you. Hence your preparation will assist in making the most of whatever time is available.

Senior staff will usually prefer to be interviewed in their offices, and these normally provide a quiet and appropriate venue. However, more junior staff and those who wish to discuss particularly sensitive issues may be prefer to be interviewed away from their immediate workplace. Finding an appropriate venue that is private, quiet and available may require some forethought. For example, you might be able to find a quiet café nearby.

Telephone interviews are occasionally unavoidable if you cannot justify travel expenses, but wish to include an important actor in your study. However, lacking the rapport normally gained through the non-verbal interaction of a successful face-to-face interview can prove a serious obstacle. Few interviewees are prepared to volunteer sensitive information to someone they have not met and cannot see at the other end of a phone line.

Structuring interviews

A normal interview goes through a series of stages. These may be characterized as: introductions; completion of ethics paperwork and obtaining permission to record, if these are necessary; establishing rapport and putting the interviewee at his or her ease; prepared questions, often asked of all interviewees to gather comparative data; then more open-ended questions; an opportunity for the interviewee to raise any matters which may have been overlooked; and concluding remarks and thanks. Some thought about each of these stages should enable an interview guide to be both complete, and sequenced appropriately. Those with substantial experience in interviewing candidates for jobs will see the many similarities here. Unlike most job interviews, however, a researcher should remain open to allowing an interviewee to go off in unexpected directions – an interview guide should not become a straitjacket.

Returning to the job interview analogy, for it is in some ways a useful one, appropriate body language and furniture placement can be important, too: no one wants to feel that they are being interrogated by the Gestapo. A good book on body language will cover such points as sitting at an angle to an interviewee rather than head-on, appropriate placement of furniture (not possible in someone else's office, of course), and unconscious body gestures (such as arms folded or mouth covered).[22]

To a greater extent than with most job interviews, however, a research interview should normally be structured to facilitate a two-way exchange of information.

The relationship between interviewer and interviewee is one of mutual discovery rather than unidirectional observation. The quality of the results depends very much on the depth of mutual understanding achieved by researcher and subject, which must be accomplished despite the tensions inherent in a psychologically stressful and socially artificial context.[23]

Controlling interviews

In everyday professional life, some people seem able to guide a conversation or discussion so tactfully that those involved seem unaware of this; others fail miserably. In an interview, too, there is a spectrum from controlling a discussion so tightly that an interviewee feels constrained, through the ideal middle ground, to a rambling, ill-focused conversation that omits important points while taking excessive time.

Give your interviewee some space by asking some open-ended questions; asking appropriate follow-up questions ('What happened next?' 'What was the result of this?'); and exploring unexpected but relevant contributions. Perhaps most important, allow your interviewee some time: don't always jump in the moment he or she stops speaking. Thoughtful pauses in a conversation allow others to share control of it if they wish.

Ensure understanding by practising reflective listening, repeating back to the interviewee your summary of what has just been said ('OK, so what happened was . . .' 'Have I understood this correctly? You think . . .'). You might even think of this as the verbal equivalent of appropriate body language, as you concentrate on exactly what is being said to you.

Keep it relevant by using your interview guide ('Thanks for that. The next question I wanted to ask you was . . .') and attempting to relate answers to the information you came seeking ('And how did that affect the training programme?'). Once again, body language can be very helpful here: we all know the significance of glancing at a watch. By nodding at the end of an answer and then picking up your interview guide, for example, you are signalling that this was all you needed on a particular point.

What makes a good interviewer?

A good interviewer will be thoroughly prepared before each interview; will put people at their ease; will ask only one question at a time; will ensure each question is clear and unambiguous; will listen both to what is said and what is not said; will not attempt to put words into respondents' mouths; will react only with interest – or, where appropriate, sympathetic concern – to what is volunteered, never with surprise, disapproval or shock; will not contradict a respondent even when information known to be incorrect is supplied; and will certainly never begin to argue. No doubt some such paragons exist.

Just as in the observation process (see Chapter 7), when you commence a series of intensive interviews you are likely to experience uncertainty, confusion and nervousness; this is when you are bound to make at least some mistakes; and at this stage you will have least rapport with your subjects and are most likely to be misunderstood. Hence the value of pilot interviews. In talking about starting observation, we suggested that you needed to ease yourself into the context, place yourself carefully, be approachable and friendly, receptive, and dress and behave appropriately. These guidelines need not be repeated here, but remain just as relevant.

Recording interview data

It is because intensive interviewing is such a demanding task that many interviewers use a tape recorder, with handwritten notes merely to record future questions or note particularly important points. Brenner has pointed out that tape recording removes a source of potential distraction, and frees the interviewer to guide the interview, check that answers are complete and consistent, and plan future questions.[24] It also allows for subsequent transcription for analysis using software such as NVivo (see Chapter 12).

However, tape recording has several drawbacks, of which four warrant serious consideration.

- It can significantly reduce the likelihood of interviewees volunteering sensitive or embarrassing material. Some may even not agree to be interviewed if they are to be taped. It is always necessary to obtain permission to tape record someone's comments, and always worth suggesting that you will turn off the tape recorder at any point if requested – as was done in the Research Scenario 8.1 above. In our experience, some interviewees will ask for this and then reveal quite sensitive information.
- Some recorders can be visually intrusive or noisy – and the act of changing a tape is always distracting.
- Unless you are tape recording in a quiet office, background noise can be surprisingly obtrusive. In the course of the study reported in Research Scenario 8.1, I taped many staff in empty common rooms and apparently quiet restaurants, only to be surprised how noisy was the clatter of dishes in the

background. It does not help that, in many instances, people lower their voices when passing on especially interesting information!

- Because, as noted earlier, we can talk so much more quickly than we can write, much spoken conversation is extremely wordy. It can take hours to listen to taped interviews, many more hours if these are to be transcribed, yet their relevant information content may be able to be summarized quite briefly.

On the other hand, we all know the tricks that a faulty memory can play on us. Sometimes we hear what we hope or expect to hear, rather than what has actually been said; very often we hear and remember only some of what we are told. For this reason, it always sensible to tape record an interview if this is feasible: you can always choose not to use the tape if you are certain your notes record all that is needed. If you are undertaking a team research project, tape recording has the additional benefit that those not present can also hear crucial interviews, and check that your own interpretation of them is complete and justifiable.

Recording equipment

Two comments about equipment may not be out of place. The first of those comments has to be, make sure it is unobtrusive. A recorder has to be small, quiet and generally inconspicuous. Settings should not require adjustment, and hence you will need one with either automatic level control or (preferably) voice-activation. Since changing tapes is distracting, choose one which will take long tapes, ideally of an hour's duration.

The second comments relates to back-up supplies. Make sure you have spare tapes and spare batteries, and a labelling system that will unambiguously identify each tape – and, even more importantly, not allow you accidentally to tape over a completed interview. One of us has not forgotten interviewing a most senior library staff member using dying batteries. When replayed the recording started off normally, but then the pitch of her voice started to get higher and higher and her words faster and faster as the tape had slowed more and more, until finally it disappeared up in a kind of squeak. The worst of it was that I did not realize that the tape had stopped until the interview was over. Although I was able to reconstruct much of what I had been told, some was lost.

To transcribe or not to transcribe?

If you tape record, should you also transcribe the tapes? We have seen many research project funding applications where the majority of the funds requested were to enable transcription of tape recorded interview data; we have had postgraduate students who have started to transcribe data, and found this such a burden that they considered giving up their research altogether. It is a time-consuming and soul destroying task. If every word in the interview is likely to be important, or if you are likely to be challenged to produce your evidence, then you may have no choice. An intermediate option, recommended by Strauss[25] and adopted in Research Scenario 8.1, is to write up your interview report while it is fresh in your mind – that very day, if at all possible – and then simply *listen* to the tape recording of the interview. This will give you the opportunity to correct any mistaken impressions, enable you to transcribe any short, highly pertinent observations, and not preclude later transcription – or partial transcription – if required. If you are planning to analyse your data using NVivo or similar software, a summary using the words of the interviewee, rather than a full verbatim transcript, may be all that is required.

If you choose not to record, or cannot record because of the nature of your investigation, then it is *essential* not only to take adequate notes while you are interviewing, but to schedule adequate time at the conclusion of each interview for the salient points to be recorded while they are most fresh in your mind. If you have access to a laptop computer to do this, so much the better. Research Scenario 8.2 describes just such good practice.

Whether you tape record or not, if important but non-verbal events take place during an interview (perhaps when an interviewee seems very concerned about some questions) these should be noted as soon as possible after the interview, since they will not necessarily be evident in an audio-only recording. Likewise, if there is an emotional component to an interview (such as distress or anger on the part of an interviewee) this too should be noted.

Record keeping

Regardless of whether you tape record your interviews, it is good practice to keep a full record or database of all the interviews you conduct. Such a record would include, at a minimum, three items of information: who, when and where.

- Who? This includes the names of the interviewees, their position or level as relevant, and any pseudonyms you chose to give them when writing up your research. This will enable you to check that any references or attributions you make to individuals are correct.
- When? This includes the dates and time taken for each interview. You may well wish to document how long you have spent on a case study, including the number of hours of interviewing involved.
- Where? If an interview has been recorded, note the tape number and counter or time readings for the start and end points of the interview on that tape. If it is then transcribed, make note of a reference to the transcript. Once again, this will enable you to check details. Because one of the strengths of the qualitative research approach is that theory can be developed as an investigation proceeds, you may well wish to return to an interview you have previously dealt with to see if some new perception might be supported by it, though unnoticed at the time.

All of these records help build up Yin's 'chain of evidence', which strengthens the credibility of your study.[26] Equally important, by organizing your research data in such a way you will not only make it easier to write up your research, but will be less likely to make mistakes when doing so.

In Research Scenario 8.1 interviews were tape recorded. In Research Scenario 8.2, presented below, Jenkins decided not to tape record his interviews and discusses the reasons for this decision.[27]

RESEARCH SCENARIO 8.2

INTERVIEWING IN A PUBLIC POLICY AREA

The author was interested in Crown Land policy making in New South Wales over the period 1965–1991, and established 'that the Crown land policy process is highly political and value-laden . . . . The process has been characterized by conflict, bargaining, negotiation, compromise and incremental policy development, interspersed with marked policy shifts according to the party political ideology of the government of the day.'[28] As many departmental files had been lost, destroyed or were incomplete, he decided to undertake this study by means of a series of interviews with current and former staff.

Deciding who should be interviewed was not straightforward. Because of the complexity of the study, not all the major players were apparent at the start, and one interviewee could suggest other people who should be interviewed. It proved impossible to predict in advance who would be a useful interviewee.

Interviews were arranged by telephone rather than by letter, which enabled Jenkins to mention other staff who had agreed to be interviewed, explain the need to cross-check the information he had been given so far, respond to any queries and stress the importance of the personal insights the potential interviewee could provide. All those he approached agreed to be interviewed.

It was decided not to tape record interviews, partly so as not to inhibit interviewees and partly because of the possibility of mechanical failure of the recorder. 'I was confident that my note taking was efficient, and that I could rely on my short term memory to rewrite, organize and reflect on my notes at the conclusion of the interview.'[29] However, Jenkins found that it typically took three to four times as long to write up such reports than for the interviews themselves. Jenkins arranged no more than two interviews per day, with several hours each day free from other commitments in order to be able to write up these reports.

Questions were prepared and learned by rote so that they could be used naturally in each interview. Some but not all interviewees asked that their identity be kept confidential; others that some remarks be 'off the record'.

One particular problem arose when two officers unexpectedly arranged to be interviewed together rather than separately. 'It was difficult to stop interjections from one as the other responded. It seemed that each interviewee was filling gaps for the other as glances were exchanged and rejoinders called for.'[30]

Review of Chapter 8

This chapter started by discussing the advantages and disadvantages of interviewing as a research methodology. Advantages include its speed and flexibility, personal approach to data collection and richness of data. However, it can be very time-consuming, care must be taken to ensure the reporting of data is not too selective, and anonymity is lost. Most importantly, the interviewer is a principal determinant of the value of any interview.

There are two kinds of interview: structured or survey, which was not discussed in this chapter, and unstructured, in-depth or intensive. In undertaking the latter, you need to decide who should be interviewed, what questions to ask, and when and where the interviews should take place. Other important considerations are how to record them, and whether they need to be transcribed. Finally, a record of the names, dates and times of interviews, together with tape and transcription details if applicable, should be maintained.

Where to now?

Once again, we suggest that you review the focus questions at the start of this chapter. Then you might wish to turn again to the knowledge management case study which concludes this volume, 'Human resources in knowledge management' (Chapter 14 below), and consider these questions:

- How did she record these interviews? Would you have chosen the same approach, and why, or why not?
- Were 'member checks' undertaken? If so, how?
- Did she use some of her interview data in this report? If so, did the data help persuade you of the credibility of the conclusions she reached?

Further reading

As always, there is a wealth of good material available online, along with the '.com' dross. J. K. Doyle has written a basic introduction to interviewing techniques, which also includes focus groups (see our next chapter), available at www.wpi.edu/Academics/Depts/IGSD/IQPHbook/ch11.html#11 – follow the chapter by clicking on 'forward'. One site that fleshes out the discussion in this chapter with examples is C. G. Boeree's *Qualitative Methods Workbook*, www.ship.edu/~cgboeree/qualmeth.html, another e-text prepared for an American university course. (This covers a range of qualitative approaches, including phenomenology and observation.)

Further details of interviewing as a qualitative research methodology may be found in M. Q. Patton, *Qualitative Research and Evaluation Methods*, 3rd edn (Thousand Oaks, CA, Sage, 2002); and in chapters on interviewing in general library science research texts – for example, R. R. Powell, *Basic Research Methods for Librarians*, 3rd edn (Norwood, NJ: Ablex, 1997). Other useful titles include V. Minichiello et al., *In-depth Interviewing: Researching People*, 2nd edn (Melbourne:

Cheshire, 1995), and M. Brenner, J. Brown and D. Canter, eds., *The Research Interview: Uses and Approaches* (London: Academic Press, 1985), which covers intensive and survey interviewing. Finally, V. J. Janesick, '*Stretching' Exercises for Qualitative Researchers*, 2nd edn (Thousand Oaks, CA: Sage, 2003), recommended in the previous chapter, also includes interview examples and exercises.

Notes

1 Chatman seems to have a penchant for the unusual in her information-seeking and information user studies. See, for example, her detailed study, *The Information World of Retired Women*, New Directions in Information Management, 29 (Westport, CT: Greenwood, 1992), and also the briefer 'Alienation Theory: Application of a Conceptual Framework to a Study of Information Among Janitors', *RQ*, **29** (3), 1990, pp. 355–68. See also J. C. Durrance, K. E. Fisher and M. B. Hinton, 'Information Grounds and the Use of Need-based Services by Immigrants in Queens, New York: a Context-based, Outcome Evaluation Approach', *Journal of the American Society for Information Science and Technology*, **55** (8), June 2004, pp. 754–66.

2 M. Brenner, J. Brown and D. Canter, eds., *The Research Interview: Uses and Approaches* (London: Academic, 1985), p. 4.

3 V. Minichiello, et al., *In-depth Interviewing: Researching People* (Melbourne: Cheshire, 1990), p. 19.

4 Examples include W. A. Belson, *The Design and Understanding of Survey Questions* (Aldershot: Gower, 1981); and Brenner, Brown and Canter, op. cit.

5 M. Q. Patton, *Qualitative Evaluation and Research Methods*, 2nd edn (Newbury Park, CA: Sage, 1990): pp. 288–9.

6 N. R. Anderson and N. King, 'Managing Innovation in Organisations', *Leadership and Organisation Development Journal*, **12** (4), 1991, pp. 17–21; P. Ranganath Nayak and J. M. Ketteringham, *Breakthroughs!* (New York: Rawson, 1986), p. 6.

7 G. Zaltman and R. Duncan, *Strategies for Planned Change* (New York: John Wiley and Sons, 1977), p. 45.

8 E. G. Guba, 'Criteria for Establishing the Trustworthiness of Naturalistic Enquiries', *Educational Communication and Technology Journal*, **29** (2), 1981, p. 85.

9 S. Zuboff, *In the Age of the Smart Machine: The Future of Work and Power* (Oxford: Heinemann, 1988), p. 425.

10 M. Brenner, 'Intensive Interviewing'. In Brenner, Brown and Canter, op. cit., pp. 158–9.

11 Ibid., p. 161.

12 P. Clayton, *Implementation of Organizational Innovation: Studies of Academic and Research Libraries* (San Diego, CA: Academic, 1997).

13 J. Reynolds and J. B. Whitlatch, 'Academic Library Services: The Literature of Innovation', *College & Research Libraries*, **46** (5), 1985, p. 414.

14 Brenner, op. cit.

15 Ibid., p. 157.

16 R. Fidel, 'The Case Study Method: A Case Study.' *Library & Information Science Research*, **6**, 1984, pp. 273–88; reprinted under the same title in *Qualitative Research in Information*

Management, eds. J. D. Glazier and R. R. Powell (Englewood, CO: Libraries Unlimited, 1992), pp. 37–49.

17 A. M. Pettigrew, *The Awakening Giant: Continuity and Change in Imperial Chemical Industries* (Oxford: Basil Blackwell, 1985), p. 41.

18 T. M. Skrtic, 'Doing Naturalistic Research into Educational Organizations'. In *Organizational Theory and Inquiry: The Paradigm Revolution,* ed. Y. S. Lincoln (Beverly Hills, CA: Sage, 1985), p. 214.

19 L. Stenhouse, 'Using Case Study in Library Research', *Social Science Information Studies,* **1** (4), 1981), pp. 221–301.

20 R. K. Yin, *Case Study Research: Design and Methods,* rev. edn (Newbury Park, CA: Sage, 1989), pp. 102–3.

21 Guba, op. cit., pp. 85–6.

22 These points are covered by, for example, A. Pease in *Body Language* (Avalon Beach, NSW: Camel, 1981).

23 M. Sandler, 'Qualitative Research Methods in Library Decision-making'. In *Qualitative Research in Information Management,* eds. J. D. Glazier and R. R. Powell (Englewood, CO: Libraries Unlimited, 1992), p. 183.

24 Brenner, op. cit., p. 154.

25 A. L. Strauss, *Qualitative Analysis for Social Scientists* (Cambridge: Cambridge University Press, 1987), p. 267.

26 Yin, op. cit., pp. 102–3; also see Guba, op. cit., p. 87.

27 J. Jenkins, 'Interviews and Interviewing: A Case Study in Geography and Public Policy', *Australian Geographic Studies,* **34** (2), 1996, pp. 261–6.

28 Ibid., p. 261.

29 Ibid., p. 265.

30 Ibid., p. 264.

9 Group discussion techniques

FOCUS QUESTIONS
- What are the advantages and disadvantages of focus groups as sources of qualitative data?
- What are the advantages and disadvantages of the nominal group technique as an alternative source of data?
- What factors might lead you to choose one of these techniques over the other?

Group processes in organizations

Group processes are fundamental to human communication and to the management of organizations. If you are investigating an organization, groups rather than individuals are central to organizational culture and much of the work of the organization. Groups of one kind or another dominate organizational life: staff meetings, senior executive groups, committees, task forces, governing bodies, user groups. Each of these can have a major impact on the choices an organization makes and the manner in which it implements these choices. It is therefore appropriate to consider gathering qualitative research data from groups of staff and clients, as well as from individuals.

A particular advantage of using groups in this way is that a variety of perspectives and explanations may be obtained from a single data-gathering session. The sessions may be straightforward to set up, especially if a pre-existing group is used, and usually take less than two hours to complete. In a group situation many people are prompted to say or suggest ideas which might not occur to them on their own: we are a social species. Finally, participants frequently express a high degree of satisfaction with the outcomes of such processes.

The disadvantages often are all too apparent. A group can be dominated by a strong individual, perhaps a senior manager, with the result that its members acquiesce to a single viewpoint and perhaps do not even bother to mention their own convictions. Much the same thing can happen if membership of the group is heterogeneous – consisting of both professional and non-professional staff, perhaps, with the professionals assuming (incorrectly) that they know everything, or of professionals and users, with the professionals again tempted to make the same mistake. Or a group can run away with an appealing idea suggested early in discussion and fail to consider alternatives that may be equally valid.

A well managed group discussion can minimize such possible problems and extract data which makes a substantial contribution to many types of research project. It can also enable a group to focus on priorities for action, and so be a powerful management tool in its own right. As this is a text on research and not management, such applications are outside our present scope; several are discussed by both Clayton and Olsen.[1] Both items also discuss a wide range of group processes. In this chapter we consider only two of the most popular and useful group processes used in qualitative research.

One of the words that appears most often in the discussion below is *facilitator*. If those who take part in a group discussion are to be allowed to put forward their own ideas, then the role of the researcher or facilitator is merely to enable this to happen, and as transparently as possible. Of course, you will have ideas, opinions and experiences of your own; these can appear elsewhere in your research report. In facilitating or managing a group discussion, however, they are irrelevant: the aim must be to encourage the participants to talk on issues related to the research project, and as far as possible, uninhibited by anything you say or do.

Focus groups in information settings

A focus group session is a small group discussion (often consisting of six to 12 participants), guided by a facilitator and used to gain an understanding of participants' attitudes and perceptions relevant to a particular topic. It is thus the simplest method by which you can gain data from a group: in essence, all you need to do is sit down with it and talk about the areas which are of interest. Needless to say, such simplicity is more apparent than real.

The normal process is to prepare a number of questions related to several facets of the topic under investigation. An example of one set of questions actually used in a recent study appears below in Research Scenario 9.1 (page 146). Usually a researcher would discuss these with research colleagues or a supervisor in order to ensure that the questions are clear and unambiguous and that all aspects of interest have been covered.

If the facilitator is inexperienced or harbours any doubts about the approach, and assuming there is sufficient time, it is normal to then undertake a trial run or pilot discussion with a comparable group not included in the actual research. If you have not used this technique before, then such a test flight is also essential to build up your own self-confidence: this is one technique in which a high degree of self-confidence is essential. You need to be comfortable talking to and working with groups of people – experience which many information professionals already have, of course. In addition, because it is a qualitative research technique, as the research itself proceeds ineffective questions are likely to be rephrased as you ease your way into the thinking of respondents.

These prepared questions are then supplemented with follow-up questions or 'probes'. The intention is not to obtain simple 'yes' or 'no' responses from participants but to address any ambiguities, obtain more detailed information and provoke a thoughtful discussion among those present about the research topic. Such a probe might be phrased, 'Can you tell me why you think that?' It will be apparent that focus groups require sensitive facilitation in order to enable all group members to participate meaningfully. Experienced facilitators use a variety of tactful questions to ensure this, from 'Can I pick up on something that the previous speaker said?' to 'That raises another important area which I'd like to move on to.'

Recording the data

A particular problem with focus group discussions is recording the data obtained. A successful facilitator will frequently provoke an animated discussion, with perhaps several people talking at once – and not all the most insightful comments will necessarily be the loudest. There are four commonly adopted ways of recording such discussions: tape recorder, notes taken during the meeting, notes made immediately after the discussion, notes taken by someone else during the discussion.

- *Tape recorder.* With a lively discussion and several people talking at once, as noted above, it can be difficult or impossible for someone else to transcribe such a tape. Its principal use will probably be to serve as an *aide-mémoire* to the researcher/facilitator. Even then, you will possibly find that much cannot be understood.
- *Notes taken during the meeting.* These are *essential*. Nothing else can record what you, the researcher, obtain from such a discussion as it proceeds. However, for one who is asking many of the questions, listening carefully to what is said, prompting further comment on this and guiding the overall discussion, more than rudimentary note taking is out of the question.
- *Notes made immediately after the discussion.* These too are essential: they can help supplement and clarify what will probably be the very sketchy notes you were able to make during the discussion itself. It is good practice to schedule yourself an uninterrupted block of time at the conclusion of each group session to enable this.
- *Notes taken by someone else during the discussion.* If your assistant is fully briefed on the purpose of the session and what you are hoping to obtain from it, this can be most valuable, not least in giving you another perspective on what took place. Once again, it is good practice is to schedule a debriefing session immediately after each discussion.

A variant on this last approach is, in fact, adopted by many of commercial organizations which make use of focus groups – for example, in planning advertising campaigns. Rather than have an additional person or several people in the same room as the group, which might be distracting for it, observers typically sit behind a one-way glass window set into a wall of the discussion room. Participants see this as a mirror. Some companies even videotape focus groups through this glass. Leaving aside the ethics of such concealment, it seems unlikely that many information researchers will have such a purpose-built venue available.

From what we have said it will be apparent that your own notes made both during and after a session are likely to be most useful, but if you can obtain a volunteer note-taker to sit in on the session, do so. Further discussion of note-taking as part of the research process appears in Chapter 11.

RESEARCH SCENARIO 9.1

THE INFORMATION AND COMMUNICATION NEEDS OF UNDERGRADUATES

A recent study was carried out by one of us in order to identify the information and communication needs of undergraduate students at a university. The findings of this study were intended for use both in formulating the goals of the relevant area of the university, and in helping determine priorities for services. From the outset it was decided that the data obtained by this project and the recommendations arising from them would be sought in a relatively quick and inexpensive manner. It was not intended that hypotheses be tested, nor was it thought necessary that either every undergraduate or even a stratified random sample of undergraduates should be consulted as part of the process. It was also decided not to survey students on a 'volunteer' basis, as it was thought important to gather opinions from students who did not necessarily have a particular point of view. Self-selected participants expose studies to a very real risk of bias in response. Instead, students would be sampled in natural groupings – lecture groups or tutorial classes.

One of the methodologies chosen was focus group discussions. Questions were suggested by the senior manager and members of the area's management team, and trialled with a group of postgraduate students involved in this project. The questions eventually used were:

- What information will you be accessing?
- How will you be gaining access to it?
- What services do you expect to be in place to facilitate access?
- How will you be communicating with staff and other students?
- What services would you like to see?
- What services would you be prepared to pay for?
- Are there any other issues which you would like to mention?

These questions prompted lively discussion among most of the undergraduate groups, with times when more than one student started speaking at once. Tactful restraining rather than tactful encouragement was needed.

Only a couple of the several discussions held were tape recorded. Unfortunately, two factors severely limited the usefulness of these tape recordings: the poor quality of the equipment available, a standard portable compact cassette recorder, and the fact that each session was taped in an unsuitable venue, currently being used at the same time by other students involved in the project. However, the notes made at the time and afterwards by those facilitating the sessions were useable.

One of the conclusions from this study was that the methodology adopted was appropriate. It provided undergraduates from across the university with an opportunity to make an input: on the one hand students did not appear to have any reservations about contributing, and on the other, by accessing students in tutorial and lecture groups, it appears that the views obtained were almost certainly representative to a large extent of the undergraduate population as a whole. Because students were in class groups and knew each other, they were very happy to discuss each of the issues raised and raised a variety of perspectives on these.

Note the difficulties experienced with the venues used for these groups. Most texts suggest something along the lines recommended by Crocker: 'select an appropriate setting for conducting the sessions. A comfortable, non-threatening atmosphere is instrumental to the disclosure of information. There should be easy access to the meeting point for participants and it should be free from external disruptions such as telephones.'[2] If natural groups are used, however, as here, then the researcher will have little control over the venues.

Advantages of focus groups

One of the advantages of focus groups is that participants and facilitator can find it an enjoyable and interesting experience. Of course, not all sessions can be expected to be equally successful: some can seem slow and laboured, even if the total time taken hardly differs from more productive sessions. Beyond the likelihood that the experience will prove positive, other advantages include speed, transparency, interaction, flexibility, open-endedness and the ability to note non-verbal communication.

- *Speed.* Focus group sessions require only moderate time commitment from both participants and facilitator. Depending on how many questions are to be asked, and how complex or controversial the matters canvassed might be, between one to two hours will be sufficient for most discussions.
- *Transparency.* Participants can see at a glance what is being done, and almost invariably accept that the methodology is appropriate. In turn this encourages them to relax and contribute fully to the discussion.
- *Interaction.* Participants are encouraged to interact with each other and not merely respond to the facilitator; in this way a range and complexity of attitudes and beliefs can emerge. For example, a facilitator might ask one participant to comment on or react to the contribution of another.
- *Flexibility.* Focus groups offer an opportunity for immediate feedback or clarification on suggestions, with the contributions of other group members included.

- *Open-endedness.* The facilitator can allow a group to explore aspects of a topic unanticipated by a researcher. It is a technique particularly appropriate when the possible range of answers is not known in advance.
- *Ability to note non-verbal communication.* Focus groups enable a researcher to 'take into account not only what is said, but gestures, facial expressions, and other forms of non-verbal communication that may reveal depth of meaning.'[3] Loud laughter or moans of mock anguish accompany many a successful session.

Finally, as a non-written research technique, focus groups are one of the few which permit investigation of groups whose writing skills are limited. Such groups might include children or the illiterate, both of whom are important subjects for information research.

Disadvantages of focus groups

The problems associated with recording focus group sessions have already been noted. Other aspects of focus group sessions that are fraught with potential problems may include getting people together, dominating personalities, wanting to be agreeable and finding a typical group.

- *Getting people together.* The example quoted above in Research Scenario 9.1 was fortunate, in that it made use of existing groups, meeting at their normal place and times. Some other focus group discussions, such as with a school parents and friends meeting, may also be able to be held at the time and place the group normally meets. However, if a group is asked to come together simply in order to enable the discussion to take place, some participants will be late and others never show up at all.
- *Dominating personalities.* As noted in the introduction to this chapter, a very real hazard of such a relatively unstructured process is the domination of a group by a few vocal members. The skills of the facilitator/researcher in drawing out other members of the group will be important in this regard.
- *Wanting to be agreeable.* There is a natural human tendency to prefer to agree rather than disagree with one's peers; again, sensitive facilitation can help minimize this.
- *Finding a typical group.* If the entire staff of an organization or a section within it can be included, perhaps at a staff meeting, fine; but, as with Research Scenario 9.1, if a sample is taken it must be representative. A common approach is to choose a number of 'purposive' samples, which in total represent most of the groups comprising the population (see the discussion of purposive sampling in Chapter 8). Here, focus groups might include professionals and non-professionals, full-time and part-time staff, senior and junior staff, those newly appointed as well as long-serving members, men and women, and so on.

However, perhaps the most serious limitation to the focus group technique, at least for a beginning researcher, is one already noted in passing: that it requires a relatively self-confident, self-assured facilitator, one who is fully briefed on the topic to be explored. The success or failure of most focus group discussions can be linked directly to the skills and expertise of the facilitator. Most of us know whether we are more of an introvert or extrovert: this is a technique unsuited for introverts. It can help enormously if you are experienced at chairing meetings, and generally at working with groups of colleagues. If you are experienced at this but inexperienced with focus groups, do consider it seriously. For anyone new to the technique, our best advice has to be two-fold: conduct a pilot session or sessions first, and do not rely solely on this method. It is, in fact, ideally suited for use in supplementing other qualitative techniques.

Storytelling
One development of focus group technique which has been enthusiastically adopted by some qualitative researchers is storytelling. David Snowden, in particular, has undertaken a considerable amount of research in knowledge management using this technique.[4] There are obvious links between the stories repeated in an organization and organizational culture; storytelling 'circles' are groups from within an organization who share some common past experience of interest to the researcher. As a research method, a storytelling group shares all the advantages and, sadly, also all the disadvantages of a regular focus group (although Snowden does also mention virtual storytelling). Recording the stories told can be a particular problem.

The nominal group technique in information settings
One of the advantages of nominal group technique (NGT) is that it is less affected by the experience or inexperience of the facilitator. It is a technique that is relatively straightforward for an untrained person to carry out although, as with anything, practice makes perfect and it is obviously necessary to undertake some kind of a pilot session first.

As noted in Chapter 3, unlike a focus group, a nominal group need not be homogeneous. Participants may be a group in name only, hence the name of the technique. Another name occasionally given to the technique is a 'quality brainstorm', and indeed it does make use of many of the principles of brainstorming.

How NGT works
In NGT a question is put to a group, which then deals with it in four discrete steps. Ideas are:

1 written down by each individual, silently
2 reported by everyone in the group and noted on a board or chart for all participants to see (and with no discussion allowed at this stage)

3 discussed, clarified and evaluated
4 voted on to establish relative importance, from which a group ranking can be
   derived.

If required, the third and fourth steps may be repeated to enable participants to re-evaluate voting patterns and so increase the accuracy of the outcome.

Looking at each of these steps in turn, the first serves to focus each participant (and the group as a whole) on the nominal group question. One proven approach is not only to put the question up on a board or overhead transparency for all to see, but also to repeat it at the top of a sheet of otherwise blank paper given to each participant. Typically, five minutes is allowed for this stage.

The next stage closely resembles a brainstorming session, except that it is a little more controlled. The facilitator goes around the group, asking each person in turn to suggest an idea. These are then written up for all to see. If an idea is repeated, ask for another; if it appears to overlap with one already suggested, ask if it is the same or not, and accept the judgement of the person suggesting it. If someone says that he or she has nothing to suggest, or that his or her ideas have already been put forward, allow this person to pass. If an idea is very wordy or clumsily phrased, ask its author to rephrase it more briefly – or accept a suggested way of doing this from other participants. It is important that the facilitator is *not* seen as dominating the session, imposing his or her own ideas, or rephrasing points so that those who suggested them do not recognize them as their own. Group ownership of the ideas suggested is needed. The facilitator's role is merely that: to act as an almost transparent facilitator of the group process. Only when the group starts to discuss the merits of an idea just suggested should the facilitator intervene; discussion can take place during the following stage.

One of the ways in which this second stage resembles a brainstorming session is that one idea can spark another – an incident usually referred to as 'piggybacking'. Research into group processes has supported the commonsense notion that, by building on each other's ideas, a successful group can suggest more than the sum of ideas of its individual members.[5]

In the third stage these ideas are discussed. Here, it is useful to take another colour of pen, and number each of the items as it is discussed. The facilitator takes charge of this stage, but only in terms of process: typical questions will be 'Does everyone know what this idea means?' and 'I'm not sure whether this idea is the same as that one. What do you think?' – and here, if any participant says the idea should be separate, leave it as separate. This stage permits the group to discuss and consider each of the ideas it has proposed in turn, taking advantage of the group's total knowledge.

The facilitator then hands around a number of blank cards, perhaps five per participant. Participants are then asked to decide upon the five most important suggestions the group has made. Using an example written up on a board, the facilitator asks that one suggestion be placed on each card:

```
┌─────────────────────────────────────┐
│                                     │
│   8.    Guide for new users         │
│                                     │
│                                     │
└─────────────────────────────────────┘
```

This example is for item 8; participants might prefer merely to write simply '8. Guide'. They are then asked to rank the five items which they have selected. This is done by asking them to identify the one of most importance, then the one of least, then of those items still unranked the most important, and so on till all are in rank order. This ranking sequence is suggested as the easiest way of ensuring that all participants make careful, considered decisions about their rank order.

Votes for each item are then recorded by participants on their cards. With five choices the first ranked items needs to be given five votes, the second four votes, and so on down to the last item which is given a single vote. Votes are then recorded on each card, either with the number of votes circled or underlined:
Again, it is best for this to be demonstrated by the facilitator. Recording the rank

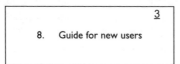

can be a source of grief for an inexperienced facilitator. Unprompted, many participants will label their priority number 1 as '1'; others will fail to make it clear whether they are intending to give three votes to item 5, or five votes to item 3. Total confusion is guaranteed!

Finally, the cards are gathered, shuffled to preserve anonymity, and a group member is asked to read out item numbers and votes ('item 7, three votes') while the facilitator records these on the board. A preliminary tally of votes is then made – a wonderful opportunity to display in public any limitations in one's simple arithmetic – and the formal session is at an end. Groups almost invariably express interest in and surprise at what they have voted for, and by what margins.

A full description of this process is given in Delbecq, Van den Ven and Gustafson.[6] If you are unable to watch an experienced facilitator using the technique, we strongly recommend you read their description: they walk the reader through the complete process, giving verbatim transcripts of what a facilitator might say at each stage, explaining the purpose of each step and discussing problems commonly experienced. Their purpose is to enable a complete novice to conduct a successful NGT session with no additional guidance.

Uses of NGT

One of the writers has used NGT for many years. It has been used as part of the preliminary research work leading to quantitative questionnaires with non-information organizations and with undergraduate students as an adjunct to the focus group method described above as Research Scenario 9.1. It has been found to be a particularly versatile and capable tool, partly because it combines elements of so many other group processes. The unique advantage of NGT is that it gives the benefits of both individual and group participation. Individual participation comes in the idea generating stage, with its silent, concentrated thought, as well as in the evaluation stage where, if people are not personally convinced that an idea is good they do not have to vote for it. The benefits of the group approach come from the discussion of ideas and the 'piggybacking', allowing the presentation of individual ideas to spark the generation of additional ideas.

NGT is a relatively quick process, usually taking no more that 90 minutes with a group of strangers. With students it can be completed in 50 minutes to fit into a regular class time. It has the advantage of showing priorities. As these are in numeric form (total votes cast for each alternative) they may be manipulated statistically if that will be useful to you, as it is very likely to be if you are undertaking subsequent quantitative research. Many techniques that require ordinal data, such as Spearman's rank correlation and Kendall's measure of association (standard tests in inferential statistics), are suitable. The technique also provides the words of the participants themselves rather than the words of the researcher. If you are involved in questionnaire design, this can be essential in obtaining valid responses.

RESEARCH SCENARIO 9.2

THE INFORMATION NEEDS OF ACCREDITED COACHES[7]

Clark wanted to investigate the information needs and information-seeking behaviour of accredited sports coaches. While coaches might not seem a group likely to have important information needs, this is not so. At the top international level, preparing athletes for the Olympic Games and similar competitions, coaching is a highly scientific, highly competitive and serious concern.

Very little previous research had been carried out into the information needs of coaches. Thus, although the principal component of Clark's project was to be a quantitative survey, it was far from clear what questions should be asked. What were the concerns of coaches? What did they see as their information needs? What information sources did they currently use, and how satisfied were they with them?

Clark decided to carry out NGT discussions with coaches from the sports she intended to survey: swimming and track and field. However, she first undertook a pilot NGT with tennis coaches so that she could be sure that the question she was using was appropriate, and to ensure that she felt comfortable using the technique. A colleague who was experienced in using the technique attended this session as an observer and assistant, and to provide subsequent comment. The question she asked her pilot group was, 'What information resources and services would you like to have for your coaching?'

This question was intended to obtain as broad as possible a range of comments from participants about information resources and services. Earlier interviews and informal discussions with coaches had suggested that using the words 'library' or 'information centre' would have restricted the range of items mentioned. Hence a very general question was piloted; it proved successful and was not changed for her other groups.

NGT sessions were held during national conferences and workshops for each sport. Coaches were happy to attend sessions, and numbers of participants ranged from 11 to 15. The only impact of these larger numbers appeared to be that the sessions were slightly longer than anticipated, at about two hours. Participants appeared very happy with the process, and continued to talk about the issues raised afterwards in informal discussion, which Clark also found helpful.

The subsequent survey prepared by Clark was based on the findings of her NGT sessions with the swimming and track and field coaches, and in this she was able to secure a response rate of 69 per cent. Her own comment on the value of the NGT sessions was that the sessions were 'highly successful as a means of identifying ideas and key issues in relation to sport information resources and services for coaches'.

This discussion suggests that four uses of NGT are particularly beneficial in an information setting:

- It can help identify the problems or concerns of participants, as with Research Scenario 9.2 (above). This can be particularly valuable if these are not really known in advance.
- It can aid in establishing priorities. If funds are limited, as is often the case, which issues are most pressing? If there are too many items to include in a questionnaire, which are likely to be most important to its recipients?
- It can bring together a diverse group, perhaps of clients and professionals, or of very widely differing categories of client.
- It can be used as a pilot research technique, again as with Clark's study in Research Scenario 9.2.

Advantages and disadvantages of NGT

The advantages of NGT were mentioned above in the description of the process. To reiterate, there are five major advantages:

- It uses individual knowledge, expertise and judgment.
- It makes use of a group's ability to suggest a variety of ideas and assess these.
- It is fast.
- It generates a numeric priority ranking.
- It uses the terminology of participants.

One particular advantage of NGT is that, if the suggestions and votes of participants are recorded on a chart at the end of a session, all the facilitator has to do is take it away to have a full and useable record of group outcomes.

Another advantage of the NGT, particularly over focus groups, is that it is very much more difficult for a senior, aggressive or dominating individual to steamroller group results. Of course, in the discussion stages such an individual may have much more to say than other group members. But in the end, if the other participants are not convinced by that person's arguments, in the final, secret voting stage they will give their own opinions. The originators of the technique, Delbecq, Van den Ven and Gustafson, rightly pointed out that this also enables its use in mixed groups of professionals and clients or consumers in situations such as strategic planning.[8] Ultimately, if the clients are not persuaded by the professionals, they vote according to their convictions.

The single greatest disadvantage of NGT is that it can only be used to address a single issue at a time. It is a truism in research that if you ask the wrong questions, you cannot hope to get the right answers. If you ask a poorly phrased or inappropriate nominal group question, your results will be of little or no value. Hence it is vital that you pilot test your NGT question; preparation for an NGT session is considered below.

Another potential disadvantage is that the group should consist of no fewer than five and no more than about a dozen participants. With fewer than five participants it is difficult to gain sufficient group momentum for participants to spark ideas off each other, and the group lacks the resources to suggest many issues. With more than about a dozen, the process becomes drawn out, and individuals start to lose the feeling that their own contribution is of importance.

As with focus groups, finding a suitable time and place to meet can be a problem. To a much greater degree than with focus groups, though, to be really effective all the participants have to start together. Latecomers either oblige the entire group to wait for them before a start can be made or will find it very difficult to understand what is going on and so to contribute.

If a whole series of NGT sessions is held, as may be the case when a broad range of opinions and perspectives is required, another potential difficulty arises. Combining the results of a number of NGT sessions into a single consolidated list of issues is far from straightforward. Indeed, it is an acknowledged difficulty with the process.[9] The usual approach is merely to identify the issues that were raised as high priority concerns by a number of the discussion groups. It has to be recognized that this procedure is essentially subjective and, further, that it is quite possible that a suggestion made by a single group – as indeed by a single individual in a focus group discussion – might well be of special insight or worth further exploration.

It has also been pointed out that with NGT 'the quality of the ideas is likely to vary greatly. Some may be shallow, uninformed, or impractical. Therefore, NGT is usually a starting place and needs to be used in conjunction with a technique for idea development.'[10] Similar comments could be made about the results of many unstructured discussions, including focus groups. Here again, as with focus groups and qualitative research generally, much will depend on the skill with which the results are interpreted.

Online group discussion

Recently, there has been considerable interest in the use of electronic brainstorming (EBS), focus group and NGT sessions. Chase and Alvarez conducted both face-to-face and online focus groups sessions and compared the similarities and differences.[11] As well as its evident value in undertaking research into online behaviour, they suggest online focus groups 'would be particularly effective for addressing sensitive issues' and suggest choice should take into account the preferences of participants. Certainly, all these online alternatives offer possible solutions to the problem of gathering an appropriate group in a single place and time and, for focus groups, of recording the discussion.

Preparing for an NGT session

We assume that anyone intending to undertake a nominal group session as part of a research project will carry out at least one pilot session. More than one pilot may, in fact, be desirable if the initial choice of question proves unsatisfactory; if the first 'real' session is important, you would want to go into it confident that your question was appropriate.

How do you choose a nominal group question? In most cases this is done by looking at the research question underlying your project as a whole. Simply phrased, in normal language, this should go to the heart of what you want to know. Develop several alternative wordings, and discuss these with colleagues, your supervisor or other knowledgeable individual. Avoid complex, multi-part questions that take several lines of type; these are more likely to confuse than elicit valuable suggestions. A good question, then, has these characteristics:

- It is relatively short.
- It is simple to understand.
- It is directly related to the research question being investigated.
- It is open-ended.

As Delbecq, Van den Ven and Gustafson point out, 'In the end, a good NGT question is one which evokes the types of responses sought.'[12]

Choice of participants is the next concern. As with focus groups, these may be pre-existing groups such as a relevant committee or perhaps a management group. However, since one of the advantages of NGT is that it can bring together individuals who do not necessarily work or interact together regularly, individuals from a variety of backgrounds or professional areas can be invited to take part. In discussing focus groups we mentioned purposive samples; here, a purposive sample may be of individuals who together will be broadly representative in some relevant ways.

Naturally, not all those invited will attend. In a work situation, most probably will. However, our experience has been that clients often are not highly motivated to take part in information agency research studies. University undergraduates, for example, can be very casual about such things. Tell clients that you will be providing tea, coffee and fruit juice as well as cakes and chocolate biscuits (and then make sure you remember to do this); invite a dozen participants – and then hope that at least six will turn up not too long after the session was supposed to commence.

To carry out the session you will need an appropriate venue. As well as being somewhere easy to find and where you are unlikely to be disturbed, this should enable you to arrange chairs and tables in a semicircle or hollow square around a vertical surface of some kind on which the nominal group question can be displayed, and where group suggestions can be written up. A blank wall and bluetack or masking tape make a perfectly satisfactory substitute for a whiteboard.

Finally, NGT is a technique with some simple but inflexible stationery requirements. Never commence a session without these five essentials:

- answer sheets with the question at the top (if you accept our suggestion on this)
- pens for participants (only some will bring pens)
- a chart and something to fasten it up, even if a whiteboard is available, since this enables you to retain full details of items suggested and the votes each attracted without any subsequent transcription
- several colours of pen to write on the chart
- 5 × 3 inch (12 × 8 cm) cards, grouped into batches of five, for the final voting stage.

We do not suggest that NGT, any more than focus group, is appropriate as a sole data-gathering technique. However, either or both these approaches are likely to be valuable in complementing more commonly employed data-collecting methods such as the interview, and deserve more serious consideration than they have so far received in information research.

Review of Chapter 9

Because organizations use groups as an integral part of their management, and because we are a social species, it can be valuable to gather data from groups as well as from individuals. Focus groups are the simplest way in which to obtain research data from a homogenous group associated with an organization. However, this is a technique very much reliant on the self-confidence and expertise of the facilitator and, at least for the novice, may well require supplementing by other data-gathering approaches.

By contrast, the NGT requires participants to proceed through a series of prescribed stages. This has advantages both for the facilitator, who is less likely to influence the outcomes through relative inexperience, and in terms of the written, prioritized outcomes it produces. However, only a single question can be addressed by the group, so a pilot session to check this is essential.

No single methodology will be appropriate to all needs. Despite their other minor disadvantages – essentially those associated with gathering together any group of participants – experience suggests that focus groups and NGT are both highly appropriate for information research. It is surprising that there appear to be so few reports of their use in this area.

Where to now?

After you review the focus questions that appeared at the start of this chapter, you may wish to turn to Clayton's account of his use of NGT in a college library,[13] and see if you can answer the following three questions:

- Was the use of NGT in this study an example of qualitative or quantitative research?
- How did the researcher achieve reliability and validity in his investigation?
- Could focus groups have been used instead of NGT?

Further reading

An impressive online guide, *Research Methods Resources on the WWW: Qualitative Group Methods,* is provided by the School of Library, Archival and Information Studies at the University of British Columbia (www.slais.ubc.ca/resources/research_methods/group.htm). As well as covering both focus group and NGT, this site also covers Delphi, a closely related technique not discussed here because of its quantitative focus. The site links to a large number of full-text articles, and as we write appears to be kept right up to date. Additional information on focus group techniques in particular is provided by M. Lewis, *Focus Group Interviews in Qualitative Research: A Review of the Literature: An Online Full-text Guide* (www.scu.edu.au/schools/gcm/ar/arr/arow/rlewis.html).

A recent overview of the use of focus group in libraries is provided by M. Von Seggern and N. J. Young, 'The Focus Group Method in Libraries: Issues Relating to Process and Data Analysis', *Reference Services Review*, **31** (3), 2003, pp. 272–84. This article also includes a useful bibliography. An example of its use in evaluating web design is provided by R. F. Dennison, J. Jackson, H. V. Leighton and K. Sullivan, 'Web Page Design and Successful Use: A Focus Group Study', *Internet Reference Services Quarterly*, **8** (3), 2003, pp. 17–27. Other introductions, incorporating examples of the technique in use, are provided by A. Goulding, 'Joking, Being Aggressive and Shutting People Up: The Use of Focus Groups in LIS Research', *Education for Information*, **15**, 1997, pp. 331–41; and K. M. Drabenstott, 'Focused Group Interviews'. In *Qualitative Research in Information Management*, eds. J. D. Glazier

LIVERPOOL JOHN MOORES UNIVERSITY
LEARNING SERVICES

and R. R. Powell (Englewood, CO: Libraries Unlimited, 1992), pp. 85–104. More detailed guides are R. Krueger, *Focus Groups: A Practical Guide for Applied Research* 2nd edn (Thousand Oaks, CA: Sage, 1994) and M. Bloor and others, *Focus Groups in Social Research* (London: Sage, 2001). Despite its evident marketing focus, *Focus Groups: Supporting Effective Product Development*, ed. J. Langford and D. McDonagh (London: Taylor & Francis, 2003) provides a great deal of highly practical advice on running focus group discussions.

A complete 'how-to-do-it' guide to the nominal group technique is provided by its originators, A. L. Delbecq, A. H. Van den Ven and D. H. Gustafson, *Group Techniques for Program Planning: A Guide to Nominal Group and Delphi Processes* (Glenview, IL: Scott, Foresman, 1975). This is strongly recommended to those unable to watch a colleague demonstrate the process. A simpler overview appears in S. L. Gill and A. L. Delbecq, 'Nominal Group Technique (NGT)'. In *Group Planning and Problem-solving Methods in Engineering Management*, ed. S. A. Olsen (New York: John Wiley, 1982), pp. 271–87. As noted, examples of its use in information research are unfortunately rare. The one recent exception is D. Havelka, 'A User-oriented Model of Factors that Affect Information Requirements Determination Process Quality', *Information Resources Management Journal*, **16** (4), Oct–Dec 2003, pp. 15–32. Some other, much older library examples are cited in P. Clayton, 'Nominal Group Technique and Library Management', *Library Administration and Management*, **4** (1), 1990, 24–6. A recent use in higher education is reported by S. C. Jones, 'Using the Nominal Group Technique to Select the Most Appropriate Topics for Postgraduate Research Students' Seminars', *Journal of University Teaching and Learning Practice*, **1** (1), 2004, pp. 20–34.

Notes

1 P. Clayton, 'Group Processes for Libraries'. In *Australian Library and Information Association, 1st Biennial Conference, Conference Proceedings* (Perth: Promoco Conventions for ALIA, 1990), vol. 2, pp. 447–59; S. A. Olsen, ed., *Group Planning and Problem-solving Methods in Engineering Management* (New York: John Wiley and Sons, 1982).

2 K. Crocker, 'Focus Groups', *AIMA Newsletter*, **10** (2), 1995, pp. 2–12.

3 O. Baskin and C. Aronoff, *Public Relations: The Profession and the Practice*, 3rd edn (Boston: Little Brown, 1992), p. 111.

4 D. J. Snowden, 'Storytelling: An Old Art in a New Context', *Business Information Review*, **16** (1), 2000, pp. 30–7; D. J. Snowden, 'The Art and Science of Story or "Are You Sitting Uncomfortably?" Part 1: Gathering and Harvesting the Raw Material', *Business Information Review*, **17** (3), 2000, pp. 147–56; D. J. Snowden, 'The Art and Science of Story or "Are You Sitting Uncomfortably?" Part 2: The Warp and the Weft of Purposeful Story', *Business Information Review*, **17** (4), 2000, pp. 215–26. The first of these articles provides a justification for the technique but little advice on its execution; for that, see the second in particular. See also D. Clandinin and F. M. Connelly, *Narrative Inquiry: Experience and Story in Qualitative Research* (San Francisco, CA: Jossey-Bass, 2000).

5 J. Hall, 'Decisions, 'Decisions, Decisions', *Psychology Today*, November 1971, pp. 51–4, 86, 88. Hall points out that the well-known group exercise, 'Lost on the Moon', demonstrates this.

6 A. L. Delbecq, A. H. Van den Ven and D. H. Gustafson, *Group Techniques for Program Planning: A Guide to Nominal Group and Delphi Processes* (Glenview, IL: Scott, Foresman, 1975), Chapter 3.

7 This research scenario is based on the work of N. Clark, A Study of the Information Needs and Information-seeking Behaviour of Australian Accredited Coaches in the Sports of Swimming and Track and Field. MA thesis, University of Canberra, 1995.

8 Delbecq, Van den Ven and Gustafson, op. cit., p. 108.

9 S. L. Gill and A. L. Delbecq, 'Nominal Group Technique (NGT)'. In *Group Planning and Problem-solving Methods in Engineering Management,* ed. S. A. Olsen (New York: John Wiley and Sons), p. 287; and C. M. Moore, *Group Techniques for Idea Building*, Applied Social Research Methods Series, 9 (Newbury Park, CA: Sage, 1987), p. 127.

10 Moore, op. cit., p. 35.

11 L. Chase and J. Alvarez, 'Internet Research: The Role of the Focus Group', *Library & Information Science Research*, **22** (4), 2000, pp. 357–69. See also A. R. Dennis and J. S. Valacich, 'Research Note: Electronic Brainstorming: Illusions and Patterns of Productivity', *Information Systems Research*, **10** (4), April 1999, pp. 375–7.

12 Delbecq, Van den Ven and Gustafson, op. cit., p.77.

13 P. Clayton, 'The Role of Users in Library Planning II: A Research Report', *Australian Academic & Research Libraries*, **20** (3), 1989, pp. 129–38.

10 Historical investigation*

Sidney J. Shep

FOCUS QUESTIONS
- What are the distinguishing characteristics of historical investigation?
- What are the range and nature of historical sources?
- How does the researcher interpret historical evidence?
- How can historical research be combined with other qualitative methods?

Why historical investigation?

The noted American bibliographer and book historian G. Thomas Tanselle once said that 'History is a subject about which everyone seems to have a heated opinion, including the determination to ignore it.'[1] Chapter 3 noted that historical research in the information profession has been employed primarily to build organizational case studies and recover life histories celebrating the profession's heroes and heroines. This chapter will demonstrate the ongoing relevance and importance of historical research to address key issues, both past and present, in the context of library, archive, knowledge management and other information services.

Definitions of history and methods of historical practice are multiple, often contradictory, and vehemently defended. John Tosh, in his eminently readable work *The Pursuit of History: Aims, Methods and New Directions in the Study of Modern History*, notes that history is both what happened in the past and how that past is represented in the writings of historians.[2] It is a disciplined and systematic form of enquiry, which combines the strengths of both humanities and social science research. History places the nature, value and interpretation of historical information sources centre-stage. As such, it enables valuable links to be made between past and present: between the variety of human mentalities or achievements and their relation to current manifestations; between the historical impact of change and its future implications; between the social, political or popular construction of what happened and its relationship to specific events.

In any organization it is impossible to understand the present situation without an appreciation of the past, of the organization's history. Moreover, if one is concerned with change, historical perspective is vital both in providing a realistic

---

* This is a revised version of a chapter originally written by Professor Lyn Gorman.

idea of what might be feasible and in revealing any distorted representations of the past that may be obstructing change. As an example, a collection manager who is contemplating a significant shift in collecting priorities would be well advised to gain some historical understanding of the long-term development of the present collection profile, the reasons for the collection's strengths and weaknesses, the existence of any vested interests likely to oppose change and so on. This historical understanding is best gained by consulting the institutional memory – whether through documents and/or people – and considering the historical context of past decision-making.

There are as many approaches to historical research as there are types of historical records. Historiography (the study of the writing of history) is frequently separated into various genres or 'sub-branches': political, constitutional, social, economic, labour, urban, rural, history of international relations, history of ideas, women's history, and cultural history, to name a few. Each 'sub-branch' evokes both a range of topics or issues addressed and a specific theoretical or methodological approach. Examples from some of these should illustrate the ongoing relevance of historical investigation for information professionals.

- Perspectives gained from institutional history may be important in a library or archive where there are pressures to implement substantial changes in collection focus and acquisitions policy; such changes may imply the marginalization of special collections that historical research demonstrates should continue to be given high priority.
- The understanding of trends revealed by research into economic history may be a prerequisite to informed budgetary decision-making and to mounting convincing arguments about funding.
- Historical data on an information service's evolving client service priorities may be essential as a basis for decisions concerning services to, say, particular ethnic groups in a multicultural social context.
- Research on gender balance, informed by historical understanding of broader trends in women's employment, may supply important data about the implementation of equal opportunity legislation for information personnel.
- Historical investigation of the impact of information technologies may inform an investigation of changing information culture, or be the basis for decisions on co-operative collection development among institutions or on planning 'the library of the future'.

The techniques of historical investigation complement other qualitative approaches discussed in this book as well as a number of quantitative methods. This chapter will outline how historians, situated in the present, gain access to the distant or immediate past, what kinds of records are available, and how to collect and interpret those records. Finally, it will demonstrate how, as Shiflett remarks, 'the role of historical study must be interactive with other forms of research'.[3]

Characteristics of historical investigation

As with qualitative research, it is difficult to find a simple and agreed definition of 'history' or 'historical investigation'. Indeed, definitions and emphases change over time. While one age may see history as grand narrative telling the story of past ages, another may emphasize its social, and thus practical, role and stress the analytical aspect, which elucidates causes and consequences. Similarly, historical methods have been scrutinized according to whether they share the rigour and objectivity of scientific research or whether they are more subjective, reflecting the preoccupations of the time and space in which they are practised. The establishment of the Social Science History Association in 1974 signalled an important milestone in straddling the perceived divide between quantitative and qualitative research. It also highlighted the complexity as well as flexibility of new approaches to historical investigation.[4]

There are several key points that distinguish historical investigation.

- History is concerned with the past, but historians can never recreate that actual past. Temporal and spatial distance from the original or primary event(s), coupled with a range of mediating factors including the historical focus and interpretive frameworks of the researcher, mean that 'history' is a re-telling of a version of the past by historians who can only use evidence that has survived from that past. Echoing Hayden White's influential pronouncements, the material culture historian David Kingery notes, 'All history is fiction; we can never "know" the past.'[5]
- The writing of history depends on how a researcher collects, evaluates, prioritizes and interprets the surviving records. E. H. Carr, in his now classic work entitled *What Is History?*, stresses that history 'is a continuous process of interaction between the historian and his facts'. Carr and others, especially postmodernists, have argued about the status of historical 'facts', particularly whether they exist objectively and independently of the interpretation of the historian.[6] However, the important point here is that there is constant interaction between interpretation and facts: some facts will be more important than others depending on the historian's focus; the historian selects from among available facts; history is indeed 'an unending dialogue between past and present'.[7] Arthur Marwick puts it another way: 'the past as we know it from the interpretations of historians based on the critical study of the widest possible range of relevant sources, every effort having been made to challenge, and avoid the perpetuation of, myth'.[8]
- A third characteristic follows from the second: given the importance of interpretation, it is evident that historians bring to historical research certain pre-existing interpretive frameworks shaped by their own social and historical background. We do not study the past from a vacuum or from a position of complete neutrality. Our own and our society's concerns and priorities influence the way we look at the past and the aspects we consider worthy of historical attention. Furthermore, some historians have clearly articulated

theoretical standpoints, perhaps Marxist or non-Marxist, feminist or non-feminist. The most conscientious practitioners are aware of their biases and prejudices, acknowledge them, and accommodate them in their work; they are never completely erased. Likewise, one needs to approach the products of other historians' efforts critically, being alert to the way a theoretical position or set of motivations may affect how a topic is approached, what issues are researched and what neglected, and how the results are reported. The fine line between history and social memory or between history and propaganda, for instance, can be better understood when the role of history as an agent in shaping consciousness is recognized.[9]

- Historians balance their temporal and spatial dislocation by using empathy and imagination to interpret historical records and, through them, to build historical contexts. The 19th-century historicist movement originating in Germany countered attacks of antiquarianism by claiming that 'the main task of the historian [is] to find out why people acted as they did by stepping into their shoes, by seeing the world through their eyes and as far as possible judging it by their standards.'[10] Modern historians declare the specific contemporary filters that have a strong effect on this utopia of seeing, but use empathy and imagination to insert themselves, as far as possible, into the historical context. As a result, they share the same goal as qualitative researchers as outlined in Chapter 1; that is, to understand those being studied from their own perspective, from their own point of view.

If we define 'history' as 'the representation of the past in the work of historians' or 'the past as we know it from the interpretations of historians based on the critical study of the widest possible range of relevant sources', and note the importance of both the interaction between the historian and the sources, and the historian and the broader contemporary context, how do we conduct historical research? The process consists of four phases:

1 Identifying and locating relevant sources.
2 Assessing the nature and value of these sources, applying the critical method discussed below.
3 Interpreting the evidence found in the sources.
4 Communicating the interpretation in written form.[11]

Identifying and locating historical sources

Sources are the raw material of historical investigation, the evidence of the past activities of individuals, organizations, societies, nations or whatever the unit of investigation might be. In what is now referred to as 'traditional history', 'sources' meant exclusively 'written sources'. However, the scope of historical enquiry expanded dramatically in the 20th century. Rather than concentrating on political and military events, elites and decision-makers and the role of the state, history now has as its subject matter the whole range of past human experience. In particular, social history has come to dominate the historical endeavour; approaches that take a 'bottom-up' or even micro-historical perspective have become popular, and historians have aspired to write 'total history'. As a result, the range of source material relevant to historical enquiry has expanded virtually without limit.[12] It now includes not only written records but also physical remains (archaeological finds, buildings, transportation systems, and so on) and the shape of the landscape revealed by aerial photography and satellite imaging; the products of communications media and popular culture artefacts (such as films, recordings of radio and television programmes, posters and cartoons) as well as literary and artistic works; oral history and oral traditions; and many more.[13] The revolution in communications technology means that historians of the 21st century will also need to consider electronic documents and archives, digital resources and the contents of the 'virtual library' among their sources.

Historians often organize this diversity of source material into two types, primary and secondary, although at times the distinctions are not always transparent. *Primary sources* are the 'raw materials', those original sources that came into existence during the period to which they refer, the sources which are in direct or close temporal and spatial proximity to the events or people in which the historian is interested. Some examples of primary data are: documents or records written by participants or witnesses of an event; remains or relics associated with a person, group or period; oral testimony often obtained in a personal interview, which may be recorded on tape or transcribed. *Secondary sources* are critical accounts, filtered by an intermediary, drawing on and interpreting primary sources. They are often written by professional historians about a period in the past but can also include reflective pieces including newspaper accounts and commentaries after the fact. However, there are certain materials that do not fall neatly into one category or the other: autobiography is a hybrid which may include first-hand experience, personal correspondence contemporaneous with the lived experience, as well hindsight, reflection and memorial reconstruction if written some time after the events in question. Electronic documents are also problematic as the traditional distinction between 'original' and 'copy' does not apply. Moreover, the increasing availability of web-based, digital surrogates of primary sources as an answer to the information profession's concerns about preservation and access raises important questions about the original context of the source material, its modification in the virtual environment, and the new skills researchers need to extract contextual as well as content-based information.[14]

The second distinction concerns the nature of the evidence that may be derived from the sources. This is usually described as *witting* and *unwitting testimony*. Some sources are created for posterity; that is, they contain a message deliberately recorded, or information or impressions that the creator of the source intended to convey. Official government-commissioned war histories are examples of such 'witting' testimony. Other sources may contain completely unintentional messages or provide insights which the originator was not conscious of conveying

– hence 'unwitting' testimony. Soldiers' private war diaries would be instances of individual responses to specific events isolated from full knowledge or endorsement of the war machine. Some historians argue that the sources of 'unwitting testimony', created with no thought of posterity, are more valuable. From them – by 'reading between the lines' – the historian may, for example, gain valuable information on prevailing attitudes or assumptions or on the underlying structures or frameworks within which events occurred.[15]

In the context of information services, what sources is the historical researcher likely to use? The answer to this question will depend on the particular research problem, but the following list will provide some idea of the likely range of sources produced within the institution or by current or former staff. Although many are written and published, other media sources and the wealth of unpublished material not in the public domain can also contribute valuable material and insights, such as:

- official written sources including documentation on the institution's establishment, its aims and objectives, formal minutes of meetings, budgets, and so on
- surveys and reports on aspects of the institution's operations (for example, on composition of the collection, or on user attitudes)
- autobiographical accounts, memoirs, reminiscences, private diaries and recorded interviews by key personnel
- legal documents such as wills referring to bequests to the collections
- handbooks, guides, bibliographies or other works of reference prepared by staff for particular client groups
- day-to-day records on loans, materials circulation and client services
- the physical infrastructure including photo documentation which represents the accretions of building programmes over the years and perhaps changes in interior design to respond to evolving service delivery or technological change.

Beyond the specific institution, relevant sources may include:

- national, state, or civic archives, or the archives of a parent organization
- published or unpublished records of library associations and other professional bodies on matters of professional relevance
- articles in the national or local press on the history of a particular information service or on broader relevant issues.

It is essential to note that when a researcher contemplates historical investigation of a particular problem, he or she does not immediately plunge into the primary sources. The fact that a problem has been identified implies that some preliminary research and thinking have already been done, even if it has not been done in exactly the same context. However, as with other research, the normal sequence in historical investigation is to do a thorough search of existing secondary sources and to become well acquainted with writing on and around the problem before examining the primary sources. Printed and online bibliographies and databases, often termed tertiary sources, are useful in the initial identification of secondary sources which, in turn, are themselves likely to provide further leads via notes and bibliographies.

The research problem will to a certain extent determine the breadth of the initial search. If one is researching an issue in a particular library, archive, or information service where no previous research on the topic has been carried out, try to identify comparable studies in other institutions. Even if the findings of existing research are out of date or have little relevance for your own investigation, the literature may contain valuable hints on methodology, types of source material and so on. If one is researching an issue with wider social implications (women's employment in libraries and archives, for instance), read broadly to begin with (on women in the workforce, trends in women's careers, the implementation of equal employment opportunity legislation, for example) before narrowing the research focus to the particular institution. The better informed one is on the topic and related issues, the more meaningful will be the primary sources. Moreover, reading broadly, then narrowing down the focus, is part of the iterative process used to define, redefine and refine your research problem. It also assists in generating hypotheses, and identifying and testing assumptions.

After ascertaining which sources you would ideally like to consult, you need to locate and gain access to them. Unlike secondary sources, primary sources are usually unique items housed at specific institutions, frequently dispersed between a number of repositories, or through accidents of time and place, not necessarily found at the most logical one(s). As a result, primary source hunting may involve at least three discrete exercises, each a function of where and how the material is deposited, as described below.

- *Applying to use formally archived material.* Most archives have clear policies regarding access and use. They may include restrictions on the use of official material if it is less than 30 years old; businesses may have deposited commercially sensitive information, which is embargoed or subject to special provisions; culturally sensitive material may be only available to those with links to or permission from an indigenous group; personal papers can have restricted access provisions, which require additional time by the researcher or institution to contact the individual or estate and to negotiate initial access as well as publication use.
- *Applying to organizations such as professional associations.* Because such bodies may not have any formal access policies, a lot may depend on making contact with the 'right person'. It is also wise in such situations to clarify the extent to which one is free to quote material directly from the organization's papers, especially if it is relatively recent and refers to living individuals.
- *Approaching an individual or family.* When private papers are held by an individual or within a family, you will need to seek their permission to use the materials.

In this case, too, a clear understanding of the researcher's freedom to quote from the sources is advisable.

Locating your initial selection of primary source material often opens up further possibilities and you should be aware of the importance of serendipity as well as methodical searching in historical investigation. Many institutions lack time and/or financial resources to catalogue their collections down to the individual item level. Consequently, browsing through related materials where possible or alerting staff to your specific area of research can frequently result in additional and highly fruitful leads. Once a selection of primary sources has been located, the researcher must approach them with methodological rigour. The fact that a source exists does not necessarily mean it is a piece of valid historical evidence or relevant to the research problem under investigation.

Using the sources

In the manner of a forensic analyst, historians use a number of critical methods to establish the authenticity, veracity and validity of the data collected, whether from primary or secondary sources, before these sources are given the status of historical evidence. What is commonly referred to as *external criticism* involves establishing the authenticity of the source so that forgeries or hoaxes are eliminated. In some disciplines, tests may include analysis of handwriting, language use, ink, paper, cloth or bones. Once a document, relic or oral testimony is found to be genuine, its accuracy or worth has to be evaluated. This involves a process of *internal criticism*, which interprets the content of the source. The bias, viewpoint, or knowledge of an 'eye-witness' or reporter, for example, has to be determined before the account can be used as evidence. Thus, what we consider to be historical 'fact' has already gone through a process of intense scrutiny; it is not an unconsidered or uncontested piece of information accepted as evidence without rigorous testing. Marwick elaborates on these two processes in a series of seven questions which share affinities with other qualitative research methods such as discourse analysis and content analysis:

1   Is the source authentic; is it what it purports to be?
2   Where did the source come from; what is its provenance?
3   When was the source produced; what is its date; how close is its date to the events related; how does it relate chronologically to other sources?
4   What type of source is it? (a private letter? an official report? a public document of record? and so on)
5   Who created the source; what were his or her attitudes, prejudices, vested interests; for what purpose was the source created; to whom was it addressed?
6   To what extent is the author in a position to provide first-hand information on the topic of interest to the historian; what is the role of hearsay?
7   How was the document understood by contemporaries; what exactly did it say?[16]

LIVERPOOL JOHN MOORES UNIVERSITY
Aldham Robarts L.R.C.
TEL. 051 231 3701/3634

Some of these questions may seem more relevant than others to the information professional, who is unlikely to be confronted with momentous questions about the authenticity of human remains uncovered during an archaeological dig or some equivalent of the faked 'Hitler diaries'. However, one wants to be sure that any source is what it purports to be. Furthermore, the questions about content and reliability are important, as they help the researcher to judge the value of any particular source. They should also assist in the identification of bias or the operation of culture-bound assumptions or stereotypes.

The sources available to the historian are never complete. History has often been characterized as a huge jigsaw puzzle – without all the pieces. There are many types of historical records, and each has its own rationale for being. What was created for one particular reason can be preserved for another, or disposed of for a completely different reason. The distinction between a record, created in the course of an institution's day-to-day activities, and an archive, that particular record which has been selected and preserved for posterity, is pertinent. Flood, fire, earthquake, and other natural disasters can impact on the survival rate of the documentary record; the material out of which the record itself is made can likewise determine its survival rate. The chance that there may be no extant records at all is an equally daunting prospect. Nevertheless, it is important to locate as many relevant sources as possible. The more sources used, the fewer the gaps to be filled. The greater the variety of sources, the more the historian will be able to give due weight to competing viewpoints or multiple perspectives and develop a more finely textured understanding of the complexity of the past. A wealth of sources also enables cross-checking to establish the reliability of individual sources. As with other research methods, such triangulation provides more scope and validity for testing hypotheses, making generalizations or formulating conclusions.

The critical method discussed above was developed in relation to documentary sources, but the same spirit of analysis and criticism should be applied to other types and formats of source material. To information professionals working in already advanced electronic environments, the critical method may seem rather archaic as it makes no provision for electronic sources. The speed with which the internet is developing presents both potential benefits and problems for historians. On the one hand is the prospect of access to a daily-expanding wealth of sources in locations to which the researcher may not have been able to travel (perhaps works of art held by the Louvre in Paris accessible on the Louvre Web Museum, or holdings of the Vatican Library converted to digital form for the internet); and the range of electronic sources is constantly expanding – text, photographs, drawings, sound, moving images, multi-dimensional representations of objects. On the other hand, 'the familiar world of paper documents at the heart of their profession is giving way before their eyes to electronic archives where records float in the ether without smell or touch or certainty about their origin, or about their authenticity.'[17] Historians working in a virtual information setting need to consider specific issues related to their source material:

- questions about the authenticity, accuracy, integrity and validity of electronic documents; these are crucial, given the ease with which electronic documents can be modified (Is an electronic document the 'first original'? Is the person named as its author in fact its creator?)[18]
- judgements concerning the significance and quality of electronic sources, particularly if they lack the contextual information to which historians generally refer[19]
- issues concerning understanding and interpretation of sources which differ fundamentally from traditional primary sources; Deegan refers to 'the virtuality of the medium', to 'dialogic text', to the problem of determining when a work produced electronically, with multiple authorial voices, has been finished, to the object of the historian's study as 'a virtual object stored in a highly mutable form' and to 'the changing nature of artefactuality in the world of networked scholarship'[20]
- how to cope with the immense volume of material becoming available in electronic form; here, selection is even more important than hitherto; those who attempt to keep up-to-date with all available information in their field will risk overspecialization and never find time to 'organize, analyse, synthesize – in other words, create'.[21]

Recording the sources

In addition to approaching historical sources critically in whatever form they occur, it is essential that you develop a competent form of note taking. When it comes to writing up research findings, it is vital to have well organized, accessible notes, which record the evidence from the sources. This provides the basis for historical interpretation. Different forms of note taking suit different researchers: some prefer handwritten records on large index cards; some enter notes directly into a computer database; some use a bibliographic software package to keep references and notes together. It is inappropriate to be too prescriptive on this matter, but there are useful general guidelines:

- It is essential to include a precise and comprehensive reference to the source on each note. This ensures that you are certain where the material came from, and that it can be correctly cited in the final written account.
- There is a related point about citation conventions: if you are not familiar with the correct way of referring to a particular type of source – archives, for example – you should discuss this with an experienced researcher or archivist, or consult an appropriate handbook or a reputable secondary work which cites similar material. This should be done before the research begins so that appropriate details can be recorded at the time.
- Historical investigation should be based on sound chronology. Therefore, it may be useful to establish a separate chronology or timeline on which to note significant events in date order.[22]

- You need to decide on the level of detail to be recorded in notes. In general it is inefficient to take long discursive notes whose relevance to particular aspects of the research problem is not clear. Notes taken under subheadings that reflect a breakdown of the research problem are easily organized. However, if you are using material to which it may be difficult to gain access a second time, more detailed notes will be appropriate – they can be edited down later if necessary.
- Finally, it is important to set aside time regularly to review notes and reorganize them if appropriate. During the research the sources may suggest further questions which require more detailed investigation. In this case it is important to return to one's notes on these issues; extract material relevant to sub-questions; decide if further research is needed to expand on the new questions, and so on.

It is also useful to consider additional organizational strategies, particularly when large amounts of information threaten to overwhelm the researcher and pre-empt the critical detachment essential to information processing and interpretation. A separate reflective journal to record impressions, insights, responses, and intuited observations while researching in the archive becomes an invaluable repository of ideas and comments to revisit throughout the writing process. In this way, it functions in many respects like the ethnographer's field book.

If research is methodical and note taking is concise, well organized and comprehensive, the writing process of any historical investigation should not be too onerous. The products of historical research, whether in the final form of an essay, a book, an exhibition, a television documentary, or a website, are the result of a process of writing, which is closely allied to the interpretative processes of conscious and critical thinking and reading. Carr counters the assumption that historians first collect all their data, then start writing, by advocating the necessary intertwining of critical thinking and critical writing: 'I am convinced that, for any historian worth the name, the two processes of what economists call "input" and "output" go on simultaneously and are, in practice, parts of a single process. If you try to separate them, or give one priority over the other, you fall into one of two heresies. Either you write scissors-and-paste history without meaning or significance; or you write propaganda or historical fiction, and merely use the facts of the past to embroider a kind of writing which has nothing to do with history.'[23]

Oral history

There is one form of historical research which requires further comment both because it presents particular challenges to the historian and because it is often mentioned as relevant to research on libraries and information services: oral history. It is discussed in this section because of the importance of oral history as a technique rather than as a separate branch of history.

'Oral history' refers to study of the recent past through the testimony of participants with first-hand experience. It is useful to distinguish between *oral history*, which relies on personal experiences but where an attempt is made to situate these within a larger context; and *life history*, which refers to spoken autobiography in which the informant relates at some length the parts of his or her life which seem most interesting and important.[24]

Oral history has become more popular in recent decades for two main reasons:

- First, some see oral history as a corrective to elitist 'traditional' history, providing almost an 'oppositional methodology' whereby 'witnesses can now also be called from the underclasses, the unprivileged, and the defeated. [It] provides a more realistic and fair reconstruction of the past, a challenge to the established account . . . [and] has radical implications for the social message of history as a whole.'[25]
- The second reason derives from social historians' interest in *mentalité*, or mental attitudes, perceptions, popular states of mind (an emphasis growing out of the work of the French *Annales* school). Oral testimony can provide valuable data on popular memory or crowd psychology, or insights into the complex workings of social memory.

In a library, for instance, one can envisage the use of oral history techniques in various research areas. For example, oral testimony might supplement other sources on user attitudes to changing service provision policies, or user reactions to changes in online public access catalogues or access to electronic databases; or a researcher might use a number of life histories to gain insight into the relationship between gender and workplace culture.

Oral testimony may provide valuable material to supplement written records. It may assist the researcher in gaining an overall perspective on available documentation, and draw attention to aspects whose importance was not apparent in written sources. It may fill out written accounts of institutional processes with subjective assessments relating to motivation, relationships, the implementation of written policies, and so on. It may convey a feeling for the mood or atmosphere of the time which is not disclosed by written sources. Finally, in an age when ephemeral electronic communication is becoming the norm, and fewer written records are generated in many areas of decision making and policy formulation, oral testimony may assume greater importance as filling the gaps in the documentary record.

The interview, whether individual or in focus groups, is the means by which oral testimony is elicited. Since Chapter 8 has dealt with the interviewing process and techniques in some detail, it is not proposed to discuss these again here.[26] However, it is important to point out that oral history has specific problems of authenticity, reliability and interpretation.

- Although oral testimony is a first-hand account by a person who participated in the events recounted, memory is never 'pure'. Memories or recollections have been filtered through experience and subject to the influence of hindsight; they may have been affected by information from other, including written, sources. They may have been distorted or oversimplified, perhaps because the individual's or broader social attitudes or values have changed, or because subsequent experiences have influenced the individual to view the past nostalgically, through 'rose-coloured glasses'. Some aspects of past experience may have been suppressed or subject to complete memory loss; others in which the individual was emotionally involved may have been remembered vividly. The individual may, consciously or unconsciously, claim more credit in a particular event for purposes of self-aggrandizement or self-vindication. By exercising excessive discretion, perhaps to protect their own or the reputation of others involved in an event, they may render their testimony of little value.

- These memories are generally recounted in an interview situation which itself affects what is said and how it is said. The relationship between interviewer and interviewee cannot be ignored. Moreover, interviews in a group setting can be impacted for better or worse by the group dynamic, whether the interviewees are acquainted or not.
- The reminiscences of individuals may not represent those of any larger collectivity. The sample may be entirely unrepresentative.
- The historical reality of the past is always more than the sum of selected individual experiences. To escape the problem of triviality, the historian needs to relate oral history to a larger framework.[27]

Finally, anyone undertaking oral history research should be aware that ethical issues are involved, and that questions relating to privacy and confidentiality need to be addressed. You should ensure that you are thoroughly acquainted with relevant formal provisions or conventions that apply within an institution. It may be, for example, that there is a formal policy concerning research involving human subjects. It might be argued that collecting oral testimony is very different from conducting scientific experiments on 'human guinea pigs'. However, you need to ascertain if the institutional policy covers oral history research.

Even if there is no written policy, you need to clarify certain issues with interviewees. For example, if the oral testimonies are tape recorded, who will own the tapes and have copyright on the material? If the interviewee is to have ownership rights, you need to clarify the extent to which you will have 'fair use' of these materials (not just at the time and immediately after interviews but also in the longer term). If oral testimony contains references to other living people, there may be issues of confidentiality especially if there are implications for individual reputations. If any controversial and damaging material were to come to light, there may be the possibility of a libel suit. Most oral historians also negotiate archive deposit of the original or edited interview as well as transcript or abstract in order to preserve the material long term and make it available to other historians. Again, access issues must be addressed with the interviewee and format specifications of the institution must be adopted.[28]

Interpreting historical information

The preceding sections have discussed the range of source material relevant to historical investigation and the appropriate methodology for using these sources in a critical manner. The next step is to consider what you do with the evidence from these sources.

The sources have been studied in order to shed light on the original research problem. In the process there may have been some reformulation of the problem, because, in the nature of the historical enterprise, there is 'give and take' between the historian and the sources. The latter may suggest the need to modify, reject or replace initial research questions, or possibly even fundamentally shift the focus of the entire investigation. However, you will reach a point where all the relevant sources have been studied and where you are satisfied about the validity of many facts which have a bearing on the particular problem being studied. It is at this point that both selection and interpretation become important.

Historical investigation involves more than collecting many facts and 'piecing them together' like a collage or assemblage. It is also not a simple accumulation of facts in order to produce a chronological narrative: establishing a chronology is an essential part of the research process, but it is not an end in itself. Above all else, the historian is concerned to understand *why* events occurred and what their consequences were. The establishment of causative relationships is an important aspect of historical research; it is this that helps to make the past intelligible. There has been much debate over the relative importance in history of long- and short-term causes, and of individual actions, contingencies, and 'accidents'. What is important for our purposes is that history is more than just a concatenation of 'facts' or events. It includes the historian's effort to bring some order to events, to prioritize some over others, to establish links among them, to explain how and why things happened and what their outcomes were. The historian requires the following skills or qualities in interpreting the evidence revealed by the sources.

- Powers of abstraction, conceptualization and synthesis are essential to identify patterns and show relationships among past events.
- Imagination is required to fill gaps left by the sources since they are always incomplete or fragmentary.
- Empathy is important in enabling the historian to look at events or issues from the perspectives of people in the past, and to identify prevailing value systems.
- Broad and deep experience of human nature and intuition are crucial in enabling insight into human mentality and motivation in the past.
- Self-awareness is essential to understanding how the historian's own values, perceptions and priorities may influence the judgements he or she makes on the basis of the evidence from the past.
- Finally – and this relates to the next section – the historian needs to be skilled in logical argument and written communication in order to convey the results of his or her interpretation to a wider audience.

An important element in the dialogue between researcher and sources is the role of informed intuition and speculation. Depending on the subject area, there may be few records; those which have remained may not be representative of place, period, or certain people. If there are too many records, the process of selection may not be immediately apparent from, or guided by, the extant archive. In each instance, the historical researcher fills in parts of the jigsaw puzzle or provides an organizational framework by the judicious and justifiable use of the probable. At times these conjectures point to new, untapped sources; at times, they help test, refine or reformulate the research question or hypothesis. An example will perhaps illustrate the process of interpretation. Research Scenario 10.1 is a generic example of a modern challenge to the information professional. While vastly oversimplified, it demonstrates the importance of historical investigation to the practical implementation of international aid programmes as well as the need for the researcher to engage with sources both shrewdly and imaginatively.

RESEARCH SCENARIO 10.1
POST-WAR RECONSTRUCTION

It is a common military strategy to target and destroy cultural repositories of the enemy. Whether the burning of the ancient library at Alexandria or the bombing of the National Library and Archive in Sarajevo, such activities, now termed 'libricide',[29] have been equated with cultural genocide. In other words, by damaging collective memory as embodied in national heritage collections, it is assumed that the identity of the collective itself will be erased.

You have been brought in by UNESCO to assist in the post-war reconstruction of a national library collection in the Near East. A considerable proportion of the collection has either been destroyed or removed by looting, and despite being a signatory to the 1956 Hague Convention,[30] the occupying forces did not have the protection of cultural property in the event of armed conflict on their military agenda. However, an international campaign has been mounted to inventory, locate, recover, salvage and restore as much of the collection as possible, and to replace where possible any of the lost items.

This scenario assumes that collections reflect the cultures that created them, change over time, and are deeply affected by local contexts, be they political, religious, racial, and so on. Whatever your personal beliefs might be regarding the moral and ethical implications of the military action described in the scenario, as a historian, you must remain dispassionate in order to recover a range of historical evidence, judge its authenticity, understand its relevance, and interpret its significance for your project. Where sources are unavailable or questionable, your experience working with the extant evidence will enable you to make decisions informed by empathy and imagination.

Here, the initial challenge for the researcher would be to establish a list of the original collection. Physical evidence such as card catalogues, computer print-outs, published bibliographies, internal and official reports, budget exercises, and any collection appraisal documentation will need to be sourced, should it be extant. Oral histories of any surviving institutional employees and long-term users will assist in reconstructing parts of the collection. Plugging into the international research community and their networks may also bring forward lists of works used and/or cited in publications. Given the value of some of the items, the international Museum Security Network[31] could alert you to any sales or purchases.

Assuming that there will be gaps in the reconstructed list, the next challenge is to explain how and why the original collection came into existence. This will assist in rationalizing how those gaps can be filled in sympathy with the aims of the institution during its century of collection development. The researcher needs to have insight into and understanding of not only the practicalities of library collection development but also changing social and cultural attitudes with respect to gender and race relations, education, national heritage, and so on, as well as an appreciation of influences working within the institution to shape collecting policies. External influences such as political regimes, religious affiliations, and economic development are important factors, which impact on institutional policy and colour the nature and range of the evidence. Imaginative 'leaps' will be required to cover periods for which there is little or no evidence; intuition and judgement will be essential in attempting to prioritize various influences in explaining cause and effect, and change over time. Your final recommendations about the level of post-war reconstruction possible would then be conveyed logically and convincingly in the form of a written report to UNESCO.

Writing history and integrating historical and other qualitative data

This chapter began by arguing that history has an important social role. It follows that the results of historical investigation must be communicated coherently, concisely and in a manner that engages the reader. The historian may have used a wide range of relevant sources and come up with a satisfying interpretation which responds to the initial problem. However, unless he or she can disseminate the results of the research in a convincing manner, the impact of the historical investigation will not extend beyond the researcher.

The dual aspect of the historical enterprise – the effort to establish what happened and the attempt to explain why things happened in the way they did – explains the twofold task in historical writing as well as the two predominant styles of writing:

- to convey a sense of time or to show chronological development, using a narrative or descriptive writing style
- to analyse and explain the interrelationships of the events studied, to detect underlying patterns, to unify the various elements in a satisfactory whole, which provides a response to the initial research problem, using an analytical style or an approach by topic.

The historian's ability to achieve a satisfactory balance between these two modes will determine how successfully he or she has both re-created and interpreted the past, and how effectively this re-creation and interpretation will be communicated. To some extent this is an oversimplification as there will generally be a measure of descriptive writing as well as narrative in the re-creation of the past.

Again, a hypothetical example will illustrate these points. Suppose that a researcher has been commissioned to write a centenary history of an archive in a large and prestigious university. Such a history would be expected to provide a thoroughly researched and detailed institutional history with appeal to a wide readership. Being a centenary history, it would convey a sense of chronological development over the past 100 years. For this a narrative account would be appropriate, showing establishment and development during specific periods identified as meaningful on the basis of the evidence. However, the history should do more than narrate key events. It should also be concerned with historical process – why certain developments occurred, underlying motivations, the impact of individual personalities, or broader institutional pressures, or the general educational climate, changes in tertiary education and so on. It should reveal the causes of what are identified as turning points, those causes possibly including short-, medium- and long-term influences; it should give priority to those which are seen as more important; it should attempt to explain even gradual transformations whose origins may not be easy to ascertain (for example, gradual shifts in social attitudes regarding the value of tertiary education). Thus, interwoven with the narrative of events there should be an analysis that reveals the historian's perception of the significance and relationship of events, of the nature of causation in the working of the institution, of the impact or consequences of change. Such analysis should also locate the particular archive not only within its own larger institutional context but also within the wider national (or even international) context.[32]

The original purpose of the historical investigation and the audience for which the final 'history' is written will influence the extent to which a researcher provides detailed documentation. If the results are written up for publication in an academic journal, then certain conventions concerning notes or references and bibliography will apply. If the results are integrated into a larger report for internal use only, little formal documentation may be needed. Two general points about documenting historical research are worth making: one is that the historical account will fail to convince if the evidence on which the interpretation is based is not apparent or is inaccurately referenced. The other is that it is general practice to provide sufficient information on one's sources so that a subsequent researcher can locate them to verify certain details or to conduct further research on the topic. This highlights the collaborative dimension of historical investigation, but also reinforces one of the overarching principles of research, that it be repeatable.

The nature of the enquiry and the intended audience will also guide the manner in which the results of historical investigation are integrated with the results of other qualitative investigation or, indeed, quantitative data. For example, the history of a special collection has been written as a 'free-standing' account for publication in a local historical journal. It might then be recycled to form the first component or background section of a larger report concerning the current collection profile, which aims to make recommendations for future strategic development. It might also provide the background documentation for a preservation assessment survey. In another instance, the oral testimonies of women information professionals solicited for an institution-specific history might be integrated into a larger sociohistorical account of the relationship of gender and library culture.

Another example, with a preservation management focus, is likely to be encountered in today's information workplace.

RESEARCH SCENARIO 10.2

PRESERVATION MANAGEMENT STRATEGIES

You have been asked to carry out background research for a preservation assessment survey[33] of a local university's special collections department. Your findings will assist the collection manager to plan a co-ordinated, long-term preservation management programme and its implementation. Because the building in which the collection is housed leaks, has no climate control, and is situated on the banks of a river which often floods, the urgency with which this report has to be completed is compelling.

This increasingly common research scenario (10.2, above) involves a number of tasks suitable for historical investigation. Work such as this relies upon collaboration with past and present information professionals, curators and conservators, and features direct contact with a range of historical records as well as the material artefacts of the collection. Initially, you must trace the historical development of the collection, which includes significant monographic material as well as personal papers, archives and manuscripts. Multiple donors were responsible for the collection as it took shape over time, but perhaps the acquisition records went missing when the collection was moved to its present location. University annual reports, alumni news and borrowing records should be available; here, possibly the first curator kept an extensive diary of day-to-day activities and the most recent past curator is still alive and willing to be interviewed.

Provenance research[34] using physical evidence such as bookplates or annotations, plus the content and context of the unique items, should assist in one aspect of the preservation assessment report, the formal collection appraisal. An accurate assessment of the value of the collection and its relative worth internationally will enable strategic leverage for funding requests to implement change. If undertaking such a project, you might also work collaboratively with a team of freelance conservators to assess the current physical state of the collection, its storage and handling, as well as the environment in which it is housed.

Review of Chapter 10

This chapter has presented the social utility of historical investigation in the context of information services, not in providing precise 'lessons' based on past experience, but rather in developing an historical perspective which contributes to understanding the present situation and to developing realistic approaches to change. It has indicated the considerable scope of historical investigation and the enormous variety of historical sources. It has provided guidelines on identifying and locating relevant sources. It has described the critical method that character-izes historical use of these sources, and it has indicated new methodological problems arising for historians as we move increasingly into an 'electronic age'. It has discussed the role of interpretation in historical investigation and the requisite qualities in the researcher. Finally, it has outlined the manner in which historians communicate their findings. The illustrative examples have suggested that historical investigation is pertinent to many problems whether they relate to micro or local levels, national or global contexts.

Where to now?

Three important aspects covered in this chapter were historical methodology, historical sources and their use, and oral testimony as historical evidence. To test your understanding of these aspects, you might like to consider the following questions.

- Why would you consider using historical methodology in research on inform-ation services?
- Suppose that you were to include historical investigation as a component of research on the collection strengths and weaknesses of a particular library or archive. What sources would be relevant to this investigation? How would you use these sources?
- Do you consider that oral history might contribute valuable insights to a particular aspect of library or archive history? How would you go about collecting oral testimony? What problems would you anticipate in using such evidence?

You might also consider how historical investigation might be integrated with other qualitative research techniques discussed in earlier chapters of this volume, in particular with interviewing.

Further reading

For additional material on the content of this chapter, J. Tosh, *The Pursuit of History: Aims, Methods and New Directions in the Study of Modern History*, rev. 3rd edn (London: Longman, 2002) is perhaps the most useful general text on historical research.

Although much that has been written on libraries and information services is historical in approach, there are few works on historical methodology specifically in this area. Specific examples of institutional histories, however, exemplify the methodology in practice; good examples are: P. R. Harris, ed., *The Library of the British Museum: Retrospective Essays on the Department of Printed Books* (London: British Library, 1991); Edward Miller, *That Noble Cabinet: A History of the British Museum* (London: André Deutsch, 1973); and W. A. Mumford, *History of the Library Association 1877–1977* (London: Library Association, 1977). You might also refer to the works of Raymond Irwin and Thomas Kelly, two of the more notable historians of English libraries: R. Irwin, *The Origins of the English Library* (Westport, CT: Greenwood, 1981); and T. Kelly, *A History of Public Libraries in Great Britain, 1845–1975*, 2nd edn (London: Library Association, 1977).

The interdisciplinary journal *Libraries & Culture* has an excellent range of articles, which position information collections in relation to cultural and social history. There are also a number of library history special interest groups, such as those organized by IFLA or ALA, and they are in turn contributing to the various history of libraries projects around the world. The Society for the History of Authorship, Reading and Publishing (SHARP) maintains a list of them as well as contact information at www.sharpweb.org/index.html#projects. SHARP is also the leading academic organization for book history and print culture, two emergent areas that build on the solid bibliographic studies foundation originating in the information profession.

In addition, the following contain relevant material: C. H. Busha and S. P. Harter, *Research Methods in Librarianship* (New York: Academic Press, 1980); C. McCombs and C. H. Busha, 'Historical Research and Oral History in Librarianship'. In *A Library Science Research Reader and Bibliographic Guide*, ed. C. H. Busha (Littleton, CO: Libraries Unlimited, 1981), pp. 72–111; O. L. Shiflett, 'Clio's Claim: The Role of Historical Research in Library and Information Science', *Library Trends*, **32**, 1984, pp. 385–406; and R. E. Stevens, ed., *Research Methods in Librarianship: Historical and Bibliographical Methods in Library Research. Papers Presented at the Conference on Historical and Bibliographical Methods in Library Research, Conducted by the University of Illinois Graduate School of Library Science, March 1–4, 1970*, Monographs, 10 (Urbana: University of Illinois, Graduate School of Library Science, 1971).

Notes

1   G. T. Tanselle, 'Printing History and Other History', *Studies in Bibliography*, **48**, 1995, p. 269.

2   J. Tosh, *The Pursuit of History. Aims, Methods and New Directions in the Study of Modern History*, revised 3rd edn (London: Longman, 2002), p. xix.

3   O. L. Shiflett, 'Clio's Claim: The Role of Historical Research in Library and Information Science', *Library Trends*, **32** (4), Spring 1984, p. 387.

4   H. J. Graff, 'The Shock of the "New" Histories', *Social Science History*, **25** (4), Winter 2001, pp. 483–533.

5   W. D. Kingery, *Learning from Things: Method and Theory of Material Culture Studies* (Washington: Smithsonian Institution Press, 1996), pp. 6–7.

6   R. J. Evans, *In Defence of History* (London: Granta Books, 1997), p. 148.

7   E. H. Carr, *What Is History?* (Harmondsworth: Penguin, 1961), p. 30.

8   A. Marwick, *The Nature of History*. 3rd edn (Basingstoke: Macmillan Education, 1989), p. 13.

9   Tosh, op.cit., pp. 1–25.

10 Ibid., p. 8.

11 For an elaborated six-point schema see C. H. Busha and S. P. Harter, *Research Methods in Librarianship: Techniques and Interpretation* (New York: Academic, 1980), p. 91.

12 P. Burke provides a concise six-point comparison of 'traditional' and 'new' history in P. Burke, ed., *New Perspectives on Historical Writing* (Cambridge: Polity, 1991), pp. 3ff.

13 For a fuller discussion see Marwick, op. cit., pp. 208–10; Tosh, op. cit., pp. 54–82. Researchers may find Burgess' survey of various types of personal documents (life histories, autobiographies, diaries and letters) useful, although he writes from a sociological rather than historical standpoint: R.G. Burgess, *In the Field: An Introduction to Field Research* (London: Unwin Hyman, 1984), pp. 123–41. His section on the evaluation of personal documents is useful; it covers authenticity, distortion and deception, availability and sampling, presentation (pp. 137–9).

14 W. M. Duff and J. M. Cherry, 'Use of Historical Documents in a Digital World: Comparisons with Original Materials and Microfiche', *Information Research*, **6** (1), October 2000, available at http://informationr.net/ir/6-1/paper86.html. For another perspective see M. Hedstrom, 'Electronic Archives: Integrity and Access in the Network Environment'. In S. Kenna and S. Ross, eds., *Networking in the Humanities: Proceedings of the Second Conference on Scholarship and Technology in the Humanities Held at Elvetham Hall, Hampshire, UK, 13–16 April 1994* (London: Bowker Saur, 1995), p. 82.

15 See Marwick, op. cit., pp. 216–220.

16 Ibid., pp. 220–8.

17 A. Rabinovich, 'Historians Told to Byte the Papyrus', *Computer Age* [Melbourne], 30 May 1995.

18 See, for example, J. Sassoon, 'Photographic Meaning in the Age of Digital Reproduction', *LASIE* [Library Automated System Information Exchange], **29** (4), December 1998, pp. 5–15.

19 Hedstrom, op. cit., pp. 81–3.

20 M. Deegan, 'Networking and the Discipline'. In Kenna and Ross, op. cit. see also S. Sukovic, 'Humanities Researchers and Electronic Texts', *LASIE* [Library Automated System Information Exchange], **31** (3), September 2000, pp. 5–29.

21 W. Crawford and M. Gorman, *Future Libraries: Dreams, Madness, and Reality* (Chicago: American Library Association, 1995), p. 81.

22 Hill suggests three strategies for organizing archival data in 'sociohistorical' research: spatiotemporal chronologies; networks and cohorts (data on interpersonal contact, intellectual influence, financial support, political action, organizational affiliations, etc.); and backstage perspectives and processes (information on motivation, personal preferences, etc.): M. R. Hill, *Archival Strategies and Techniques*, Qualitative Research

Methods, 31 (Newbury Park, CA: Sage, 1993), pp. 59–63.

23 E. H. Carr, op. cit., pp. 28–9.

24 D. Henige, *Oral Historiography* (London: Longman, 1982), pp. 2, 106. See also Smith's comments on life histories and group biography (p. 295) in his chapter directed at qualitative researchers interested in using biographical method and 'life writing': L. M. Smith, 'Biographical Method'. In Denzin and Lincoln, op. cit., pp. 286–305.

25 P. Thompson, *The Voice of the Past: Oral History* (Oxford: Oxford University Press, 1978). For a range of issues, techniques, and case studies, see *The Oral History Reader*, ed. R. Perks and A. Thomson (London and New York: Routledge, 1998).

26 In a work on contemporary history Seldon's chapter on interviews includes clear advice on their conduct: A. Seldon, ed., *Contemporary History: Practice and Method* (Oxford: Basil Blackwell, 1988), pp. 3–16.

27 For a defence of oral history see Thompson, op. cit.; for a critique of the methodology plus an appreciation of the value of oral history in studying the formation of popular historical consciousness see Tosh, op. cit., pp. 295–309, 319–20; see also Henige, op. cit., especially pp. 110–11. R. G. Burgess, ed., *Field Research: A Sourcebook and Field Manual* (London: Allen and Unwin, 1982) includes brief chapters on oral sources and life histories.

28 Seldon sets out four possible options regarding access by the interviewer and by other researchers to interview records, permission to cite material from them and ownership of the material during the life of the interviewee and after his or her death: Seldon, op. cit., pp. 12–13. Henige also offers some guidance: op cit., p. 111. However, these comments are no substitute for knowledge of the rules or conventions applying within your own research situation.

29 R. Knuth, 'Libricide: The State-Sponsored Destruction of Books and Libraries'. In A. Kent, ed.. *Encyclopedia of Library and Information Science*, vol. 72 (New York: Marcel Dekker, 2002), pp. 234–44; see also her *Libricide: The Regime-Sponsored Destruction of Books and Libraries in the 20th Century* (Westport, CT: Praeger, 2003).

30 See www.unesco.org/culture/laws/hague/html_eng/page1.shtml.

31 See www.museum-security.org/index1.html.

32 For an Australian example, see the manner in which the history of the libraries is integrated into the broader institutional history of the University of Melbourne: J. Poynter and C. Rasmussen, *A Place Apart. The University of Melbourne: Decades of Challenge* (Carlton: Melbourne University Press, 1996). This work also provides insights into historical interpretation of source materials.

33 J. N. DePew, *A Library, Media, and Archival Preservation Handbook* (Santa Barbara: ABC-CLIO, 1991), pp. 235–51. and P. N. Banks and R. Pilette, eds., *Preservation Issues and Planning* (Chicago: American Library Association, 2000).

34 D. Pearson, *Provenance Research in Book History: A Handbook* (London: British Library, 1998).

11 Recording fieldwork data*

FOCUS QUESTIONS

- What are the goals and objectives of recording fieldwork data?
- What are some of the options for recording fieldwork data?
- What are the characteristics of field notes, reflexive notes and expanded notes?

'The primary purpose of gathering data in naturalistic inquiry is to gain the ability to construct reality in ways that are consistent and compatible with the constructions of a setting's inhabitants.'[1] In information service settings, most information professionals develop skills to observe and assimilate their users' behaviour. This chapter presents an overview of specific techniques to formalize these skills. Particular emphasis is given to providing examples of fieldwork methods for collecting data in information organizations or settings.

Overview of data recording

Qualitative research seeks to understand a particular social phenomenon in its natural setting. For our purposes, the social phenomena to be studied are those occurring within the context of information services. The objectives of qualitative research are to discover, describe and analyse the complexities of common phenomena through observation and involvement in a research setting. It is the role of the qualitative researcher to scrutinize commonplace occurrences because, when observed for prolonged periods, common phenomena can reveal remarkable levels of complexity. For example, in an archive a user is seated at a terminal but gazing out the window – a common enough phenomenon. Is he thinking through the significance of the records he has just retrieved, or is he planning a more detailed search strategy? Is he perhaps wondering why he has so far failed to retrieve anything of value, and what he can be doing wrong? Perhaps he is waiting for assistance from one of the archivists, or he may be simply bored with his research, and thinking about taking a break.

In other words, fieldwork is the disciplined study of a particular social world where the fieldworker learns from the participants themselves, seeing the

---

* This is a revised version of a chapter originally written by Dr Mary Lynn Rice-Lively.

world through the eyes of its inhabitants. From the perspective of a learner, the qualitative researcher collects field data through careful observation, prolonged engagement, documentation of observations and, finally, data analysis. This chapter explores techniques of data collection in fieldwork.

As noted in Chapter 6, the researcher first must seek prior approval from a person in authority to obtain access to the research setting. Of equal importance, observations must be made with the full permission and co-operation of any individuals involved, and not just that of the person who gave formal approval. If confidentiality is required, study participants must be guaranteed that confidentiality and be assured that their identity, behaviour and comments will not be attributed directly to them and that the setting for the study will not be identified. One way to assure study participants of the confidentiality of an investigation from the outset is to distribute a letter briefly describing the study and your role in it. Figure 11.1 presents an example of such a letter. In a social enquiry it is crucial to develop trust between the researcher and the study participants at the onset.

TO: Records Management Division Staff
FROM: C Castlemaine, Corporate Affairs
DATE: 1 October 2004
SUBJECT: Records Management Division Project

This is to inform you that Professor A. N. Other, a senior member of the Department of Information Management at Horatio Alger University, will be conducting research in the Records Management Division (RMD) of Excellent Corporation. His study will focus on the service ethos in the RMD as staff and users interact with each other and with new technologies in the course of information processing and seeking. The study will in no way interfere with the transactions in the RMD, nor will study participants be required to do additional work to participate in the research, beyond agreeing to communicate with Professor Other using e-mail, telephone, and through occasional short personal interviews.

Professor Other will use data from observation and transcripts of interviews for the study. Please understand that the study involves no invasion of individual rights or privacy, nor does it incorporate any procedures or requirements which may be found ethically objectionable. No individual messages or contributions to the study will be attributed.

If, however, you find any procedure or requirement ethically objectionable in the future, you have the right to contact the following person and report any objections, either orally or in writing:

Head of Department
Department of Information Management
Horatio Alger University
Newtown, Wessex WX1 1HA

Thank you for your participation and co-operation. Should you have questions or comments please contact me either by telephone or e-mail.

Charlotte Castlemaine
Director, Corporate Affairs
Excellent Corporation
(0000) 456 7890 office
(0000) 22 777 666 mobile
ccastle@excellent.co.uk

Figure 11.1   Research project letter to study participants

Chapter 6 also considered choice of data collection technique. Every technique requires a set of tools, the most important of which are the researcher's mind, creativity and ability to make decisions. In fieldwork the researcher becomes the 'human research instrument'. As the keystone to collecting fieldwork data, the use of a human research instrument requires the researcher to use innate abilities for cognition, intuition, and flexibility to discover the 'flesh and blood' behind observations, the interior texture rather than the external form of participant interactions.[2] In information settings the researcher is well placed to observe and analyse complex social settings, and qualitative research methods are especially suited to exploring what information users do and think. Through intentional observation you can discover what your subjects think and why they respond to particular situations as they do. Simultaneously, as the researcher, you must seek to understand the context of events in which individual or social behaviour or events occur.

While there is no exact formula for selecting data collection techniques, a strength of the human research instrument is the ability of the researcher to experiment, evaluate, redirect and refine the use of any given technique in any given situation. A researcher should choose a data collection technique for a particular situation, but also remain flexible enough to change the approach if the technique seems to interfere with productive, comfortable interaction in a particular social setting. In other words, use experience and intuition to determine what is appropriate for you, your respondents and your place in the social setting.

This should be applied to every data collection technique used in a project. But remember that each method of data collection has advantages and disadvantages, and that using more than one method is often desirable. However, Aldridge and Levine issue a caveat about the benefits of combining methods (mixed methods): 'If we regard a questionnaire as a measurement from point A, and an interview as a measurement from point B, can we now determine point C – namely, data about a respondent? Are social data like that?'[3] They go on to answer this by suggesting that collecting opinions about an issue in an interview and a questionnaire do not allow us to determine the respondent's opinions definitively. They further suggest that 'the act of measurement affects the thing being measured'.[4] Finally, 'we may simply conclude that an open-minded use of a variety of methods will do no harm, and will tend to enrich our understanding of the social world.'[5]

Bearing this in mind – that every data collection technique is essentially a pale reflection of reality – the qualitative researcher documents a study using field notes, the goal of which is to collect information from a social setting that will contribute to understanding the behaviour and interactions of study participants. The data you collect should facilitate the reconstruction of a believable account of what you and others observed and experienced in a particular social setting. What follows are descriptions of various note-taking techniques and formats.

Field notes and note-taking techniques

What are field notes? They are the recorded account of what a researcher observes, hears, experiences and thinks when collecting data. They describe people, places, activities, interactions and dialogue. They also include the researcher's own ideas, reflections and observations on what is occurring.

Field notes are usually characterized as descriptive and non-evaluative. Non-evaluative note taking avoids the use of judgemental adjectives and conveys respect for the setting's culture and for individual participants. The fullness of these notes depends on the accuracy and completeness of what you write. Cresswell recommends that notes be taken without 'narrow specific regard for your research problem'.[6] In other words, jot down as much as you can, recognizing that you will expand the notes in greater detail at a later time. These details may contribute to understanding the entire descriptive fabric of a setting or social situation.

The discipline of note taking

Observing and note taking are acquired skills that must be developed and that require regular practice if they are to be maintained. Your ability to observe accurately and record fully improves with practice; the first few times can be both daunting and disheartening.

It is important that you begin your research with a strong commitment to write something every day relating to your study. By incorporating into your routine as a researcher a daily discipline of journal writing (or 'journalling'), you formalize your reflections on the study. Writing is thinking – as Wallas phrased it, 'How can I know what I think till I see what I say?'[7] Although field notes are often rough and full of incomplete sentences, the very process of writing about what you are experiencing and observing provides the opportunity for new insight into your enquiry.

The process of writing field notes also requires some initial reflection, and a clearer understanding of the researcher's intervention in the recording process. As Wolfinger reminds us, little attention has been paid to the practical detail of note taking. He uses field notes from various sources to show that, regardless of any formal strategies for note taking, the researcher's tacit knowledge and expectations often play a major role in determining which observations warrant annotation.[8] Thus a conscious awareness of your tacit knowledge before you begin note taking should help the process proceed more smoothly, with richer, more relevant notes being the result.

Field notes and the reflexive journal

Should you actually use a journal? To answer this question, each researcher must decide what is most convenient, accessible and appropriate to the particular situation. A worthwhile suggestion is that first-time researchers experiment by using some configuration of the following approaches:

- bound journals (more than one)
- hole-punched paper and a looseleaf binder

- a small tape recorder and a good supply of audio tapes
- a laptop computer or PDA.

Many researchers use looseleaf notebooks, as these require one to carry paper at all times, saving the bound journal for private reflections, making mental notes and documenting the chronology of the study. Furthermore, the large looseleaf binders give the flexibility of expanding and rearranging documentation of the study (artefacts, documents and expanded field notes). Thus one might well find it appropriate to use a looseleaf paper in the field, a bound journal for reflexive notes, and looseleaf binders for arranging materials.

Because each of us has unique information gathering and processing styles, every researcher must make an informed decision after experimenting with a variety of formats. For example, start by experimenting with a journal format and, if this is not satisfactory, in your next study use a looseleaf binder. Alternatively, data can be recorded very quickly into a laptop with a simple word-processing package. It is less efficient to record data by hand, as they cannot be manipulated (cut and pasted) in the way they can on a computer. Once you have selected your field journal format, of whatever kind, what kinds of notes comprise field notes?

Types of field notes

Field notes should be both observational (describing the place, people, activities, conversations) and reflexive or analytical (noting ideas and issues that emerge from the observations). The primary concern initially is to describe what is observed; reflecting on what is observed comes later and increases as the observations increase. In the observational notes you as an observer try to record accurately and objectively what occurred. You should record in as much detail as possible. For example, it adds little if you state that a setting was 'institutional and sterile', but rather more if you describe the setting as containing 'neutral-coloured' computer hardware, 'electric blue' chairs, and fluorescent lighting contrasting markedly with the soft autumn light coming in through the open windows. In other words, record such details as might be of use in understanding the setting. Initially this means that you may well record more than you need; that's fine, as it is better to err on the side of completeness, because you can never revisit a scene that has already occurred. Do not be vague or abstract in your descriptions.

Your *observational notes* will cover five aspects of a setting:

- *People*. What did the subjects look like? How were they dressed? How did they speak and behave?
- *Places*. What was the configuration of furniture, doors, windows in the room? What was on the noticeboard, bookshelf, desk? Use both sketches and verbal pictures to describe the setting.
- *Researcher*. How did you behave in the setting? What did you say? Given the researcher-as-research-instrument in qualitative research, it is important to

describe yourself in the research setting and not just those individuals being observed.

- *Words.* Who said what? In an information setting this is probably the most crucial question to address in observational notes. Note the actual words that were spoken, the tone used, the gestures and facial expressions. Use inverted commas only if you are absolutely certain that you are quoting verbatim; otherwise record the dialogue as normal text.
- *Actions.* What actually happened, and in what sequence? How did events unfold? Who did what to whom?

If observational notes seek to be objective, your *analytical notes* can be described as 'subjective'. That is, here you record ideas, impressions, feelings and perceptions, and generally reflect on what you saw and heard and try to begin making sense of it. Reflection is confessional and speculative. You should record what went wrong and what worked well, consider relationships that seem to have some importance, indicate what you might need to do as a result, and so on. These must be distinguished in some way from the observational notes: some researchers use a heading (for example, 'Comment'), others use different coloured pens, and so on.

Analytical notes might cover three aspects of an investigation:

- *Themes and patterns.* From the very beginning you should analyse what you observe. What patterns are there? Why are people behaving in a certain way? What effect is the environment having on behaviour and dialogue? How does it 'feel', and why? What do you see or hear that suggests additional observations that might need to be made?
- *Methodology.* What are you learning about procedures and data collection techniques as you go along? What works and does not work in this particular investigation? What problems are you encountering, and how might these be solved? Methodological analysis is an important aspect of reflection, as the qualitative researcher does not persist with an approach without tailoring it to the situation.
- *Researcher-as-research-instrument.* What ethical problems are you facing, and how can they be resolved? What is your attitude to what you are seeing and hearing? How are your assumptions being challenged? All of these are part and parcel of your 'baggage' as a research instrument, and need to be dealt with in analytical notes rather than in the field so that you impinge on the setting as little as possible.

Some investigators recommend using two journals: a field journal to record observations and events while in the field, and a reflexive journal as a place for these reflections and insights. The field journal not only documents the details of a study, but also serves as the chronological record of an investigation. Descriptive note taking requires a balance between focus on detail and stepping back to see the whole scenario. Reporting an exchange or observation from a respondent exactly as it occurred, as recommended above, not only contributes to the depth of a study but also adds to its trustworthiness and sense of time and place. Samples of some descriptive note taking appear below in Research Scenario 11.1.

Although formal data analysis occurs later in a study, the process of qualitative research includes a cyclical process of data collection and reflection. The analytical or reflexive journal serves as the place to capture these insights. Writing in such a journal formalizes your thinking by noting insights relating to the study or patterns of behaviour or interactions that begin to emerge. Among other things, the reflexive journal is a place to note flashes of insight that occur at unlikely times. For this reason, keep your journal and a pen close at hand at all times during your study. In addition to a reflexive journal, you also might use a tape recorder. The recorder provides a place to dictate thoughts when writing is not convenient (for example, when commuting to and from work). The private exercise of journal writing stimulates meta-conversations – the researcher engaged in self-conversation. It is a place to reflect on doubts as well as insights or speculations with regard to your investigation. Furthermore, journal writing every day not only formalizes your reflections on the study but also exercises your writing skills. An example of just such reflexive journalling also appears in Research Scenario 11.1.

RESEARCH SCENARIO 11.1

SAMPLE FIELD NOTES AND REFLEXIVE JOURNAL NOTES

This scenario draws from a notional study of the changing role of collection managers in academic libraries. During the past four decades collection managers have become accustomed to the rapid pace of change due, in part, to the increased use of information technology. But have the functions, skills and expectations of collection managers been affected by the use of new technologies? Our study addresses this question by exploring the role(s) of collection managers in tertiary libraries and looking at the effects, if any, of networked information technologies on that role. Focus groups, individual interviews and follow-up questions via e-mail are used to collect data; and field notes, expanded interview transcripts and notes, and reflexive notes are to be used during the data collection process.

Of particular importance are the focus groups. Here the sessions will be recorded on audio tape, with observational notes as a means of documenting seating patterns, social and communication interactions and other phenomena. Here are some sample notes.

Cover note

> Focus Group Number 1
> Monday 30 August 2004, 14:00 hrs
> Library Meeting Room, L103
> 10 invited participants
>
> Comment: first focus group meeting of the project, probably extensive notes will need to be made.

Observational note

> Mon. 30 August 2004, 14:00 hrs
>
> Nine of the ten invited participants arrived and chatted quietly among themselves. A section of the large, comfortably appointed meeting room had been arranged in a circle of chairs around a large, low table. As the group gathered, some people talked amiably, while others wandered around the room to become familiar with their surroundings.

Methodological note

> During the first focus group the participants sat around the circle grouped together with familiar colleagues (usually those doing the same type of work in the library). Need to prepare a seating arrangement for the next session so that participants will be forced to mingle more.

Theoretical note

> Based on what participants said in Focus Group 1, I am beginning to see how the role of collection manager is evolving. For the older, more experienced members of the group, collection management used to be collection development. Then their jobs were pretty exclusively involved with developing in-house collections. But the younger members insist that collection development is just a small part of their work, and they are more concerned about access and all that this involves – licences, pricing, suitable platforms, etc.

Eight steps to better field notes

There are eight steps that will help you take better field notes:

1 When beginning an observation or interview session, start the notes with a clear indication of which session, where, when and the time: e.g. Library Meeting Room, L103, Monday 30 August 2004, 14:00 hrs.
2 Foreshadow data analysis by presenting notes in easily manipulated 'chunks'. Specifically, allow for coding by keeping paragraphs short and limited to a specific idea, event, and so on. Whenever there is a change of any kind, this is a signal for a new paragraph to permit a new code to be used later on.

   Leave plenty of space for later notation – large left hand margins, for instance. Consider numbering paragraphs or lines (all word-processing software has this facility), which will make it easier for you to process, manipulate and move data later on.

3 Make notes on everything at the beginning, as you will not know what is important or unimportant until you are well into the project. Even then, be cautious in deciding not to record something. It is better to have too much data.

   Later in the project you may well be able to determine with some confidence that a particular relationship or scene is of no interest to you. Your notes will become more selective as you progress, as it is no longer essential to record everything in the same detail as at the beginning of the project.

4 Make notes as soon as possible after completing a session. If you cannot do it immediately, at least outline what occurred as a reminder for later recording in detail.

5 Record the observation rather than discussing or reflecting upon it. Discussion before recording only confuses the events.

6 Allow plenty of uninterrupted time for recording your observations; remember it can take up to four times longer to record than to observe.

7 When working, do not worry about memory lapses, but put down what you can remember. Memory tends to return as you work, so you will continually go back and fill in gaps. It is best to follow chronology in observational notes and leave thematic arrangement to the analytical or reflexive notes.

8 Record dialogue as accurately as possible, and indicate when you are only approximating what was said.

As you are the research instrument in a qualitative investigation, you will react to specific events or will want to analyse particular situations based on your own perceptions and experiences. The use of a specific place, such as the reflexive journal, to express these emotions and reactions formalizes your identification of particular biases that will undoubtedly influence your investigation. The following section explores the concept of error and bias as viewed by many qualitative researchers.

Error and bias in note taking

Qualitative research has long been the object of criticism based on the prominence of the researcher and the possible significance of researcher bias.[9] This dismissive view arises largely out of the prevailing positivist paradigm, and its inherent incompatibility with the emerging naturalistic paradigm. This is aptly described in some detail by Lincoln and Guba in Chapter 1, 'Postpositivism and the Naturalistic Paradigm', of their 1985 work, *Naturalistic Inquiry*,[10] and tidily summarized in their Table 1.1, which contrasts positivist and naturalist axioms. Thus the positivist states that reality is single, tangible and fragmentable, while the naturalist see that realities are multiple, constructed and holistic. To the positivist enquiry is value-free; to the naturalist, value-bound; and so on.

   While objectivity is the goal of quantitative research, the naturalistic paradigm argues that objectivity is an illusion. Instead, most qualitative researchers acknowledge that there are multiple realities and that together the researcher and the study participants influence and mutually shape a reality. While risking bias and reactivity, the qualitative researcher works to control bias through the practice of building trustworthiness. Qualitative researchers maintain that the demon-stration of trustworthiness in an investigation corrects the natural biases of the researcher.

Many qualitative researchers claim that objectivity is impossible and view researcher bias as a resource rather than a weakness of a study. When joined with the perceptions of study participants, a researcher's bias contributes to a new, mutually constructed reality. Wolcott argues that bias in qualitative research is a misnomer. Rather than view this factor as something we should guard against, he maintains that bias is crucial to an investigation, because researcher bias is a manifestation of the cultural self.[11]

As a qualitative researcher, the information professional must be candid about personal perspectives and experiences in the 'person-as-research-instrument' statement. This statement may be an appendix to a research report, or it may be embedded in the report. Acknowledging that objectivity does not exist requires that the researcher build a credible study. You must demonstrate that the research data are reliable and valid. For example, in the collection of fieldwork data, careful documentation of the chronology of a study and noting the data collection methods used in a particular setting will strengthen the replicability and confirmability of an inquiry. Such documentation is grounded in the principle that it is better to retain or document too much than to record too little. Further, such careful record keeping establishes the 'audit trail' of the study, or what Yin calls the 'chain of evidence – that is, explicit links between the questions asked, the data collected and the conclusions drawn'.[12]

In summary, the qualitative researcher works to control bias through the practice of building trustworthiness. To build a trustworthy study you must establish credibility among participants, and there are many techniques for achieving trustworthiness. Lincoln and Guba[13] suggest five such techniques:

1 Be prepared for prolonged engagement in the field of study. In qualitative research it is rarely a matter of 'quick and dirty', but rather 'long and slow'.
2 Be persistent in your observations. It is only through persistence that you will be able to identify relevant events and relationships. Even experienced investigators find that persistence is essential, as every setting has unique features and dynamics.
3 Be ready to undertake mixed methods. Not only should data collection methods be subjected to this approach in order to help ensure legitimacy of your observations, but the data sources, settings and other variables should be varied in order to see phenomena from a variety of perspectives.
4 Be modest enough to seek peer debriefing. Discussing all aspects of a qualitative investigation with a colleague or another researcher as you proceed will help to

review perceptions, methods and analytical techniques. Such debriefing will give additional and expert perspective as events unfold.

5 Be democratic enough to allow for member checking or review. Remember that reviewing with study participants allows you to confirm data and their interpretation, and this helps to overcome certain aspects of research bias.

Having established techniques for building a trustworthy study, in the following sections we explore data recording techniques in participant observation, intensive interviewing and focus groups.

Data recording in participant observation

The role of the participant observer is to enter a social situation with a commitment to engaging in interactions as appropriate and to observe the activities, people and details of the setting. The choice of an appropriate position on the participation continuum was discussed in Chapter 7. For example, in the knowledge management case in Chapter 14, would you characterize the researcher as 'observer-as-participant' or 'participant-as-observer'?

Participant observation seems to involve more pitfalls and what Labaree calls 'hidden dilemmas' than other techniques. Labaree maintains that a common assumption about being an insider participant observer is that this 'offers a distinct advantage in terms of accessing and understanding the culture'.[14] Not so, he says, because 'these advantages are not absolute and the insider must be aware of ethical and methodological dilemmas associated with entering the field, positioning and disclosure, shared relationships and disengagements'.[15] Every participant observer must be prepared to grapple with these issues if the data collection and analysis are to be meaningful.

Participant observation requires concentration (focus), the ability to refocus when something new or of interest moves into view, and the ability to see the panoramic view of a setting. One way to achieve explicit awareness is to observe yourself observing. Try to identify what draws your attention to a particular scene. Why does the scene or interaction seem important? Force yourself to refocus your attention to what you are *actually* seeing, rather than whatever motivated you into this particular setting or field of enquiry – what you came hoping to see.

Fetterman recommends beginning qualitative research by describing a panoramic view – what some call the 'grand tour' of a research setting.[16] Try imagining the bird's eye view of a scene, looking down at the whole setting. If you have difficulty beginning this on your own, have a participant show you around the study setting. Listen to the participant's descriptions of the place and note what is pointed out as important. When documenting a 'grand tour' from the perspective of another person, include extensive details. Carefully scan a setting (something like an environmental scan) as though you were seeing it for the first time (which may in fact be the case). Describe each of the participants in verbal snapshots that include gender, age, ethnicity and what they are wearing. Capture in your notes the images, as well as the sounds and aromas of the place. If possible, use metaphors or phrases to describe the setting. Using metaphors offered by the participants themselves is a powerful way to lend authenticity and meaning to your case report.

Include in the notes your physical location and whether your observations are being made unobtrusively. Be sure to note if members of the social group know what you are doing. Recording the chronology (date, time and place of each observation) and making a rich and accurate description of the scene contributes significantly to the confirmability of your investigation. Incorporate sketches or drawings in your notes to recall a particular setting or to refine and use as illustrative material in your case report. Graphic illustrations will assist you in recalling a particular situation and contribute to a subsequent reader's ability to visualize a scene or setting. This is illustrated in Research Scenario 11.2.

RESEARCH SCENARIO 11.2
THE ACADEMIC LIBRARY REFERENCE ROOM

As a restrained observer of behaviour and events in an academic library reference room, you, the information professional-researcher, are sitting quietly and unobtrusively observing and documenting interactions between information-seekers and the reference staff. You note in your field journal the body language of a particular student as she interrupted the work of staff at the reference desk. With the goal of reconstructing this scene for a reader, you describe in detail this scene as follows:

A young woman dressed in jeans and a red pullover and wearing a backpack, apparently a student, pulls open the door to enter the brightly lit reference room in the main library of Horatio Alger University (HAU). She stops, briefly glancing around at the shelves that line the room. Turning to face the reference desk (actually a 1.5 metre high counter) in the centre of the room, she walks the 50 paces from the entrance toward the counter marked by a hanging sign: INFORMATION. At the counter are two staff members, a man in his late 20s and a woman with greying hair. Both people, sitting on stools, gaze intently into their respective computer screens. The reference counter is equipped with four computer terminals, shelves of books and two counter-level stools.

To create the above scenario, you draw sketches of the reference room in your field notes to accompany your detailed descriptions of what people are wearing, their facial expressions, what words are exchanged, the tones of the conversations. All of this descriptive information is an attempt to capture as vividly as possible the atmosphere of the setting and the interaction among participants.

Observation provides only one slice of a social setting. As a participant observer, you also must address any unanswered questions that arise. In particular, what are you not seeing? Thus field notes on the above Research Scenario might feasibly include four questions:

- Was this the first place the information seeker asked her question?
- Had she already queried her peers before going to the reference desk?
- Why did she hesitate and look around the room before approaching the desk?
- What might you, as the observer, be missing?

Because a researcher's attention can focus on only one event at a time, it is important to acknowledge that at a later time other data collection methods will be employed to help answer questions and gather more data on the context.

In addition to interviews with study participants, an alternative data source might be a collection of artefacts from the study setting. Artefacts are physical items that can be considered part of the cultural record of a place or people. Examples of artefacts might be documents, works of art, tools or almost any other physical evidence of a setting or social situation. These might include handouts that describe library services and hours, guides to indexes (print and electronic), tips for online searching, a map of the location, and so on.

As noted above, observation provides only one perspective of a social setting. The use of focus groups facilitates constructing yet another view. The following section explores interviews and focus groups and how to collect data by exploring the perspectives of study participants.

Data recording in interviews

While participant observation is a largely passive experience in a social setting, the goal of interviews in qualitative research is to create a more active interaction or dialogue with a study participant. Spradley refers to interviews as 'a conversation with a purpose'.[17] The situation and purpose of the interview should dictate the interview style (whether formal or informal, planned or spontaneous). This section focuses on data collection techniques during interviewing, rather than on interviewing techniques per se. Fuller discussion of interviewing techniques appears in Chapter 8, which first introduced the whole question of how best to record interview data. Additionally, you may wish to consult one of the guides mentioned at the end of this chapter.

Qualitative research is both an art and a science. Interviewing requires the work, first, of an artist and then of a scientist. For example, during intensive interviewing the researcher must ask appropriate questions, recognize when to deviate from planned questions in order to explore a new topic or issue, manage the recording technology (tape recording and note taking) and be an attentive and active listener.

Your initial goal during interviewing is to make the respondent as comfortable as possible with the interview process. Therefore, when beginning an interview, inform the participant that you will be taking notes and recording the interview. If for some reason the informant requests that you not record the session or that you turn off the machine during portions of the interview, by all means comply with this request.

Wolcott observes that some researchers do little or no formal interviewing but rely instead on informal, spontaneous conversations.[18] Whether spontaneous or formal, the goal of the interview is to enable and encourage the respondent to answer questions explicitly or implicitly related to the study. In situations of spontaneous or unplanned interviews where you may not be able to take notes or record the interaction, you must make notes about the exchange immediately following the encounter.

Experience indicates that informants usually do not find the presence of a tape recorder intrusive. Furthermore, the device can serve as another pair of ears, recording comments made during interviews or focus group sessions that the researcher might have missed. The use of tape recording in interviews requires planning. If your interview is an hour, use tapes which will cover the whole hour without changing sides (for example C120 if using compact cassette tapes). The goal is to focus attention on the respondent and to minimize interruptions due to technical or mechanical problems. Remember, however, that the tape recorder is a mechanical device, and mechanical devices (recorders and tapes) malfunction, so do not depend exclusively on them. Every researcher has experienced the disappointment of losing a valuable recording of an interview due to malfunctioning equipment.

A final suggestion is to leave the tape recorder running after you end the interview – often the respondent will explore new and interesting insights into a particular issue or question once the interview has ended. Alternatively, ostentatiously turning the machine off can encourage an interviewee to proffer sensitive observations previously withheld.

As indicated above, note taking during an interview requires a challenging balance of listening, thinking and writing. With practice you will develop your own form of shorthand that can be expanded into fuller notes at a later time. Collecting field data through interviewing presents an excellent example of the need for note expansion. First, your interview notes must be converted into full notes. Expanded notes will include the questions you asked and the respondent's replies, the context of the interview and a description of the respondent. The following section considers the task of converting notes taken in the field into fuller notes that will become the descriptive record of your study.

Data recording in focus groups

Chapter 9 introduced focus and nominal group techniques, and considered some of the advantages and limitations of these methods of data gathering. The nominal group technique results in the generation of a set of written group outcomes, and so is not considered further here. A focus group, however, does not, and the recording of contributions to a focus group discussion is rarely straightforward.

The intention of a focus group is to promote self-disclosure in an environment where people are encouraged to listen to the opinions of others as they form their own views.[19] The keystone of focus groups as a data collection method is the construction of quality questions. Krueger recommends that you prepare no more than ten questions.[20] Experience shows that ten questions will fill more than an hour in a normal focus group. The questions asked in focus groups should be open-ended, allowing the respondents to determine the direction of their responses and stimulating their thinking.

Clearly, focus group questions require thoughtful preparation. First, to construct quality questions you must immerse yourself in the study setting in order to acquire sufficient background to develop questions. Plan to cover a range of relevant topics that take account of the participants' personal contexts. Second, prepare participants by informing them of the purpose of your study and how the data will be used (see Figure 11.2). The next step is to plan for data collection during the focus group meeting.

The primary means of capturing data during focus groups is through the use of tape recordings and note taking by an observer. As noted in Chapter 9, the participation of more than one researcher in focus groups permits one person to moderate the session and the other to function as a note-taking observer during the meeting. The basic data source, however, is usually audio tape transcripts. For this reason, testing the acoustics, recorder microphone and seating arrangements before a meeting is essential. Morgan suggests using media experts to help design a successful recording session.[21]

While videotaping can also be used to collect data, the following comment identifies some concerns with this method:

> Videotaping is obtrusive and simply not worth the effort. I have found that it invariably changes the environment and affects spontaneity. Videotaping usually requires several cameras plus camera operators who attempt to swing cameras quickly to follow the ensuing conversation. The fuss and fury of videotaping makes the focus group appear more like a circus than a discussion.[22]

Further discussion of focus groups, and the issues associated with recording the data collected during their course, appears in Chapter 9.

Through the use of participant observation, intensive interviewing and focus groups the information professional-as-researcher must practise the skills of an artist and a scientist, but the keystone to collecting fieldwork data is the researcher. As the human research instrument, the researcher must employ the skills of a *bricoleur*, using the resources of personal experience, information from the environment or situation to construct meaning or an interpretation of the event, the *bricolage*.[23]

The expansion of field notes
Conversion into full notes

Writing provides a path for assimilating ideas and experiences gained during fieldwork, and notes taken in the field are incomplete until they have been

TO: RMD Focus Group Participants
FROM: Professor A. N. Other
SUBJECT: RMD Project Information
DATE: 5 October 2004

This is to inform you that Professor A. N. Other, Department of Information Management, Horatio Alger University, is about to begin collecting data for the project of which you were informed on 1 October 2004 by Charlotte Castlemaine. You have been selected to participate in one of three focus groups designed to discuss issues related to the study. The forums will be informal and require no advance preparation.

Your focus group session is scheduled as follows:

DATE:
PLACE:
TIME:
DURATION:

Professor Other will audio-record the sessions and use data from tape transcripts for the study. Please understand that the study involves no invasion of individual rights or privacy, nor will it incorporate any procedures or requirements which may be found ethically objectionable. No individual messages or contributions during the focus groups will be attributed.

If, however, you find any procedure or requirement ethically objectionable in the future, you have the right to contact the following person and report any objections, either orally or in writing:

Head of Department
Department of Information Management
Horatio Alger University
Newtown, Wessex WX1 1HA

Thank you for your participation and co-operation with this project. Should you have questions or comments please contact me either by telephone or e-mail.

A.N. Other
Professor of Records Management
Department of Information Management
Horatio Alger University
(0000) 123 4567 office
(0000) 027 654 321
ano@bogus.hau.ac.uk

Figure 11.2   Research project letter to focus group participants

expanded once the researcher is away from the constraints of the field. Wolcott recommends that instead of leaving everything in abbreviated note form, it is useful to take the time to draft expanded pieces written in rich detail immediately following a field visit.[24] Often expanded notes will be written in such a way that they can be incorporated in a final project report. Kleinman and Copp recommend a particular format for note taking.[25] They suggest taking notes on only half the page, leaving space in the margin for reflection or analytical comments. These 'notes on notes' facilitate the expansion of the incomplete notes made in the field. The 'notes on notes' may be added in ink of a different colour.

Your field notes document the study. Converting these notes into fuller, descriptive text is essential to the reconstruction of what you and the study participants experienced and observed. Obviously, there is a variety of notes that can be taken during a study. Building on the work of Glaser and Strauss, Richardson describes four categories for note taking.[26] These are listed below, followed in each case by an example.

- *Observation notes* are as concrete and detailed as you are able to make them. They provide accurate renditions of what you see, hear, feel, taste and smell.

> Tue. 31 August 3:00 pm
>
> During my visit to the RMD today my goal was to wander around and note the seating arrangements in the department, and the gender, age and other visible attributes of the staff. As you face the terminal area, there is a rectangular arrangement of 'cubbyhole' office cubicles, each with a computer, computer table (computers and tables are the same neutral colour) and chairs (ergonomically correct with bright red upholstery – the only colour in the configuration). There are also storage cabinets and the usual personalization of most spaces – football club memorabilia, photos, soft toys, etc. The entire room was lit by fluorescent lighting – cold and functional. During my 90 minutes in the RMD, all office cubicles (12) were occupied by staff, who seemed to be working quite frantically to locate and retrieve a large volume of information – must check if this is normal. All staff except the records manager were dressed very casually, which seems to be the norm in such settings. The manager was dressed in a smart, fashionable suit, with a colourful scarf adding to her image.

- *Methodological notes* are messages to yourself. They might include ideas on how to collect data, ideas about people to whom you might speak, what to wear, whom to phone, and so on. Such notes also can document which data collection techniques worked and which did not.

> During the next week I must contact the following staff at Excellent Corporation: James Reid-Smith, Technology Manager; Jane McVittie, Director of Public Affairs Division; Charlotte Castlemaine, Director of Corporate Affairs. It is essential that I keep these people informed of my research as well, as each of them will provide a unique perspective on the role of the RMD and of its relative successes and failures.

> When observing and collecting data, I must remember two concepts from a pair of articles I've just read. (1) The researcher must use passive and active strategies as well as interactive strategies. (2) Always be aware of and note my expectations for respondent behaviour. This will enable me to identify these expectations and to balance them by inquiring of the behaviour expectations of my respondents.

- *Theoretical notes* are hunches, hypotheses, connections, critiques of what you are doing, thinking and seeing. Theoretical notes often begin with 'I wonder why . . . ?' or 'How does . . . ?'

> Making sense of their experiences in learning about and using the latest document processing and retrieval techniques, including metadata, is a challenge for most of RMD staff. They seem to have no study time to allow them to catch up with developments. I wonder how we all struggle to articulate what is not yet clear, what does not fully make sense to us? This must fit somehow into Boulding's description of reconstructing our image of something each time we have a new or unexpected experience. Sense-making as a theory is ripe for further exploration and understanding in networked environments.

• *Personal notes* are statements of your feelings about the research, the people to whom you are talking, yourself in and during the research process, your doubts, anxieties, and pleasures as they relate to the research.

> How has the selection of respondents affected this study? First, it has been a challenge facing the unpredictability of locating a pool of co-operative, responsive and responsible (e.g., showing up for interview appointments, etc.) individuals. Second, this study has taken a tremendous amount of time. Time to observe, time to interview and transcribe taped interviews, time to reflect on what I am learning. Agar's description of the qualitative researcher as remote, distant, the 'professional stranger' is sometimes too true.

Your expanded notes will contribute to the written style of your final report. During the process of note expansion you begin to integrate the formats (field notes, methodological, and reflexive notes). This exercise is particularly useful as an analytical technique for the identification of recurring themes and patterns that emerge from the data.

Note expansion inevitably leads to analysis and interpretation and contributes to the researcher's ability to recall events and conversations. At this point it is essential to begin distinguishing between the voices and language you use in your notes. For example, among the voices used in the study described in Chapter 14 were:

• the voice of the investigator (both descriptive and analytical)
• the language of some senior staff members and the HR manager
• the language of several consultants
• the words of a couple of new staff members.

Each of these voices conveys a distinct meaning, with implications for interpretation of the study.[27] Therefore, each voice must be clearly distinguished. One technique employed to achieve this distinction is to italicize exact quotations from informants and to highlight your own interpretations or notes on what was said. The point here is to identify clearly in the expanded notes whose opinion or language is being reported.

Transcription of verbatim statements

The best way to capture verbatim statements is by using tape recording equipment. Transcription of tape recordings is a significant undertaking both in terms of thoroughness (do you transcribe everything?) and style. Many researchers choose to transcribe tapes themselves rather than commissioning professional transcription. Although very time consuming, tape transcription provides another opportunity to listen to and experience each interview session, and it enables the researcher to reflect on, evaluate and interpret events. A good keyboard operator can take from three to three and a half hours to transcribe a one hour interview. Transcription of tape recordings allows you to monitor the quality of the recording and make adjustments in equipment such as the brand of tapes or the use of a microphone. Such continuous analysis of and reflection on the data can strengthen, even redirect, an enquiry. The process may also lead to further questions for study participants. Serving as another set of ears, the tape recorder captures conversations and comments when the researcher's attention might have been distracted by another person or event.

Undertaking tape transcription yourself also allows you to evaluate what to include in the transcript and what not to include. Obviously, the ability to identify whether interactions should be included or excluded in transcription grows with experience. One evaluative criterion to use is the exclusion of anything that is not directly relevant to the inquiry's focus – professional transcribers (or research assistants for that matter) cannot evaluate this, so tend to include some quite irrelevant material.

Whether you transcribe everything from a tape recording, you must listen to every tape. Some researchers use an alternative to complete transcription – they listen to and index a recording using the calibration of tapes as they play in the recorder. Another strategy for efficient transcription is to use codes for nonverbal utterances such as those occurring during a pause or when someone is thinking (for instance, 'hmmmm' or 'ahhh') and abbreviations for names of those involved in the interview. Furthermore, there are numerous computer software programs that format transcripts or expanded notes with numbered lines, tagging pre-identified words, and so on. These computer-assisted resources that facilitate data analysis are explored in the following chapter.

Review of Chapter 11

While Chapters 7, 8 and 9 looked at different techniques of data gathering, in which the question of data recording was necessarily secondary, this chapter has focused on techniques used to formalize the data collection skills in observation, interviewing and conducting focus groups. With the goal of understanding a particular social phenomenon in its natural setting, qualitative data collection techniques facilitate discovery, description, analysis and finally reconstruction of a descriptive account of a common phenomenon.

During data collection the researcher must experiment to learn effective techniques for everything from note taking to observation, interviewing and transcription. By cultivating the disciplines of observation, note taking and writing, making both observational and reflexive notes, using persistent observation as well as triangulation of perspectives, data sources and data collection methods, the researcher works to build a study that is both credible and trustworthy.

The next step to completing a qualitative study is to begin formal analysis and interpretation of the data. The techniques for analysing and interpreting qualitative research data are explored in the following chapter.

Where to now?

Now that you have reached this point in the volume, as well as reviewing the focus questions at the start of this chapter, you may care to think about some of the issues arising from four key questions:

* What are the implications of mixed methods or triangulation for the recording of fieldwork data?
* How can adequate data recording help address concerns with error and bias?
* Why is it important to use a combination of field, reflexive and expanded notes?
* Finally, what are the links between data recording, reliability and validity?

If you are unsure of your skills in data recording, just as we earlier suggested you undertake a pilot study of a fieldwork technique new to you, you may also find it valuable to experiment with the recording of data. This need not necessarily be related to your research project: professional work often provides opportunities for recording observations, interviews or group discussions that are equally challenging. An ability to record such occasions accurately is a generally useful professional skill.

Further reading

R. L. Emerson, R. I. Fretz and L. L. Shaw, *Writing Ethnographic Field Notes* (Chicago, IL: Chicago U.P., 1995) covers the process of how one goes about collecting and writing ethnographic data. The book begins with theoretical issues, then moves into jotting, full field notes, then how to analyse field notes and write a full ethnography. It provides practical advice which is well illustrated by samples collected by the authors and their students.

Other useful guides which consider recording fieldwork data are J. Spradley, *Ethnographic interviewing* (New York: Harcourt Brace Jovanovich, 1979) and H. F. Wolcott, *The Art of Fieldwork,* 2nd edn (Walnut Creek, CA: AltaMira, 2004). For a more general discussion that places fieldwork in context, one might usefully read H. J. and I. S. Rubin, *Qualitative Interviewing: The Art of Hearing Data,* 2nd edn (Thousand Oaks, CA: Sage, 2004). A recent title is *Handbook of Ethnography,* ed. by P. Atkinson et al. (London: Sage, 2001), in particular such contributions as Chapter 24: R. M. Emerson, R. I. Fretz and L. L. Shaw, 'Participant Observation and Fieldnotes'. Some examples of qualitative field notes are included in V. J. Janesick, *'Stretching' Exercises for Qualitative Researchers,* 2nd edn (Thousand Oaks, CA: Sage, 2003); see especially the Appendices.

Notes

1　D. A. Erlandson et al., *Doing Naturalistic Inquiry: A Guide to Methods* (Newbury Park, CA: Sage, 1993), p. 81.

2　S. Zuboff, *In the Age of the Smart Machine: The Future of Work and Power* (New York: Basic Books, 1984), p. xiv.

3 A. Aldridge and K. Levine, *Surveying the Social World: Principles and Practice in Survey Research* (Buckingham: Open University Press, 2001), p. 60.

4 Ibid.

5 Ibid.

6 Creswell, J. W. *Research Design: Qualitative, Quantitative and Mixed Methods Approaches,* 2nd edn (Thousand Oaks, CA: Sage, 2003).

7 G. Wallas, The Art of Thought (New York, Harcourt Brace, 1926), quoted in K. E. Weick, *Sensemaking in Organizations*, Foundations in Organizational Science (Thousand Oaks, CA: Sage, 1995), p. 12.

8 N. H. Wolfinger, 'On Writing Fieldnotes: Collection Strategies and Background Expectancies', *Qualitative Research,* **2** (1), 2002, http://QRJ.sagepub.com/cgi/reprint/2/1/97.

9 Erlandson et al., op. cit., p. 14.

10 Y. S. Lincoln and E. G. Guba, *Naturalistic Inquiry* (Newbury Park, CA: Sage, 1985), pp. 14–46.

11 H. F. Wolcott, *The Art of Fieldwork* (Walnut Creek, CA: AltaMira, 1995), p. 164.

12 R. K. Yin, *Case Study Research: Design and Methods,* rev. edn., Applied Social Science Research Methods Series, 5 (Newbury Park, CA: Sage, 1989), p. 84.

13 Lincoln and Guba, op. cit., pp. 281–4.

14 R. V. Labaree, 'The Risk of "Going Observationalist": Negotiating the Hidden Dilemmas of Being an Insider Participant Observer', *Qualitative Research,* **2** (1), 2002, www.sagepub.co.uk/frame.html?http://www.sagepub.co.uk/journals/details/issue/j0331 v02i01.html [accessed 1 August 2004].

15 Ibid.

16 D. M. Fetterman, *Ethnography Step by Step*, Applied Social Research Methods Series, 17 (Newbury Park, CA: Sage, 1989), p. 51.

17 J. Spradley, *Ethnographic Interviewing* (New York: Harcourt Brace Jovanovich, 1979), pp. 58–9.

18 Wolcott, op. cit., p. 105.

19 R. A. Krueger, *Focus Groups: A Practical Guide for Applied Research* (Newbury Park, CA: Sage, 1988), p. 23. For a useful article on focus groups see L. Chase and J. Alvarez, 'Internet Research: The Role of the Focus Group', *Library & Information Science Research,* **22** (4), 2000, pp. 357–69.

20 Krueger, op. cit., p. 59.

21 D. L. Morgan, *Focus Groups as Qualitative Research*, Qualitative Research Series, 16 (Newbury Park, CA: Sage, 1988), p. 61.

22 Krueger, op. cit., p. 87.

23 *Bricoleur* comes from the French verb, *bricoler*. A *bricoleur* is a handyman or woman who is a professional 'DIY' person using the materials and tools available to accomplish a task or to create a *bricolage*. The researcher as *bricoleur* must perform a large number of tasks using the tools at hand. The *bricolage* is not considered a project but rather is that which is accomplished or created using tools or resources collected by the *bricoleur* for use when they might 'come in handy'. C. Levi-Strauss, *The Savage Mind* (Chicago, IL: University of Chicago Press, 1966), p. 17.

24 Wolcott, loc. cit.

25 S. Kleinmann and M. A. Copp, *Emotions and Fieldwork,* Qualitative Research Methods, 28 (Newbury Park, CA: Sage, 1993).

26 L. Richardson, 'Writing: a method of inquiry'. In *Handbook of Qualitative Research*, 2nd edn, eds N. K. Denzin and Y. S. Lincoln (Thousand Oaks, CA: Sage, 2000), Chapter 36.

27 Spradley, op. cit., p. 71.

12 Analysing qualitative data from information organizations*

FOCUS QUESTIONS
- What is involved in the process of analysing qualitative data from information organizations?
- How does the researcher achieve depth of understanding when analysing data?
- What are the roles of, and differences between, data analysis and data interpretation?
- How can computer technology assist in the analysis of qualitative data?

This chapter provides an overview of qualitative data analysis, as well as strategies for analysing and reformatting large bodies of data. Information organizations involve complex social processes; qualitative research methods are themselves complex – and for this reason are well suited to dealing with such organizations. As a result, qualitative research in information organizations frequently results in enormous quantities of rich and complex data that must be analysed and descriptively reconstructed. The greatest challenge in a qualitative study is 'not to get data, but to get rid of it!'[1]

Before beginning, however, it is worth indicating that the carefully structured approach that we discuss here is not always necessary. For some qualitative investigators, even quite inexperienced ones, it is entirely feasible that data analysis may be simply a matter of finding a quiet corner, spreading out the field notes without a laptop in sight, and writing about what was seen and heard. Many times we know instinctively, from our sensitive immersion in the particular culture being investigated, what needs to be said, and how.

Sometimes this approach works very well, as it has for generations of researchers. More often than not, however, you will need to take a more structured, conscious approach to your data analysis. In this case, you may find computer software an invaluable aid. If your data prove too great in quantity or too complex to carry in your head, this chapter suggests several approaches to making sense of it.

---

* This is a revised version of a chapter originally written by Dr Mary Lynn Rice-Lively.

Overview of data analysis

> Believing, with Max Weber, that man is an animal suspended in webs of significance he himself has spun, I take culture to be those webs, and the analysis of it to be therefore not an experimental science in search of law but an interpretative one in search of meaning.[2]

The search for meaning from data collected during fieldwork is no simple task, for now the researcher must reduce a huge volume of information into a meaningful case report. As noted in earlier chapters, qualitative enquiry places the researcher in the 'lifespace' of a group or organization, using a variety of data collection techniques to gain a full and realistic overview of events and patterns of behaviour among members of that group or organization. When conducting a study, the qualitative investigator collects data on both mundane and unusual events through the eyes and voices of the social group being studied. When fieldwork ends, the researcher begins the equally important chore of formal data analysis. While there are numerous approaches to the analysis of qualitative data, Miles and Huberman usefully summarize such analysis as a combination of:

- data reduction
- data display
- conclusion drawing and verification.[3]

To analyse qualitative data you, the researcher, must move between the role of the scientist and that of the artist. During data reduction the researcher-scientist condenses volumes of data into quantifiable analytical units; data are manipulated and reconfigured in an attempt to discover patterns and connections not previously apparent. The researcher-artist then summarizes complex data in charts, graphs and other illustrations requiring creative, interpretive skills to draw out the full meaning of relationships between units and to integrate these interpretations into a meaningful account.

These interpretive skills require that the researcher engage in both convergent and divergent thinking.[4] Convergent thinking is an information-processing activity with the goal of a single solution or a correct answer. The qualitative researcher must moderate convergent thinking and work to remain open to the ambiguity of emergent themes and patterns. This also requires divergent thinking, which is the creative process of formulating questions, referring to past experience and cues from the social setting.

Using words such as 'cautious', 'controlled', 'structured', 'formal' and 'systematic', Wolcott describes data analysis as the process in which the researcher considers units of data such as words, behaviour, events and ideas, as well as the properties of these units. From analysis you must then move to the process of interpretation, which Wolcott characterizes as 'freewheeling, causal, inductive, subjective, holistic, and systemic'.[5] Another view describes analysis as a continuum of analytical approaches to the data that ranges from sifting the raw data to find patterns, themes, properties and relationships to interpreting the findings.[6]

Data analysis may involve coding, content analysis or ethnographic analysis. Whatever the technique employed, it follows a nonlinear process of seeing a pattern, returning to the data or the study setting, and exploring or confirming the pattern or an observation with an informant. In a qualitative inquiry 'analysis facilitates the identification of essential features and the systematic description of interrelationships among them – in short how things work.'[7] In the final product of your study, the case report, you identify and interconnect the themes to tell the story of the social group in your enquiry.

Preliminary data analysis

Data analysis is the process of bringing order, structure and meaning to the mass of collected data. As suggested in Chapter 3 (see Figure 3.2, p. 37), it does not proceed in a tidy linear fashion. Rather, it is a messy, ambiguous, time-consuming, creative and fascinating process. The purpose of this process is to search for general statements about relationships among categories of data.[8]

Because of the iterative nature of qualitative data analysis, the researcher moves through the enquiry records, choosing one type of data over another or reformulating questions to achieve a better fit with the context of the study setting. From the inception of a study, the researcher has employed the iterative process of collecting data to analyse, evaluate and use information in order to collect more data, and refine that data through interpretation, and that data analysis is a dialectic rather than a linear process.[9] In other words, you have been undertaking data analysis from the moment you began to collect it. Nevertheless, for those new to the analytical process it can help to visualize this as a staged procedure (see Figure 12.1) in which the researcher begins to function consciously as a processor, teasing out key elements, establishing broad data categories, and assigning initial data units to categories.

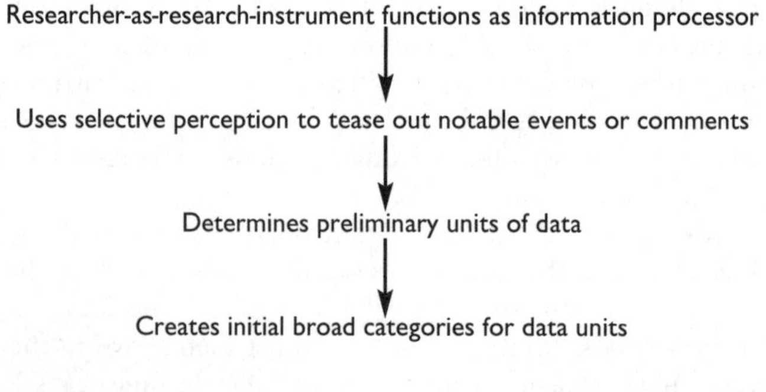

Researcher-as-research-instrument functions as information processor

↓

Uses selective perception to tease out notable events or comments

↓

Determines preliminary units of data

↓

Creates initial broad categories for data units

Figure 12.1   The preliminary data analysis process

This preliminary process is intended to begin reducing masses of data to meaningful and manageable portions. Data reduction, as Miles and Huberman view it, is a dialectic, iterative process that includes selecting, focusing, simplifying, abstracting and transforming the data.[10] They note, however, that data reduction as a process is not separate from analysis but rather a part of it, because during data reduction you analyse while sorting, discarding and reorganizing fieldwork data. What, then, is the end result of this focusing, sorting and transforming? The reward of data reduction is the emergence of patterns of behaviour or themes that eventually will contribute to the study's interpretations and conclusions.

In qualitative data analysis the primary tool is an investigator's innate human ability to confront enormous amounts of information and to make sense of it. But this tool must be honed through practice and used with patience. To begin with, then, qualitative data analysis is a test of the researcher's ability to think and process information in a meaningful and useful manner. For example, consider an investigation into the reasons why people become information professionals. An investigator might begin such a project by asking some speculative questions based on personal perceptions, conversations and background reading:

- Are people attracted to information careers because of the pleasure drawn from reading and being around books?
- Are they attracted to the service aspect of information work?
- Are they primarily interested in the ways in which information technology can be used to process and manipulate information?

These 'hunches' will guide preliminary analysis of the data just as, at the outset, they contributed to the conceptual framework for data gathering. During data analysis the working questions can be tested by confirming or challenging their validity with study participants (described in the preceding chapter as 'member checking'). Furthermore, your cognitive skills enable identification of the interconnections between separate events and observations.

Second, during the initial stages of data analysis the researcher uses a form of selective perception to tease out events or comments of note from the data. During this stage relevant terminology and notable themes are identified, and those with apparently significant characteristics and attributes guide the categorization of data. This kind of analysis must begin with the broadest of categories, such as:

- places
- events
- behaviour
- feelings.

One useful way to determine which broad categories are appropriate is to begin 'with a static picture in which you set the scene and introduce major actors one at a time, much as if you were writing a play. Continue presenting these "still shots" until you have enough elements on hand (or actors figuratively on stage) to set things in motion.'[11] This to some degree is what the first paragraph in the section 'KMP and knowledge management' in Chapter 14 sought to achieve.

As Figure 12.2 indicates, you can identify emerging data categories by a process that is fairly straightforward (but no less nerve-wracking for all that): read a unit of data, assign a category, read another unit of data, assign the same or a new category, and so on.[12] But remember at this stage that you are looking only for broad categories that will allow you to sort data; you should be doing neither more nor less. Wolcott offers some sound advice in this regard:

> Begin sorting by finding a few categories sufficiently comprehensive to allow you to sort all your data. Remember that you are only sorting. If you are having problems with what ought to be a straightforward task, you are probably starting to develop theory, regardless of how modest. You are trying to take two steps at once. Try one at a time![13]

Third, using innate creative abilities, the researcher begins to piece together the puzzle of understanding and description of the investigation.[14] Unlike the pieces of a jigsaw puzzle designed to come together in one pattern, the recombinant nature of qualitative data offers a variety of configurations. Consider, for example, the interview transcript in Table 12.1. This is based on a possible project on the acceptance of IT, using Rogers' *Diffusion of Innovations*[15] as the framework, among librarians in academic institutions. Note in particular the underlining of key phrases in the dialogue and the resulting categories in the right hand column; the broad categories identified in this interview with a particular librarian were skills, feelings, attitudes and activities.

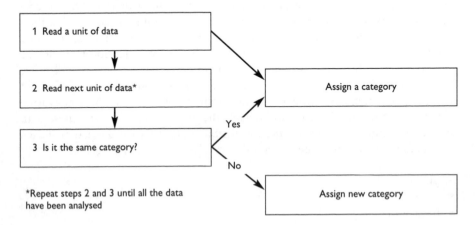

Figure 12.2 The process of identifying initial data categories

Table 12.1 Categories derived from preliminary data analysis

8 October 2004 3:50pm in Library Staff Room	Categories
Researcher: As you know, I'm studying the role of librarians in relation to IT. Now, your library has just installed a new computer network, which makes it an ideal 'lab' for gathering some ideas and opinions. Can you begin by describing how you have learned to use this resource?	
Participant 1: I'll talk to you about this, but I may <u>not be the best person</u> – <u>not representative</u> of most of the staff. Surely most of these people know more about how to use the system here than I do.	skills feelings/attitude
R: Tell me more about that.	
P1: To tell you the truth, I <u>hate computers</u>. I always <u>feel so stupid</u> when I have to <u>try to do a search</u> and make a mistake. It looks like no one else is having any trouble. I feel comfortable <u>using e-mail</u> and while <u>that is fun</u>, I am sure we all <u>waste too much</u> time <u>setting up lunch dates</u> and that sort of thing. The library administration has been <u>offering training sessions</u>. I go, and I have so many questions, but the presenters go too fast. I just become <u>confused and frustrated</u>....	feelings activity activity, feelings activity activity feelings

In a second reading of the data, usually during the detailed data analysis stage described below, you might identify new categories or decide to divide a category into two. For instance, you might need to distinguish between activity and event. Another step would be to write a sentence defining the category and clarifying the context when appropriate. After broad categories have been created in this initial reading you might then group them into like categories. Following these preliminary analytical steps, you begin to discover new ways of understanding the setting being investigated.

Qualitative data analysis is thus a complex task. Krueger notes that this complexity arises in part because the data are products of a mix of open-ended questions, observations, interviews and other unpredictable, unreplicable social interactions.[16] For this reason, when confronting the task of data analysis, you should perform at least three mental exercises:

- Remind yourself that you have been analysing data throughout the study.
- Cultivate a comfort level with ambiguity.
- Remain open to exploring multiple analytical strategies and trust that the process will tease out themes and patterns.

Formal analysis requires that you review all of the data collected (field notes, transcripts and online transactions), and it is commonly accepted among qualitative investigators that this review be undertaken at least three times.

Preferably the review readings are done over a long enough period to permit substantive gestation and reflection. With each reading new insights, patterns and connections will emerge – this is when qualitative research can be at its most exciting! Two strategies will assist you during this stage of preliminary data analysis:

- *Writing*. Use your reflexive journal to formalize reflective, creative thinking about the data.
- *Discussing*. Schedule regular meetings with a 'peer debriefer' to discuss your analysis techniques or patterns that may be emerging. (Peer debriefing was mentioned in Chapter 11 as a technique to help avoid error and bias in note-taking.)

Both strategies, the reflective practice of writing and the social practice of discussing, will focus your attention in new ways, stimulating fresh insights and revelations. In addition they will help you stay focused on the research questions, while remaining open to new revelations or approaches to data analysis and interpretation.

Preliminary data analysis thus allows the researcher to begin examining data carefully and thoughtfully, to begin breaking them into small units for easier analysis. Following this preliminary 'tinkering' with the data, which in fact often occurs during the data collection process, especially in larger, more complex investigations, the researcher is ready to delve more deeply into the now slightly ordered data.

Detailed data analysis

Essentially, this more detailed data analysis involves reconfiguring the units of data in order to view the phenomena from fresh perspectives, and watching for emergent theories pertinent to the enquiry. To achieve the required understanding of what an investigation has discovered, and to interpret it meaningfully and contextually, researchers employ numerous methods of qualitative data analysis. Among them are:

- affixing codes to a set of field notes
- noting reflections or other remarks in the margins of notes (discussed below in the section on memos)
- sorting and sifting data to identify key events, phrases, relationships between variables, patterns, themes
- confirming patterns and themes through additional data collection and analysis
- developing new theories or contributing to existing theories.[17]

As the researcher compares incidents and observations during an enquiry, the properties of the data will take on greater definition, form and depth. Key methods employed by researchers in information settings to achieve meaningful comparisons are the coding of identified events, activities and behaviour; and the content analysis of textual data. Both thus warrant discussion in the following section.

Coding and content analysis

Qualitative research data consist primarily of text (such as interview transcripts, observations and field notes). For this reason analysis demands that investigators consider the semantic relationships of words by describing and classifying terminology unique to the enquiry. According to Mead, 'data analysis involves taking constructions gathered from the context and reconstructing them into meaningful worlds.'[18]

Coding

Such classification of terminology and language constructs goes by many names. Lincoln and Guba, for example, refer to the process of analysing textual data as 'unitizing', or disaggregating data into the smallest pieces of information that may stand alone as independent thoughts in the absences of additional information other than a broad understanding of the context.[19] Miles and Huberman, on the other hand, speak of 'chunks' of data, which during analysis are assigned codes.

> Tags or labels for assigning units of meaning to the descriptive or inferential information complied during a study. Codes are usually attached to 'chunks' of varying size – words, phrases, sentences, or whole paragraphs, connected or unconnected to a specific setting.[20]

Once these small units of data are fully described, they are brought back together into new descriptive configurations (charts, tables or even narrative). Eventually through this process emerging themes and patterns shape 'the systems of meaning', giving form, order and direction to the study setting.[21]

Whether you prefer to think in terms of units or 'chunks', the coding process is the key to meaningful data analysis. Glesne recommends that you begin with a simple coding scheme.[22] Inevitably the codes will change, expand and collapse, creating a data management nightmare. The method is illustrated in Table 12.2, which shows a basic coding scheme used in a study of 'information encountering', described as 'a form of information behavior that involves accidental acquisition of information.'[23] The domain for the study included four dimensions of inform-ation behaviour:

- user
- environment
- information
- problem.

In this study data analysis involved coding of survey and interview transcript data, with the codes being developed inductively from the data.

Table 12.2 Thoughts before encountering information [24]

Code term	Code definition	Supporting quotes
Exploration	The respondent was interested in knowing what information could be found in the environment. Thoughts were not concentrated on a specific task.	'I was actually exploring – just playing to see what I could find.' 'Looking for anything anomalous.' 'What was available.'
Information need	The respondent was thinking about a specific task and information needed to accomplish the task.	'Is what I was looking for available?' 'If I needed something to open the bank account?' 'Were any of the unshelved books interesting; is the book I need among them?'
Inadequacy	The respondent's thoughts addressed a lack of confidence in the information-seeking strategy, in the skills for finding information, or dissatisfaction with the resource itself.	'I was looking for information using a really cumbersome logic.' 'I don't know much about WWW.' 'This book was kind of useless.'

While some researchers prefer formal coding schemes such as Murdock's Ethnographic Atlas, many others follow Bogdan and Taylor's view that there is no viable one-coding-formula-fits-all coding scheme.[25] That is, you will need to develop a coding framework from the data unique to your investigation and link it to the study's conceptual framework. This requires a progressive process of sorting and defining, and of coding to define and sort bits of collected data. During the coding process, remember to pull from interview transcripts, quotations that are particularly illustrative or poignant, because exact quotations lend authority to the case description, as well as humanize the study narrative.

Research Scenario 12.1 provides another example of the use of coding, here contributing to the identification of patterns of attitudes and behaviour linked to the culture of a records department.

RESEARCH SCENARIO 12.1

CODING AND CATEGORIZATION IN A RECORDS DEPARTMENT

During an ethnographic study of the culture of a corporate records department, interviews with staff in other departments revealed that these people found their records colleagues 'reserved, insular, quiet and not fitting in with the company's ethos'. My own observations of the records department documented a quiet, orderly space where staff worked quietly with their desktop computers and files. During one two-hour stretch of observation I noted only two conversations, and those were held quietly in a space away most of the other staff. Records officers repeatedly emphasized to me the need for concentration and silence. They proudly explained the complexity of their duties and how future access to an information source depended on the care and accuracy with which they abstracted and indexed them. They also explained that they were in the process of starting to work with metadata, which required special concentration, as it was quite new to them. Perhaps, if other staff fully understood the need for concentration and quiet, they might reinterpret their perceptions of records staff as attributes of professionalism, rather than insularity and quietness. These separate and quite different perceptions of records staff might not be discovered without careful analysis of the interview transcripts and identification of themes of behaviour.

In the fieldwork data I found in my field notes and in interview transcripts dozens of descriptions for quiet. The list below illustrates a few of the phrases and attributes of 'quiet' in the perceptions of records staff and other staff.

Staff	Records staff	Other staff
Types of quiet	Silence, hushed, whisper, uninterrupted	No business, slow, no phone calls
Attributes of quiet	Concentration, accuracy, peaceful, good, quality	Shy, lacking initiative and bravado

When units of analysed data are reconfigured into a whole, they contribute to the research findings and can be woven into a rich description of people, places and events of the enquiry. Scrutiny of the social situation in your enquiry becomes 'the stream of behavior (activities) carried out by people (actors) in a particular location (place)'.[26]

There are many approaches to detailed data analysis. The previous section explored one such alternative, data or text coding. In more extensive studies the use of manual coding and index cards is impractical. Fortunately, coding can be automated and further systematized through the use of computer software programs. Some options for automating the coding process are discussed later in this chapter, in the section on using computers. In the next sub-section we explore an alternative to data coding, content analysis

Content analysis

Another approach to textual data analysis in qualitative enquiries is the use of content analysis. This classifies textual material by reducing it to more relevant, manageable bits of data.[27] As noted in Chapter 3, content analysis on its own is more strictly a quantitative method as it involves measuring selected units of text and drawing comparisons. However, when used in tandem with other, qualitative data analysis methods, it offers a supplementary approach to qualitative text coding. The challenge in using content analysis is not to decontextualize a phrase or a word by removing it from its written or spoken framework.[28] Westbrook observes that the technique of content analysis coding makes intuitive sense among information professionals, because we are familiar with the process of searching for patterns in organizing and providing access to information.[29]

Content analysis can involve the use of qualitative data collection methods, either alone or in combination with quantitative analysis. Research Scenario 12.2 illustrates such a combination. It also demonstrates a difference in emphasis between qualitative and quantitative content analysis: the emphasis in qualitative analysis is less on frequency of occurrences than on the identification of themes.

RESEARCH SCENARIO 12.2

CONTENT ANALYSIS OF SURVEYS EVALUATING LIBRARY SERVICES

A study was conducted on the content of user surveys in academic and special libraries. Of particular interest were the questions, and the extent to which they focused on user perceptions and expectations, rather than merely measures of usage. About 150 surveys were collected from academic and special libraries of varying size. Additional data were gathered from 20 library administrators either in person or through telephone interviews.

First, the survey questions were examined, and those judged to be specifically oriented to user perceptions were tallied. Examples of these questions included:

- What were your reasons for visiting the library today?
- What helped you achieve your goals for the library visit?
- What hindered you from achieving your goals for the library visit?

Questions that were not counted included any that focused specifically on such matters as library hours or functioning of library services (for instance, circulation or reference). Because this categorization involved subjective decisions, several coders analysed the same survey forms and compared their categorization in order to ensure that the subsequent coding was consistent.

Second, terms that specifically referred to library users were listed and counted. For example, some questions asked about user status.

Finally, in order to supplement this quantitative analysis of the documents – the questionnaires themselves – transcripts of the interviews with administrators were analysed for expressions of interest in the user (rather than simply in library use).

As noted in Chapter 10, the strong historical research tradition in library and archival research and writing, in particular, has also involved a form of content analysis which is further removed again from the quantitative paradigm. In assessing documentary records, for example, without necessarily counting frequency of occurrence, the researcher notes the recurring themes and concerns which obviously occupied the minds of the protagonists of the time, and also perhaps those issues which did not seem to receive great attention.

Ethnographic data analysis

Another form of data analysis in qualitative studies involves use of the ethnographic analytical model. Spradley's analytical model of ethnographic analysis can provide both methodological guidance and also facilitate the 'systematic examination of something to determine its parts, the relationship among parts, and their relationship to the whole'.[30] It offers a structure for the cyclical research process used to identify behaviour patterns among study participants. The data for the study may be drawn from:

- observation field notes
- reflexive journal notes
- individual interview and focus group transcripts.

Spradley's model for domain, taxonomic, componential and theme analysis provides a practical analytical map for systematically identifying patterns of behaviour and conversational themes from data gathered during the investigative stages of research.

Domain analysis

Domains in data analysis are categories that include other categories. 'All members of a domain share at least one feature of meaning.'[31] The domain structure includes a cover term, included terms, and the semantic relationship of these terms. A cover term names a category, and included terms are specific examples or names for members of a category. The semantic relationship links the specific (included) term to the cover term. For example, in a study of public library users one domain would include people who use the library – that is, a user is a kind of person. Another domain might be places within the library where people communicate. Table 12.3 illustrates how one might analyse domains from study data.

Table 12.3 Sample domain analysis

Included terms	Semantic relationship	Cover term
Teacher Student HR manager Retired person Business person	is a kind of ————————————————→	Person
Internet chat room Conference room Reference desk OPAC	is a place for ————————————————→	Communication

Remember that the primary analytical goal of the researcher is to find patterns that exist in the research data. For example, in the records department described in Research Scenario 12.1, above, the physical room (the records department) where staff worked was a kind of place. In this place there were people (records staff, IT staff, occasionally staff from elsewhere), equipment (computers, scanners, printers and telephones), furniture (filing cabinets, shelving, tables and chairs) and instructional guides (directories, signs and books). Where does one find these details? By consulting descriptions in field notes, reviewing transcripts, field notes and field journal; from these data sources one identifies recurring patterns in study participants' thoughts and behaviour.

Taxonomic analysis

In Spradley's model the next step in formal data analysis uses taxonomic analysis to identify patterns in the organization of cultural domains. During this process the researcher begins to focus the data analysis. Spradley defines cultural taxonomies as a set of categories organized on a single semantic relationship.[32] The taxonomy differs from a domain in that it shows the relationship among all the terms in a domain. The current serials section in a library, for example, contains journals, magazines and newspapers. Each of these types of publication is a domain within the library collection. Among the kinds of magazine that library users read are the following: science, sports, literature, current affairs, education, psychology. Such a list of magazines describes a taxonomy of popular publications in the current serials section. Such a taxonomy can show the relationship between both entities with a broad category and between entities and the larger whole as a way of highlighting and explaining those relationships.

Componential analysis

Once taxonomic analysis has been completed the next logical step is to consider the descriptive attributes (components of meaning) of terms in each domain. This is referred to as componential analysis. For example, in a study of information technology skill levels among library staff the employees comprise a domain. Within that domain there are different types of employee: full-time staff and part-time staff for instance, and within those categories there are information professionals, support staff, student staff, and library school trainees. Componential analysis facilitates categorizing a group and identifying contrasting attributes. Table 12.4 shows one way of categorizing and contrasting respondents within this domain.

Table 12.4 Componential analysis of academic library staff

Contrast set	Dimensions of contrast			
	Full-time employee	Employed ten years	Employed less than three months	Information technology skills
Professional librarian	Yes	Yes	No	Skilled in some computer applications and internet
Support staff	Yes	Yes	No	Skilled in many computer applications, but not internet
Student staff	No	No	Yes	Skilled in many computer applications and internet
Library school trainee	No	No	N/A	Skilled in many computer applications and internet

Theme analysis

The final analytical strategy used in ethnographic research is theme analysis. Remember that ethnography has as its primary goal the description of the sense of a whole culture. Theme analysis seeks to discover and identify the relationships among domains and connections with the description of a study's cultural setting. Remember that from the inception of a study to the writing of the report, events and observations have been documented in the field notes. The field journal, as emphasized in Chapter 11, serves as the historical record of interviews and significant research events, as well as introspective reflections (tightly or loosely coupled to the study). The collection and analysis of the narratives of study participants provides data that complements the researcher's own observations and interpretations. All of these data contribute to the cultural description of the social setting.

Among the themes that emerged from the records department study (see Research Scenario 12.1) and contributed to the final cultural description were rules, language, rituals and routine events:

- *Rules.* Canons of behaviour included working alone, speaking softly, relating minimally to staff outside the department.
- *Language.* There were many terms and acronyms familiar to records staff that served to differentiate them from other staff – for example, discussion of specific data fields or metadata applications.
- *Rituals.* Whenever a specific section's records were completely indexed, abstracted and made accessible on the corporate database, a small party was held to signify completion of another milestone.
- *Routine events.* Morning tea was always taken at 10:30.

Each of these characteristics contributed to the cultural identity of this particular department and helped to differentiate it from other sections in the organization.

Memos and visual displays

As we have discussed, qualitative research uses inductive data analysis, a process employing abstract constructs such as hypotheses, models, or theories that evolve from the research data.[33] During data analysis one challenge for the researcher is to remain at arm's length from the flood of particulars. True, data analysis requires immersion, but the researcher also must be able to stand back and reflect on the meaning of data – an uncomfortable combination of experience-near and experience-distant as discussed in Chapter 3. Notes written by the researcher to her/himself, or 'memos', offer one way to stand back from data immersion. Strauss and Corbin define the memo as a written form of abstract thinking, and general designs, a graphic representation of visual images, used particularly to demonstrate the relationships between concepts.[34] The reflexive journal is a place in which the researcher deliberately looks up and away from empirical data to conceptual levels of an investigation.

As noted in Chapter 11, it is essential for an investigator to capture reflections and insights as they occur. During the data reduction and reconfiguration process writing memos to yourself helps to extend and expand understanding of the empirical data. For example, as part of the case study in Chapter 14 the researcher made a number of reflexive journal entries that illustrate the use of memos. These are all from the period of data collection and data analysis.

> Pay attention to the differences in project problem solving. Are there differences between senior and junior consultants, between those who've been with KMP for a long time and those who've just joined, gender differences, or differences and patterns along generational lines?

> An extremely valuable side benefit of 'chunking' in data analysis is the identification of questions not asked or topics not pursued. They literally come flying off the page.

> Note that some reluctance in sharing self-disclosing observations may be related to different personality types.

Such memos serve to flag concerns for later consideration, suggest lines of analysis to be followed during the coding stage, raise issues for discussion with colleagues, and generally act as a kind of dialogue between you and your data.

In addition to memos another important technique for understanding data is the use of figures, tables, matrices and other illustrations – although these are most easily employed with empirical data. One work referred to often in this chapter is an outstanding resource to consult when experimenting with alternative displays of significant patterns: M. B. Miles and A. M. Huberman, *Qualitative Data Analysis: An Expanded Sourcebook*.[35] Illustrations of various types provide a useful alternative when trying to simplifying complex data, and thoughtfully constructed displays facilitate easy assimilation of complex ramifications or implications from data. Among the approaches to data display, a writer might create tables, matrices, graphs or figures – examples of several such techniques appear not only in Miles and Huberman but also throughout this text.

Using computers for qualitative data analysis

By now it should be apparent that analysis of qualitative research data can be an enormous and complex task. Qualitative researchers now have access to a number of excellent computer applications that diminish some of the drudgery of managing, analysing, displaying and reporting fieldwork data. But if computers can support qualitative data analysis, they can also feed a data-collecting fetish. A warning about data overload is clearly put by Wolcott and should be recalled by every qualitative investigator whenever zealous IT missionaries enthuse over the data massaging capabilities of the latest hardware or software, as they almost universally do.

> The trick is to discover essences and then to reveal those essences with sufficient context, yet not become mired trying to include everything that might possibly be described . . . . Computer capabilities entreat us to do just the opposite; they have gargantuan appetites and stomachs. Because we can accommodate ever-increasing quantities of data – mountains of it – we have to be careful not to get buried by avalanches of our own making.[36]

By its very nature qualitative research encourages the collection of too much data, and the abilities of information technology only compound this tendency.

Consequently, technology-reliant qualitative investigators can be forced back to more quantitative methods of data analysis (which are ideally suited to manipulating very large volumes of data) or engaging in less in-depth analysis. Some experienced researchers have recognized this problematic relationship between qualitative research and information technology and have warned their colleagues accordingly. For example, John Seidel, developer of a useful software package called The Ethnograph, has expressed his concern that: 'because computer technology allows us to deal with large volumes of data, we will be lured into analytical practices and conceptual problems more conducive to breadth analysis rather than depth analysis. We are trading off resolution for scope.'[37] With these in mind, there is still much to be said in favour of the convergence of information technology and qualitative data analysis.

According to Richards and Richards (creators of NUD*IST, now NVivo, another useful software package), most qualitative researchers now work in some way with computers. Relatively few, however, use software for data analysis.[38] In our view this is an unsatisfactory situation but one which, on the basis of anecdotal evidence, seems to be improving.[39] Today, for example, most researchers would be aware that ordinary word-processing programs provide the option to count and search by word or text strings. Beyond that are facilities for spreadsheeting and graphing, and creating and managing databases. In our own research, for example, we use computer programs to save time and reduce the drudgery of such tasks as data management, tape transcription and the creation of visual displays (figures, tables and graphs). Drawing from this experience and that of colleagues, Table 12.5 suggests some of the advantages and disadvantages of using computers in qualitative data analysis.

Table 12.5 Advantages and disadvantages of computer programs for qualitative data analysis

Advantages	Disadvantages
Assists calculation and quantification	Depends on quality of data entered
Eases process of writing and rewriting	
Encourages systematic work	Risks data loss
Forces organization of data	Removes researcher intellectually from data
Focuses analysis	
Supports sorting, referencing and coding	Risks decontextualization
Facilitates creation of statistical and	Uses technical processing methods on data
graphic displays	more suited to other methods

The key to using computers in qualitative research is to know on the one hand what computers *can* do and, on the other, what you *want* or *need* to do. Miles and Huberman offer sound, extended advice on both counts. We only summarize their key points here, concentrating on the qualitative processes for which computers are especially useful: entering and editing notes, coding notes, storing and retrieving data, memo-writing and theory building, and displaying and mapping data.[40]

- *Entering and editing notes.* At the top of any qualitative researcher's list of what computers can be used for is making notes in the field, writing up or transcribing notes after being in the field, and editing and revising notes. Initial versions of notes are corrected and commented upon as a first, partial step in processing data. That is, the computer is an ideal medium for storing and processing raw material in an editorial sense. Anyone familiar with word-processing will know how much easier this is than recording and revising data on paper.
- *Coding notes.* Many more investigators are finding that some software is particularly suitable for coding notes once they have been entered and edited. Attaching key words or tags to segments of text permits later electronic retrieval and comparison of information swiftly and efficiently. Furthermore, the coding scheme can be developed and recorded as an electronic dictionary, thesaurus or authority file of key words, phrases, categories and definitions. At the same time, content analysis is easily undertaken, using coding-related techniques to count frequencies, sequences and locations of phrases and words.
- *Storing and retrieving data.* Text can be stored in a database which can then be searched using the coding thesaurus, and the selected information retrieved quickly. Furthermore, the computer can store the search results for subsequent tracking or retrieval at a later date. This is especially useful during the comparative stages of data analysis when the report is being written. Storage and retrieval facilities of computers also permit the ready linking of data – connecting relevant data segments with each other, forming categories, clusters and networks of information.
- *Memo-writing and theory building.* Increasingly researchers are finding that some software is suitable for recording and processing a range of analytical material, from early memos to final theories. In particular reflections on the conceptual meaning of data lead to theory building through the development of systematic, conceptually coherent explanations of the findings.
- *Displaying and mapping data.* Much computer software is ideally suited to displaying data in graphically organized formats such as matrices or networks. In these formats reduced or condensed data are displayed in different ways to aid interpretation. In addition diagrams can be created to depict findings and theories visually, and such diagrams are easily linked to the relevant text.

Each of these five principal areas will have a different priority in every qualitative investigation, and it is essential that the researcher be aware of these priorities. That is, each of us has different requirements when conducting a qualitative study and specific expectations of computer-assisted data analysis. Furthermore, every qualitative researcher works differently, has a unique relationship with computers and a distinctive level of techno-literacy. Therefore, we need to understand our project requirements, our hardware and software capabilities and our level of technological expertise. This understanding is enhanced by answering the following questions honestly and objectively:

- What do I require of a computer in a specific project? That is, what is the principal form of data analysis on which the project depends?
- How competent am I at using computers, and how quickly do I learn new software procedures?
- What are the strengths and weaknesses of the specialist qualitative software programs, and which is best suited to my requirements?

The first and second questions are context-specific so cannot be addressed in general terms here – they can only be answered by you on the basis of what you are doing in a project and what you know about yourself. For the third question, though, there is readily available assistance. Most traditional, of course, are the published guides to hardware and software, some of which guided the writing of this chapter and which are listed in the suggestions for further reading. When you have used this literature and its most up-to-date successors, you will have a pretty good idea of currently available software and its notional capabilities.

All of us know that this is a field in which there is constant, unrelenting change. Even such a useful published evaluation as Miles and Weitzman, 'Choosing Computer Programs for Qualitative Data Analysis', is now ten years old.[41] Any updating that we might offer here too is certain to date, and inevitably date much more quickly than the rest of this volume. To retrieve the most current information you should contact both the program developer or distributor and other users. Most developers and distributors are on the internet and have websites.

Take, as an example, ATLAS.ti (www.atlasti.com) and The Ethnograph (www.qualisresearch.com). If you access these sites you will find that both the ATLAS.ti and Ethnograph websites include a free demonstration program for downloading, which allows you to try some trial runs on both programs – a change from a few years ago, when only The Ethnograph provided a demonstration program. In addition the ATLAS.ti site also has excellent support, community and other sections. There is a mailing list to which you may subscribe, and a most useful bibliography of items about ATLAS.ti. Thus on the ATLAS site you are able to find out much more information than you had expected based on past experience, and you now tend to feel that this might be the best software for you.

But what about The Ethnograph? You remember that the web support for this program was quite useful in the past – is the same true today? Clicking on their website, you find a very up-to-date collection of features, including a demonstration, screen shots (a helpful inclusion), list of workshops, and so on. This is nearly as good as the ATLAS site, but not quite as supportive of its users. The workshop section actually takes you to a group called Research Talk Inc., which runs workshops on several software programs used by qualitative researchers – this may prove useful in the future, but for now there is nothing in your general area on The Ethnograph. Overall, it now looks as though ATLAS.ti provides the better support, and after using the demonstration program as thoroughly as possible, you decide to look more closely at this software.

You do this by contacting other users of ATLAS.ti, for hands-on experience is more valuable than any written assessment or publicity from a vendor. Using the mailing list facility on the ATLAS.ti site, you are able to make contact with a number of researchers in your field who are using this software very successfully, and this, along with some readings suggested on the website, convinces you that ATLAS.ti is your program of choice. (Interestingly, undertaking the same exercise in 1997 convinced us that The Ethnograph was the better choice – in the intervening years there seems to have been substantial user-friendly development at ATLAS.)

Miles and Weitzman's 1994 analysis offers positive assessments of several programs that have a role in computer-assisted data collection and analysis. However, in recent times some of them have fallen out of favour with the majority of qualitative researchers, among them Folio Views, HyperQual, Inspiration, QUALPRO and SemNet. Others seems to go from strength to strength and are more widely used than ever; these include ATLAS.ti, The Ethnograph and Hyper RESEARCH. Recently, NVivo seems to have attracted considerable support – see our list of further reading, below, as well as the bibliography at the end of this volume. There are also some relative newcomers that are gaining popularity: C-I-SAID and MAXqda in particular.

In 2004 Scolari, the Sage Publications software division, offers an impressive range of qualitative data analysis software. At the time of writing (late 2004) these include the following (scope notes are from the Scolari website, www. scolari.co.uk/, with our notes added in square brackets):

- ATLAS.ti 5.0. For the visual qualitative analysis of text, graphics, audio or video files.
- C-I-SAID. The new package from the developer of *Code-A-Text* for qualitative and quantitative analysis of text, audio and video files [available from www.code-a-text.co.uk/ and no longer sold by Scolari]
- The Ethnograph. For qualitative analysis of text-based data [apparently now available from www.qualisresearch.com/]
- HyperRESEARCH. For the qualitative analysis of text, audio or video files [free trial version available for downloading]
- MAXqda. For qualitative and quantitative analysis of rich text files [replaces winMAX software]
- QSR NUD*IST N6 and N4 Classic for Macintosh. For qualitative analysis of text-based data [apparently no longer distributed by Sage, but the international QSR website, www.qsrinternational.com, sits within the Scolari website; there is also an Australian site at www.qsr.com.au, which appears identical]
- QSR NUD*IST Vivo 2.0. For qualitative analysis using rich text documents with the ability to embed audio, video and other files to create compound documents [apparently no longer distributed by Sage, but the QSR website, www.qsrinternational.com, sits within the Scolari website; there is also an Australian site at www.qsr.com.au, which appears identical].

Additional information can be found online at the Scolari website and individual software sites.[42] Vendors and users also regularly offer seminars and training sessions on individual software programs; those of you who are attached to a university in some way, either as students or staff, are likely to be advised of these. Joining an online users' group is another obvious way of keeping up with developments in specific software.

Review of Chapter 12

This chapter has attempted to clarify the goals and components of the qualitative data analysis process. We introduced some of the complexity and challenge of systematically categorizing, coding, comparing and reconfiguring enormous quantities of data, all of which support the process of searching for meaning in the many patterns and themes.

Because ethnographic data analysis is so clearly structured and so frequently the model used to analyse qualitative data from information organizations, this has been considered in some detail. Furthermore, as computers are looming as ever more significant tools for analysis of qualitative data, their software capabilities were also discussed at length – but bearing in mind that in this volatile field whatever we write today may well have changed tomorrow.

Those of us overwhelmed by the task of analysing qualitative data can take some comfort in Geertz's reassuring observation that 'it is not necessary to know everything in order to understand something.'[43] Yes, the process of data analysis is time-consuming and ambiguous, but the creative search for patterns and themes in data will reward the qualitative researcher with fresh insights into the operation of information organizations.

Where to now?

This has been a long and somewhat daunting chapter, especially for anyone who feels a little uneasy at the prospect of coping with great quantities of data, whether paper-based or digital. Really, though, it is like anything else – once you survive the shock of starting, it can be relatively painless and even quite exhilarating.

Certainly the study reported in Chapter 14 did present profoundly depressing obstacles on more than one occasion, but on the whole the analysis and interpretation phases were as close to fun as one is likely to get in the research enterprise. Have another look at this chapter now, and consider what you see there about data analysis in the light of what you have just read in this chapter.

It also might be worth visiting some of the software websites listed in Note 42, downloading any demonstration programs they contain and testing them. This is an important activity, as it will give you confidence just to get the feel of how the programs work and what they are capable of achieving.

Further reading

This chapter has sought to occupy the middle ground in presenting an overview of qualitative data analysis, but most other work on this topic tends to fall into either the cursory or unnecessarily detailed category. Leaning towards the former but still useful for its 'broad brush' approach is H. Finch, 'Analysing Qualitative Material'. In *Research Methods in Library and Information Studies*, ed. Margaret Slater (London: Library Association Publishing, 1990), pp. 128–47. Altogether more detailed, but still very readable, is M. B. Miles and A. M. Huberman, *Qualitative Data Analysis: An Expanded Sourcebook,* 2nd edn (Thousand Oaks, CA: Sage, 1994).

Then we have works that evaluate software for qualitative data analysis. One group of writings seek to evaluate a range of qualitative programs. Relatively recent are M. Alexa and C. Zuell, 'Text Analysis Software: Commonalities, Differences and Limitations: The Results of a Review', *Quality and Quantity,* **34**, 2000, pp. 299–321, and S. Friese, *Comparison of Qualitative Data Analysis Software* (Stuttgart: Qualitative Research and Consulting, 2000), www.quarc.de/body_overview.html.

There is also a quickly expanding range of titles devoted to specific software applications; this has changed significantly from the last edition of the book, when there were relatively few such assessments. NVivo (formerly NUD★IST) seems to have captured the imagination of a large percentage of qualitative investigators, and there are now several titles devoted to this software. Two of these are rather similar: G. Gibbs, *Qualitative Data Analysis: Exploration with NVivo* (Milton Keynes: Open University Press, 2002); and L. Richards, *Using NVivo in Qualitative Research* (Thousand Oaks, CA: Sage, 1999). Both are quite comprehensive guides, although Gibbs is perhaps more student-oriented and simpler to follow, whereas Richards appears more comprehensive. A third NVivo title is P. Bazeley and L. Richards, *The NVivo Qualitative Project Book* (Thousand Oaks, CA: Sage, 2001), which offers a step-by-step guide to using Nvivo for analysing project data. Other NVivo-related literature is regularly reported on the Scolari website (www.scolari.co.uk/).

Notes

1　H. F. Wolcott, *Writing Up Qualitative Research.* Qualitative Research Methods, 20 (Newbury Park, CA: Sage, 1990), p. 8.

2　C. Geertz, *The Interpretation of Cultures* (New York: Basic Books, 1973), p. 5.

3　M. B. Miles and A. M. Huberman, *Qualitative Data Analysis: An Expanded Sourcebook.* 2nd edn (Thousand Oaks, CA: Sage, 1994), pp. 10–11.

4　J. P. Guilford, *The Nature of Human Intelligence* (New York: McGraw-Hill, 1967), pp. 213–15.

5　Wolcott, op. cit., p. 19.

6　R. A. Krueger, *Focus Groups: A Practical Guide for Applied Research* (Newbury Park: CA, Sage, 1988).

7　H. F. Wolcott, *Transforming Qualitative Data* (Thousand Oaks, CA: Sage, 1994), p. 12.

8　C. Marshall and G. B. Rossman, *Designing Qualitative Research* (Newbury Park, CA: Sage, 1989), p. 112.

LIVERPOOL JOHN MOORES UNIVERSITY
LEARNING SERVICES

9   D. M. Fetterman, *Ethnography Step by Step* (Newbury Park, CA: Sage, 1989), p. 88.

10 Miles and Huberman, op. cit., p. 10.

11 Wolcott, *Writing Up*, op. cit., p. 33. Another example of setting the scene is provided in the section headed 'Site of the Study' in M. Smith and P. Yachnes, 'Scholar's Playground or Wisdom's Temple? Competing Metaphors in a Library Electronic Text Center', *Library Trends*, **46** (4), 1998, p. 721. This study also provides an example of the types of coding discussed later in this chapter: see pp. 724ff.

12 D. A. Erlandson et al., *Doing Naturalistic Inquiry: A Guide to Methods* (Newbury Park, CA: Sage, 1993), p. 118.

13 Wolcott, *Writing Up*, loc. cit.

14 Miles and Huberman, op. cit., p. 9.

15 E. M. Rogers, *Diffusion of Innovations* (NY: Free Press, 2003).

16 Krueger, op. cit., p. 108.

17 Miles and Huberman, op. cit., p. 9.

18 G. H. Mead, *Mind, Self and Society from the Standpoint of a Social Behaviorist* (Chicago, IL: University of Chicago Press, 1962), p. 52.

19 Y. S. Lincoln and E. G. Guba, *Naturalistic Inquiry* (Newbury Park, CA: Sage, 1985), p. 133.

20 Miles and Huberman, op. cit., p. 56.

21 J. P. Spradley, *Participant Observation* (New York: Harcourt Brace Jovanovich, 1980), p. 86.

22 C. Glesne, *Becoming Qualitative Researchers: An Introduction*, 2nd edn (New York: Longman, 1999), pp. 132–3.

23 S. Erdelez, Information Encountering: An Exploration beyond Information Seeking. PhD dissertation, Syracuse University, 1995, p. 175.

24 Ibid., p. 175.

25 G. P. Murdock, *Outline of Cultural Materials* (New Haven, CT: Yale University Press, 1950); R. Bogdan and S. J. Taylor, *Introduction to Qualitative Research Methods* (New York: John Wiley and Sons, 1975), pp. 120–1.

26 Spradley, op. cit., p. 85.

27 R. P. Weber, *Basic Content Analysis*. 2nd edn. Quantitative Applications in the Social Sciences, 07-049 (Newbury Park, CA: Sage, 1990), p. 5; for another discussion of this method see B. Allen and D. Reser, 'Content Analysis in Library and Information Science Research.' *Library & Information Science Research*, **12**, 1990, pp. 251–62.

28 P. K. Manning and B. Cullum-Swan, 'Narrative, Content, and Semiotic Analysis'. In *Handbook of Qualitative Research*, eds. N. K. Denzin and Y. S. Lincoln (Newbury Park, CA: Sage, 1994), p. 464.

29 L. Westbrook, 'Qualitative Research Methods: A Review of Major Steps, Data Analysis Techniques, and Quality Controls'. *Library & Information Science Research*, **16**, 1994, pp. 241–54.

30 J. P. Spradley, *The Ethnographic Interview* (New York: Harcourt Brace Jovanovich, 1979), p. 92.

31 Ibid., p. 107.

32 Ibid., p. 141.

33 R. Fidel, 'Qualitative Methods in Information Retrieval Research', *Library & Information Science Research,* **15**, 1993, pp. 219–45.

34 A. L. Strauss and J. Corbin, *Basics of Qualitative Research: Grounded Theory Procedures and Techniques* (Newbury Park, CA: Sage, 1990).

35 Miles and Huberman, op. cit.

36 Wolcott, *Writing Up,* op. cit., p. 35.

37 J. Seidel, 'Method and Madness in the Application of Computer Technology to Qualitative Data Analysis'. In *Using Computers in Qualitative Research*, eds. N. G. Fielding and R. M. Lee (Newbury Park, CA: Sage, 1992), pp. 107–16.

38 T. J. Richards and Richards, 'Using Computers in Qualitative Research'. In *Handbook of Qualitative Research*, eds. N. K. Denzin and Y. S. Lincoln (Newbury Park, CA: Sage, 1994), p. 445.

39 Hard evidence supporting this is found in the work of Miles and Huberman, whose survey found that three-quarters of respondents used computer software for 'entering data, coding, search and retrieval, making displays, or building concepts', Miles and Huberman, op. cit., p. 43.

40 Ibid., pp. 43–6.

41 M. B. Miles and E. A. Weitzman, 'Appendix: Choosing Computer Programs for Qualitative Data Analysis'. In ibid., pp. 311–17. However, while the software Miles and Weitzman evaluated may have moved on, the questions they asked and the approach they adopted remain instructive.

42 The most popular qualitative research software, in addition to the Scolari website at www.scolari.co.uk, has the following URLs:
ATLAS.ti – www.atlasti.com
C-I-SAID – www.code-a-text.co.uk
The Ethnograph – www.qualisresearch.com/
HyperRESEARCH – www.researchware.com.
MAXqda – www.scolari.co.uk/
NVivo 2.0 – www.qsrinternational.com.

43 Geertz, op cit., p. 20.

13 Writing qualitative research reports

FOCUS QUESTIONS
- How does one go about writing up a qualitative research report?
- Is there a particular structure or style that should be followed?
- What are some of the ways in which a mass of data can be organized into the 'findings' of a study?
- Who are the readers of qualitative research?
- Why should research studies be published?

Finally, your data have been collected, sorted and resorted, studied, analysed and re-analysed. Now you are at the final activity of the final stage – writing it all up. You are either at the top of the pyramid (see Chapter 3, Figure 3.3, p. 38) or on the final step in the recursive cycle (Chapter 3, Figure 3.2, p. 37). But remember that nothing is final and that you will constantly refer back to earlier stages and steps during the report-writing exercise.

You should regard everything we have to say in this chapter as advisory rather than prescriptive, for every writing exercise has its own purpose and context and therefore unique stylistic requirements, organizational conventions and reader expectations. A dissertation, for example, will have quite rigid conventions for presentation and style, and these must be followed exactly. Journal articles and reports for funding bodies, on the other hand, may allow rather more leeway in presentation, but there will still be certain expectations for you to meet. It is best to begin, therefore, by having an absolutely clear understanding of what is required of you in a specific writing exercise. Then, to the extent possible, consider following the appropriate suggestions in this chapter.

The writing process

When preparing to write up the results of your qualitative investigation, remember that it helps to begin with a disciplined approach to the writing enterprise. For those new to this activity, Glesne offers a number of suggestions suitable for qualitative researchers.[1]

Basic considerations

To begin with, develop a detailed schedule and firm deadlines for your writing. Work backwards from when the completed product is due, and fit each chapter or section into a realistic time frame. Remember that there will be holidays and other unavoidable delays in your writing schedule. If you are relying on participants or referees for feedback, bear in mind that they will have other commitments. As a rough guide, you can expect the focused data analysis and writing to take at least as long as the data collection phase. As Chapter 12 has warned, it can take considerable time to become fully conversant with the data and their full meaning as part of the overall writing exercise.

As part of your schedule, have a realistic understanding of your own abilities as a writer. Specifically, at what time of day are you likely to do your best writing? During these hours how much time can you expect to devote to writing? And, given other commitments, on how many days of the week can you expect to write? How many pages or words are you likely to write at an average sitting? On average, an accomplished researcher who writes for two to three hours at a sitting can expect to produce about 1000 words of reasonable prose during that time.

An office or study is often not the best place in which to write, because there you are easily distracted by colleagues, family, telephone, fax or e-mail. Instead, it can help to have a special writing room or area in which you will not be distracted. Make it known to those who might offer distractions that you are actually working, and to a deadline (as we have attempted to do in revising this book). One of our colleagues goes to a beach-side holiday home on her own to ensure she has the solitude she needs to work, and one of us uses a study in a remote part of the house without telephone or internet connections.

Once you get into a writing frame of mind, ideas often occur at inopportune times – during a meeting, while travelling by air or walking the dog. Therefore, it helps to keep a notebook at hand most of the time, so that you can jot down these ideas. When you have free time but are away from your writing room, outline new sections in the notebook or record possible solutions to problems encountered during the last writing session.

Whenever you sit down to write, make sure you have clearly in mind the specific focus of your investigation and the themes you are teasing out. Keep asking yourself, 'What am I meant to be writing about, and what am I trying to say?' This helps to avoid the tangential writing that often occurs, especially after a long break. Sometimes thinking can be refocused if you start by editing what you last wrote. This not only gives your writing the appearance of a closely argued, logically connected series of paragraphs or sections but also can generate ideas for further sections.

Should you write on paper or at the computer? These days, most of us key text directly into the computer. This saves subsequent re-keying, as eventually you will need both the flexibility of editing on-screen, and the ability to massage the final appearance of the text. However, you should have a paper copy of the initial outline beside you at all times. This helps ensure that your writing has a consistent direction and that nothing important is overlooked. An alternative – especially useful when preparing a presentation or conference paper – may be to dictate it into a tape recorder. This can give it an overall unity and an appropriate conversational tone difficult to convey in print, but here having an outline to hand will be essential.

At the first draft stage it is important not to worry unnecessarily about grammar and syntax, even spelling, although sloppy writing at any stage will come back to haunt you. It is essential to concentrate on expressing your ideas simply and clearly, and using all the available data to do so. Very often concentration on content helps to make the words flow naturally, or at least less painfully. Many people find it easier to write if they bear in mind someone who may eventually read the result: in other words, try to think of writing as talking to someone you know.

Always work towards crisp, lucid prose. This means avoiding wordiness, passive constructions, convoluted phrases, abstract nouns, lengthy paragraphs, unnecessarily long or complex sentences, misplaced modifiers – all easy to list but equally easy to use in practice. If allowed by the conventions appropriate to your circumstances, write in the first person and the active tense – 'I then observed . . .', rather than 'It was observed by the researcher that . . .'. These techniques give your data and its analysis a sense of realism and vibrancy often missing in conventional academic writing. But this is easier said than done – one of us finds it almost impossible to write in the first person or to avoid the passive tense, and this after perhaps 25 years as a reasonably competent writer of scholarly prose.

Organizational flexibility

The most basic principle is: begin writing with a carefully planned outline, or at least an overall structure, in mind. Remember, though, that with qualitative research the development of ideas as you write is quite likely to take you down new paths; allow this to happen. What characterizes the writing process in a qualitative mould is that data are constantly being organized and then reorganized. As you work through the data time and again, you are not fitting observations or conversations into predetermined categories or patterns but rather are looking for emerging patterns and focal points, so the process by its very nature is a fluid one. Writing about your research is, after all, one of the most powerful ways in which you can think about it more deeply over an extended period.

During the data analysis stage discussed in Chapter 12 you were advised on how to go about organizing your data. You should have begun at the macro level to code all the data roughly into broad themes, focal points or categories; then, following these broad points, prepare an outline before you start writing. This helps you to see some shape to the mass of information (the data sets that exist in your database, print-outs, note cards or other means you might have used to record data) and the findings you have in mind, usually in a series of chapters as suggested below, or set of sections in a shorter work. As the writing occurs you move more intimately into the data, progressing from macro to micro levels, finding previously hidden patterns and themes. When this happens, you may need to reorganize the data sets to give prominence to emerging patterns that you feel are important. How this approach might take place is suggested in Research Scenario 13.1.

RESEARCH SCENARIO 13.1

RESOLVING CONFLICT IN A MINISTRY LIBRARY[2]

In a major project investigating management styles of senior personnel in government libraries you have been given special responsibility for a particular ministry. As a result of your data-gathering activities you have a major group of data on 'conflict resolution' among section managers in the unusually large information service within your ministry. Under 'conflict resolution' you have categorized data by conflict resolution techniques, among them 'holding section meetings', 'holding individual discussions', 'involving superiors', 'ignoring the situation', and so on.

As you write, it becomes apparent that there are two ways in which individual discussions are used. One is very confrontational and 'school masterish' in approach, seeking to resolve the conflict by directing the relevant staff member to cease specific activities that create ill will. The other approach is far more nondirective, in which the section head invites the staff member to discuss the problems, verbally reflecting on cause and effect, in the hope that this person will come to a personal understanding of an appropriate course of action. The subcategories are re-sorted accordingly, and you continue to write.

Then, as you write in depth about the nondirective approach, it emerges that male and female subordinates are treated differently in the nondirective scenario. With female staff the supervisors, usually males, take a very passive nondirective approach, almost never suggesting a course of action but rather allowing the women to devise their own solutions to the problem. With male staff, on the other hand, the supervisors are quite likely to suggest two or three course of action based on causes of unrest suggested during the conversations. Once again, then, you sort your data into new subcategories and continue to write, seeking to highlight this new pattern in dealing with conflict. 'Through this progressive coding process, you increasingly impose order on your data. Yet, at the same time, the order is flexible; it continuously changes, shaped by the ideas that your writing generates.'[3]

As you progress in this way, some initially relegated data may need to be reconsidered and incorporated as evidence. Conversely, other data that seemed crucial may now appear less relevant in relation to newly discovered patterns, and you are able to summarize this information in just a paragraph. Do not worry, as most writers new to the craft do, that you are failing to use hard-won data; there probably will be opportunities to use them in other writing at a later stage.

The important point is to keep using data as you write, and this will help you focus on the topic at hand. That is, do not allow yourself to be led astray, but stick to the information you have, using it so that there is progressively less and less of the remaining data. Conversely, do not worry about nonexistent data – if anything, you will probably have far more than you can use in a single piece of writing. And if there is a genuine gap in your data, admit it, indicating this as an area for further research. On rare occasions it may be that such a gap cannot be passed over in this way. Then, when your first draft has been finished, go back to the scene of your investigation and try to collect the missing information from those who can provide it most readily.

Structure in qualitative research reports

In practice the writing process is not as flexible as Research Scenario 13.1 might suggest. First, there are basic conventions regarding content that should be followed in any good research report. Second, there are some useful organizational strategies that help guide the presentation of ideas in qualitative studies. We look first at the structure of a 'typical' report, and then at some common organizational techniques.

The logic of structure

To the extent that we can speak of a 'typical' qualitative research report, a reader might expect to find five sections:

- introduction to the problem and its significance
- review of related literature
- discussion of research methodology and procedures
- presentation of the findings
- statement of implications and conclusions.[4]

Any good guide to scholarly writing or the preparation of theses and dissertations will provide substantial discussion of these elements. Here we only summarize the key points from the standpoint of qualitative research reporters.

It should go without saying that anything you write must have a beginning, middle and end; put most simply, this means that a written report should:

- tell them what you're going to tell them
- tell them
- tell them what you've told them.

Tell them what you're going to tell them

In doing this, a traditional piece of research will provide an introduction to the research problem, a review of related literature, and a discussion of research procedures. The introduction to the problem presents your view of why the study is significant, and why you carried it out in the first place. It offers a theoretical framework and clearly states the problem(s) or research question(s) being investigated. If necessary, terms are also defined, and limitations of the study are noted.

The literature review then places your study in context by offering an historical overview of earlier writing related to the topic, focusing specifically on both theory and methodology. The intention is also to offer a critique of the theory and findings, showing where your own study not only articulates with what others have written but also where it will offer a new, and perhaps corrective, perspective. Some prefer to integrate this in the text, but in most cases it is far less confusing to the reader if you confine the bulk of such discussion to a specific section. Then you can refer to such works briefly elsewhere in the report without having this intrude unnecessarily into the flow of ideas.

On the other hand, some of the literature review may be placed more appropriately where it is to be used. In Chapter 14, our sample case study chapter, there is no section called 'Review of the literature' (or words to that effect) but simply an introduction, which serves a similar purpose. Formal literature reviews are often abbreviated in journal article length publication of research reports. However, note that other work, especially of a methodological nature, is referred to in the following section, 'Method' (and indeed there are also subsequent citations where relevant). Because the literature is discussed in two sections, the author is able to note the methodological writings where they are most relevant to her chosen structure. (Of course, an alternative arrangement might be preferable in a different report.)

In the research procedures section, which conventionally comes next, you describe the specific methodology and procedures chosen for the investigation, linking these to what has gone before and presenting a clear rationale for their choice. Here it is necessary to describe the research focus (place and participants, including a 'researcher-as-research-instrument' statement), how data are being collected and why, and how data will be treated. Van Maanen believes that a 'method discussion' must explicitly deal with four factors:

- the assumed relationship between culture and behavior (the observed)
- the experiences of the fieldworker (the observer)
- the representational style selected to join the observer and observed (the tale)
- the role of the reader engaged in reconstructing the tale (the audience).[5]

Extrapolating from this for our own requirements, we might say that a discussion of research procedures needs to tell the readers about your participants and the setting, about you as an observer or participant (what your place on the continuum is), the approach you will take in the ensuing discussion (more on this below), and all of this in full knowledge of the audience for which you are writing (again, more on this below).

Tell them

Having dealt with all of the factors you are then in a position to present the findings, which is really what 'telling them' is all about. This is the core of any piece of research. Here, following one of the styles discussed below, you show the readers what you have seen and heard. In this section there are often lengthy verbatim transcriptions of participant dialogue, and detailed descriptions of settings or events, for these are the raw data from which findings are derived in qualitative research. You present evidence that supports or disproves your initial research questions, as well as any unexpected findings that may lead to further research, or at least remain as unanswered questions.

Rely on your field notes for concrete, descriptive examples of what you are trying to say; you will have a rich collection of data which should be used to 'prove' your case. Detailed descriptions of scenes and verbatim quotes from participants, often colourful and in the vernacular, set qualitative research writing apart from other types of research writing with rich and evocative descriptions of people, places and events. But qualitative research is more than description – it is essential that your writing be interpretive and evaluative as well. When evaluation is absent, it is not research but reportage. You have done the research to increase our understanding of a topic, and you do this by interpreting what you have found – not by being judgemental and prescriptive, but by finding meaning in words and events. Because interpretation and discussion of the findings is critical to your research, we offer our views on this subject in a separate section below entitled 'Discussing the findings'.

Tell them what you've told them

Finally, arising from your findings, by whatever technique these are conveyed in the main chapter or section of your writing, it is important to present implications and conclusions. In qualitative research in the information sector this can be the most important section, for readers tend to be looking for solutions to problems. What conclusions do you draw from the findings, and how can they be explained? Given the role of theory-building in qualitative research, are there implications in your research for theory-building? Do these implications suggest some commonly held professional beliefs may need to be modified? On a more practical level, what are the implications for professional practice? Do you recommend changes in professional practice, organizational structures, policies, procedures? The author of Chapter 14 does just that for her organization.

In other words the concluding section must be just that – a conclusion. It should not be a review of the evidence, a misplaced abstract of your study as a whole, or simply a suggestion of what research might be done next. Rather, it should draw out of your investigation the key points that readers can use to improve the information organization you were investigating. That is, your concluding thoughts should go beyond what you have seen, heard and reported to address a key question: What does it all mean, and what is the value of what I have learned?

Discussing the findings

We have said that the essence of your report is 'telling them', or discussing the findings. In this middle section of a report, which is drawn from the bulk of your notes, it often helps to follow a particular organizational approach throughout, one that is best suited both to the data and to the story you are trying to tell. Of four possible approaches, the two most often found in qualitative studies within information settings are the thematic and changing focus techniques.[6]

Thematic technique

Most common of all is the thematic or topical approach, in which the investigator follows a typology of themes or topics that either informed the investigation at the outset or emerged during data collection. The discussion of findings is then organized around these focal points, with observed relationships and events, as well as conversations, being fitted to the pattern. This approach is useful if you are developing a specific theory related to an investigation, or seeking to draw conclusions that will inform concrete actions in an information setting. An example of this occurs in Chapter 14, where the researcher has organized her findings using headings such as 'Recruitment' and 'Training and development'.

Changing focus technique

If the thematic approach seems somewhat rigid for you, then the changing focus technique may hold more appeal, as it does for many experienced qualitative investigators of information organizations. Here the researcher moves from descriptive detail to theoretical abstraction, or vice versa, and back and forth. 'Like a zoom lens, the text glides through various levels of generality.'[7] A leading advocate of this techniques is Spradley, who maintains that a writer moves quite naturally from universal statements about human nature to incident-specific observations in a single piece of writing.[8] To do otherwise is both unnatural and, for the reader, quite tedious: at one extreme the writer remains on a theoretical plane, without a clear grounding in observation and so lacking context, whereas at the other extreme a writer is so bogged down in detail that no general ideas or conclusions are allowed to emerge. Therefore, a good qualitative writer should move back and forth across the various planes or levels.

Natural history and chronological techniques

The other two techniques, natural history and chronological, are less commonly found in qualitative studies of information settings but are nonetheless worthwhile possibilities. A writer using the natural history technique tries to recreate the fieldwork process of exploration and discovery as closely as possible. This can be useful when it is important to portray a sense of time and place in dramatic fashion. Here the writer is loath to interpret, which is seen as an interruption of the natural flow of events, but rather seeks to portray events as they actually occurred. Obviously, then, description and analysis, which we feel are crucial in qualitative research within information settings, sit uneasily in this technique.

Finally, the chronological technique is similarly naturalistic, although it tends to follow a particular characteristic of the setting or participants from inception to conclusion, rather than taking a whole-canvas approach. This can be a useful adjunct to the thematic approach, as it allows the writer to show the chronological logic of a theme to good advantage.

Whatever technique you use, remember that you are writing not for the sake of writing but to convey to the readers what you saw and heard so that they will accept your generalizations when you come to make them. You want to show your readers what you found, and you want to provide them with details substantiating your findings as clearly and as unambiguously as possible. All of the discussion techniques have one element in common: they invariably rely heavily on well-documented description from your data notes to establish the veracity of whatever you are trying to convey. The difference among the techniques is the degree to which they rely on description, verbatim reporting and so on, and not whether they use such data.

Styles of writing in qualitative research

Closely related to techniques for presenting findings is the matter of writing style. Two factors should determine the style you employ when writing up research findings: how the data are shown to best advantage, and what feels comfortable to you as a writer. Of the available descriptions of qualitative writing conventions, the one that we find most suitable for information professionals is that espoused by Van Maanen in *Tales of the Field: On Writing Ethnography*; there he devotes the three core chapters to three types of 'tales' in ethnographic writing: realist, confessional, and impressionist.[9] The discussion in this section is based on Van Maanen's typology, although rather than discrete styles we prefer to view this as a continuum, with one style blending into another. This is shown in Figure 13.1.

The best qualitative writing tends to employ a combination of these conventions to convey particular ideas or situations, because each is best suited to particular intentions. For example, at one point in a methodological discussion you may want to adopt a confessional approach, as this is an excellent way in which to convey your own role in the investigation, and to indicate your particular

Figure 13.1 The continuum of writing styles

perspective (as the researcher describes in the section 'Method' in Chapter 14). Then, in the section on data description you may prefer the impressionist approach when dealing with a participant who is particularly striking in appearance or colourful in use of language – you as writer could not possibly improve on what you saw or heard, so you let the event speak for itself. But then, in the data analysis, it may be important to take a realist approach, focusing on what you regard as crucial aspects of the investigation and presenting data in light of what you deem significant.

At all costs remember that style is not your primary aim; rather, you choose a style appropriate to the ideas that have emerged in your study. 'Content is paramount – *what* you have to say, not how you say it. Style is critical but auxiliary in reporting qualitative research, necessary but not sufficient.'[10]

Realist writing

The realist researcher draws observations and descriptions from data collected during fieldwork in the information setting, using the data as a source of quite specific statements about occurrences, and often quoting very extensively from the people studied. The emphasis is primarily on reporting 'observed facts' rather than on interpretation, the attempt being to present a photograph-like portrait. In this approach, the most familiar form found in qualitative studies of information settings, the reader is likely to find particularly rich descriptions of events, activities and relationships, and rather less speculation on cause and effect.

There are four conventions that set realist writing in information research apart from other styles: absence of the author, documentary style, participant viewpoint, and interpretive authority.[11] First, the author cannot be discerned in this writing, which emphasizes the participants to the almost virtual exclusion of the researcher. Objectivity, neutrality and impersonality characterize this writing style, which implies that I, a detached researcher, am simply passing on value-free data for your information. For the new researcher this can be an awkward position, as it relies heavily on one's proven credibility as a competent investigator. In Chapter 14, our researcher has, for the most part, adopted this impersonal, apparently objective style.

Second, realist writing uses a documentary style that emphasizes the minutiae of everyday activities in the setting or in the population under investigation. However, details are not reported in slavish chronological fashion; rather they are used to support precepts that might have informed the research at the outset. Here researchers tend to use received theory to inform and structure their investigation, and in their reporting they highlight those facets. For example, in Chapter 14 the researcher may well have anticipated that coping with large quantities of e-mail could be a problem, and used statements from two consultants ('Sometimes I come in and it takes me a couple of hours to work through all my e-mails', and 'E-mail is our biggest unsolved problem') to substantiate what she started with – 'details are in a sense precoded in a realist ethnography to serve as instances of something important, usually a structural or procedural unit (i.e., precept).'[12]

Third, the participant's point of view is of major concern to the realist writer, and this is presented through extensive quotations collected during fieldwork. However, it is not just the participant's words that are important, but also the ideas and theories embedded in these words. In a view that is shared by Van Maanen and others, we see that here observation, so characteristic of realist writing in the past, is allowing room for interpretation, thereby showing a trend towards impressionist writing. The difference here is that the impressions are from the participants, and not from the investigators.

Fourth, realist writing is characterized by espousing a particular view or interpretation rather than allowing for the possibility that there may in fact be numerous, equally valid interpretations of events or interactions. This is not to say that qualitative researchers today take what Van Maanen terms a 'godlike pose' but rather that they tend to posit one set of positions as offering the 'best' explanation of events. What happens is that data are presented as facts that support a particular position taken by the researcher, and the participants are used to buttress the case.

Confessional writing

The researcher who is writing a confessional story places particular emphasis on the interpretation of data gleaned in the field. Here we are speaking not of those standalone confessions by fieldworkers about 'how they did it', but rather of personal views expressed within the context of reporting fieldwork. If realists seek to express the views of respondents without embellishment, confessional writers becomes intimately involved in the story and interpret events, activities and relationships through their own eyes. In this writing there is a greater tendency to informality, with named respondents speaking and interacting in an almost theatrical (but not fictional) manner. Much qualitative research includes at least some confessional writing, primarily in the section devoted to 'the researcher-as-instrument' and to presentation of data on setting and participants.

In an information setting, confessional writing is almost the other side of the realist coin. That is, whereas the realist investigator believes the author should be absent from the writing, the confessional writer takes pains to introduce a personal author (the 'I' of much qualitative writing). If realist writing presents the participant's viewpoint, then confessional writing presents that of the investigator. Each characteristic of confessional writing is worth noting in turn: the presence of the author, the investigator viewpoint, and an acceptance of flaws.[13]

The presence and personal authority of the investigator shows through in elaboration of the formal methodological descriptions that are so important in qualitative research. The confessional writer attempts to describe how well he or she was able to compensate for both personal shortcomings (methodological weaknesses, psychological uncertainties, social gaffes, and so on) and for methodological mis-understandings, muddling through despite these problems. No longer an expert, the investigator or fieldworker is a student and an interpreter of what is seen. For most of us, this is perhaps closer to the truth than the image portrayed in realist writing.

In the field we *do* become involved in the setting, attracted to certain people or places, angry when things do not go according to plan, and so on. This is allowed to show in confessional writing, but not to the extent that it invalidates the data analysis or conclusions. We are showing that we suffer in the field but win through nevertheless. This approach is probably not best taken by the neophyte investigator, but rather by one with established credentials. A study written totally as a confessional story probably has little place in information work; rather, a confessional approach might be taken at appropriate junctures in order to illuminate certain events or theories.

While the viewpoint represented in confessional writing is that of the fieldworker, the intention is, through the investigator, to show the perspective of those being studied. A curious kind of schizophrenia often results, with the writer ranging across the spectrum of experience-near and experience distant. 'The attitude conveyed is one of tacking back and forth between an insider's passionate perspective and an outsider's dispassionate one . . . . A delightful dance of words often ensues as fieldworkers present themselves as both vessels and vehicles of knowledge.'[14] That is, the researcher tries to convey his or her actual participation in the situation being investigated, and how this participation developed through contact with other participants, and through learning the unique behaviour patterns or relationships of the setting. A word of warning is in order here: never allow the 'I' to dominate, because this ultimately detracts from your findings. As Wolcott wisely suggests, 'keep the subject(s) of your study the focus of your reflections. The more you feel an urge to step into the spotlight, the more you should consider divorcing your reflections from the research.'[15]

Impressionist writing

The third type of qualitative research reporting is the impressionist. Here the researcher seeks to tell those stories or dramatic episodes that make a fieldwork experience memorable and that best exemplify particular themes. Using various techniques to create a dramatic atmosphere, the researcher presents knowledge gradually, allowing characters and incidents to develop in much the same way as they did during fieldwork. Interpretation is left largely to the reader, and the researcher interferes very little in the dramatic unfolding of events. The characteristics of impressionist writing are: dramatic recall, unfolding of events, use of literary devices, and the presence of 'real' people.[16]

Impressionist writing takes the form of dramatic recall, which means that events are presented in historical sequence so that the readers can enter into the real scene, through the investigator's eyes, more completely than in other forms of qualitative reporting. To a large extent there is less need for commentary or explanatory asides, which are kept to a minimum. Interpretation and analysis, therefore, are secondary to reliving the experience of the fieldworker. Consequently, and this is the second key characteristic of impressionist writing, the unfolding of events is almost a form of creative writing. As in a short story, events occur and are tied together in the mind of the reader instead of being given credence and meaning by authorial explanations (methodological notes, for example). The story told creates its own, literary credibility. To achieve this dramatic unfolding of events, the impressionist writer uses any number of literary devices to tell the story – the third characteristic of this type of reporting. The standards at work here are those of the writer, who has in mind three attributes of quality prose: interest, coherence and fidelity.

- Does it draw the reader in?
- Does it hold together naturally?
- Does it ring true?[17]

Finally, then, the impressionist writer seeks to convey fully the personalities involved in the investigation, including the researcher, who are shown to be involved and interested in what occurs. Often they are also shown to be developing their own skills as they learn to fit into the surroundings and react to other participants – many features the realist writer would not care to have known. But most important is the way in which the leading participants are portrayed. These participants become more like literary figures, personalities fully developed physically and emotionally, with unique personalities and interesting dialogue.

Impressionist reporting is not frequently used in research focused on information organizations. This is perhaps because it embodies a degree of methodological iconoclasm and seeks to make a particular point about research per se. As Van Maanen sees it, impressionist writing protests against 'the ultimate superficiality of much of the published fieldwork in the social sciences – ethnographic or otherwise'.[18] In our view this is not much of an issue in our field. Ours is a discipline in which, until recently, the norm has been quantitative research, but today qualitative research has found its place and is no longer suspect. However, one must be vigilant in how this research is presented, for reporting which appears to be highly subjective can quickly reawaken old suspicions. We suggest that impressionist writing be used rarely and with caution.

Readers of qualitative research

What you decide to use as the primary writing style must depend on one thing above all others – your readers. They should determine what is told, and how. In the case of information-based research, these readers are likely to be: examiners (academic specialists), employers (who asked for the study), colleagues and other information professionals. Except perhaps in the first group, which will be expecting certain fairly rigid conventions to be followed, for the most part your readers are going to be busy information professionals who want to read something that is interesting, jargon-free and to the point. This concept of readership should always shape your qualitative writing. Van Maanen speaks of three types of readers, only one of which can really be addressed adequately in a single written piece: collegial readers, social science readers and general readers. We think the last can be dismissed almost out of hand, as qualitative studies of information work are rarely of interest to anyone in the general community. None of us is ever likely to write a piece for *The Economist* or a quality newspaper on a day in the life of an information centre.

The 'typical' audience

At the other extreme, though, we may well be writing for collegial readers, that is, other qualitative investigators of information settings, and in particular academics asked to examine a thesis or dissertation.[19] Here one would expect to find writing that adheres to the conventions of 'the club' (if one exists), inhabited by those who are expert in qualitative research in information settings. When this is the case, theoretical or methodological language and jargon can be especially useful, because they allow one to speak in a recognizable shorthand, conveying a great deal of assumed knowledge economically. At the same time, even among club members jargon can be abused and over-used, operating as much to exclude as to explain.

In general, writing for a specialized audience of experts (that is, other information professionals conversant with the canons of qualitative research) should be characterized by clarity and attention to detail, and a balance between abstraction and concrete example – giving due attention to both the theoretical framework and the unique contribution of the particular investigation. In addition, a clear organizing structure is important. As indicated above, in a typical report we can expect to find a statement of the study's theoretical framework, a review of the literature, discussion of methodological issues, and so on. (Given this expectation, it should be clearer why impressionist writing is less common in formal academic writing.) For example, as academics we are interested in how the researcher in Chapter 14 handles the methodological aspects of her study, and how this fits into the framework of qualitative methodologies; therefore, we expect the report to address these aspects thoroughly (if perhaps briefly). In short, when writing for readers within your general circle, you must be aware of formal expectations and specific institutional requirements. To go outside these is to court unwelcome criticism.

More flexibility is allowed with the largest readership of qualitative research – that is, with Van Maanen's social science readers, whom we equate with 'typical' information professionals. Here we have in mind people who read our reports or journal articles in search of information and solutions to specific problems in the workplace. They are not experts who are immersed in the niceties of research methodologies and read with the same focus as collegial readers. Rather,

> this audience treats fieldwork as merely a method among methods, and while normally respectful of the work, this audience judges it by how well it informs their own research interests. These readers are not reading ethnography in order to be entertained, challenged, or enlightened about the nature of social science. They wish only to be informed about certain facts the fieldworker has unearthed.[20]

When we write for these people, we are really addressing our peers in the information professions, as distinct from those who may be experts in our topic. Such individuals are often described in the 'Information for contributors' section of a professional journal. For example, *Library Collections, Acquisitions and Technical Services* describes its audience as 'members of the library acquisitions, collection management, and bookselling communities throughout the world'. If we were preparing an article for such a readership, we would write to describe what we have found in an investigation, and this should be our primary aim. The conventions that apply to collegial writing are much less important here. For example, the typical information professional will look at the report in Chapter 14, which might have been published somewhere like the *Journal of Knowledge Management*, and not be especially concerned with how the researcher uses Spradley or Freedman to structure the analysis. On the other hand, such a reader will want to know what the researcher learned about HR practices in an organizational culture of this kind. Our advice when writing for this audience is that offered by Van Maanen in relation to ethnographies: what you write should be 'empirical enough to be credible and analytical enough to be interesting'.[21]

Four keywords best summarize what we have been saying about writing:

- content
- structure
- style
- readership.

When we write qualitative research, we should have foremost in our minds what it is we want to say – the message or content to be conveyed. How this content is presented depends on the structure that may be required by external factors, on the style best suited to the information and most likely to attract the desired readers. Handy hints on how to juggle these complementary factors are not our forté, but Wolcott's short and readable volume, *Writing up Qualitative Research*, is replete with just such ideas.[22] Wolcott provides a series of highly practical suggestions on getting going with your writing, keeping going and finishing – straightforward, entertaining advice that any beginner will find useful.

Writing for publication

Writing a formal research report is one thing; writing for publication is another, arguably more valuable. The first is, perhaps, a dissertation destined to be read by a tiny and highly select audience: one's supervisor(s), with luck a long-suffering spouse, and two or three external examiners. Many theses are read by no others. Alternatively, it is a research report, commissioned by an information organization and of special interest to it; copies circulate around that organization, recommendations are acted upon (we trust), and the report is then filed and forgotten.

In both cases it is more than possible that at least some general findings and conclusions may be of interest and value to a wider audience. Adding a few letters to your name ('MA', 'PhD') or completing a consultancy add to your reputation and standing in the profession; publishing a worthwhile article in a respected professional journal, or giving a timely conference paper can add, if anything, rather more. Apart from other considerations, by the time you have completed a research report or dissertation, you will also have completed something like 90 per cent of the work involved in preparing just such an article or presentation. All that remains is to re-cast it, possibly using a different authorial voice, eliminating much of the literature review and methodological detail, but retaining its essence.

Both the authors of this volume believe in gaining maximum value from the work that we do. We would term this 'killing two birds with one stone' if we were not, in fact, bird fanciers (we need not mention our poor aim). As readers of this book, you will have noticed that several of its research scenarios are based on our own experience. Work we did originally for one purpose (a higher degree, a consultancy), and which has probably already been published as a research report, is here being used for perhaps a third time as an illustration of methodology. Today, few information professionals are not busy people – why not also get the maximum value from the work *you* do?

There is also another, ethical argument. Members of our professions are frequently generous in allowing both colleagues and research students into their organizations. Their staff give time to support various research projects. Is it not reasonable to expect that some of this assistance is returned to the profession, and to the organizations which support such work? It is for this reason that many research texts describe such wider publication as the final stage in the research process. Rayward, then editor of the *Library Quarterly*, said that

> As an editor, I see as one of my major tasks the encouragement of such persons [those who have recently completed research degrees] to meet a serious professional and academic obligation to report what they discover. . . . In terms of adding to our knowledge, they tend to represent a job half done . . . . The contribution of dissertations and reports to professional knowledge is not complete until they are published either as articles or books.[23]

There are many guides to getting published in the professional literature. Rayward's is one of the most comprehensive: he discusses deciding upon an appropriate journal, the role of the editor, the refereeing process, revision (usually necessary), common deficiencies in articles submitted, and ends with the mechanics of the publication process itself. Another contribution, from O'Connor and Van Orden, concentrates on the refereeing process in particular.[24]

Journal editors generally can attest to a paucity of really worthwhile copy. As journal editors ourselves, we more often than not have to return contributions for some revision. Try to see this as positive rather than negative criticism – most submissions will be accepted for publication when revised, and be all the better for that revision. Good advice before submitting a manuscript to a journal is to look carefully at several issues: does it in fact publish the kind of article you have in mind, and in that topic area? (One test of this is whether in your paper you would have to cite some previous research reported in that journal.) Use the articles in the journal as a guide to the style and type of presentation the editor will expect, especially with regard to referencing. Has it published a guide for contributors?

Finally, whether you are seeking to publish in a journal or give a conference or seminar presentation, we would suggest that you ask a colleague to review your contribution first. Fresh eyes can often pick up points which have eluded the author. It is easy to become too close to your work.

Publication, then, is the final stage in a research project. It seems appropriate that in the final chapter of this book we turn to an example of a project which could well have been published in order to bring its findings to a wider audience.

Review of Chapter 13

This chapter has suggested that you develop a detailed schedule and deadlines for your writing. Write simply and clearly, keeping in mind the specific focus of your study. Begin with a carefully planned outline. An adaptation of the familiar 'tell them what you're going to tell them; tell them; and tell them what you've told them' approach can provide an overall structure, with the findings themselves probably presented using either a thematic or changing focus approach.

The style you adopt will depend on your audience; for a qualitative research project, some combination of realist and confessional writing will probably be most appropriate. Finally, we urge you to publish your results in order to make them available to a wider professional audience.

Where to now?

For the last time, we suggest that you review the focus questions at the start of this chapter. Then we suggest that you might analyse a published research report in terms of its organization, style and approach to discussing findings. Most accessible for this purpose is Chapter 14, to which we have referred throughout this chapter. Ask yourself the following questions:

- Is this final case study chapter written in a style that you find particularly accessible?
- Is there a logical sequence to the arrangement of sections, and of material within sections?
- Does the literature review place this project squarely in the context of similar investigations and appropriate methodological approaches?
- Do the findings match the data as you perceive them?
- Is the writer teasing out all relevant conclusions from the findings?

Further reading

One publication continues to stand head and shoulders above all others as a guide to writing qualitative research, so you need look no further than this: H. F. Wolcott, *Writing up Qualitative Research*, 2nd edn, Qualitative Research Methods, 20 (Newbury Park, CA: Sage, 2001). There is nothing like Wolcott's work specifically for information professionals.

After quite a long hiatus in the publication of such guides, there has been a slight flurry of output in recent years. Two recent works combine advice on writing with other topics, such as proposals and research conduct: P. L. Munhall, *Qualitative Research Proposals and Reports: A Guide*, 2nd edn (Sudbury, MA: Jones and Bartlett, 2000); and A. Holliday, *Doing and Writing Qualitative Research* (Thousand Oaks, CA: Sage, 2001). A third, by Ely et al., is more limited in focus and deals specifically with writing of research, especially in the field of education: M. Ely et al., *On Writing Qualitative Research: Living by Words* (London: Falmer, 1997). Those specifically seeking to publish their work might start with D. Black et al., *500 Tips for Getting Published: A Guide for Researchers and Professionals* (London: Kogan Page, 1998) – one of a series of '500 Tips' titles, but with much sound advice on such matters as targeting the right journal.

In addition to reading about writing, we advise that you read exemplary qualitative studies in order to see how others have done it. Examples of qualitative research reports specifically in information work are found in the concluding bibliography. Also very worthwhile, and quite entertaining, is C. D. Smith and W. Kornblum (eds.), *In the Field: Readings on the Field Research Experience*, 2nd edn (Westport, CT: Praeger, 1996). This particular work we recommend less for its insights into field research than for the quality of the writing about that experience – none of it relates specifically to fieldwork in information settings, but the writing is highly atmospheric and gives a strong sense of place.

Notes

1 C. Glesne, *Becoming Qualitative Researchers: An Introduction*, 2nd edn (New York: Longman, 1999), pp. 160–1.
2 This research scenario is based on a suggestion in Glesne, p. 163.
3 Ibid., p. 163.
4 This division is based on J. E. Mauch and N. Park, *Guide to the Successful Thesis and Dissertation: A Handbook for Students and Faculty*, 5th edn (New York: Marcel Dekker, 2003). A somewhat more detailed division of main parts is offered by D. R. Hittleman and A. J. Simon, *Interpreting Educational Research: An Introduction for Consumers of Research* 2nd edn (Upper Saddle River, NJ: Merrill, 1997): background, purpose, methods, subjects, instruments, procedures, results, conclusions, references (pp. 50–63).
5 J. van Maanen, *Tales of the Field: On Writing Ethnography* (Chicago, IL: University of Chicago Press, 1988), p. xi.
6 These, and the other two organizational techniques discussed in this section, are mentioned by Glesne, *op. cit.*, pp. 165–6.

7   Ibid., p. 165.
8   J. Spradley, *The Ethnographic Interview* (New York: Holt, Rinehart and Winston, 1979), pp. 207–10.
9   Van Maanen, op. cit., pp. 45–124.
10 H.F. Wolcott, *Writing Up Qualitative Research,*. Qualitative Research Methods, 20 (Newbury Park, CA: Sage, 1990), p. 48.
11 Van Maanen, op. cit., pp. 45–54.
12 Ibid., p. 48.
13 Ibid., pp. 74–81.
14 Ibid., p. 77.
15 Wolcott, op. cit., p. 61.
16 Van Maanen, op. cit., pp. 103–6.
17 Ibid., p. 105.
18 Ibid., p. 119.
19 Mauch and Birch, op. cit., offer excellent advice on what one might expect to find in a 'typical' thesis or dissertation, and general guidelines on conventions in this type of writing based on their understanding of what examiners tend to look for.
20 Van Maanen, op. cit., p. 30.
21 Ibid., p. 29.
22 Wolcott, op. cit. The quotations which follow from this brief but helpful work come from pages 13–19, 46–7 and 55 ff.
23 W. B. Rayward, 'Publishing Library Research', *College & Research Libraries*, **41** (3), (1980), pp. 210–19.
24 D. O'Connor and P. Van Orden, 'Getting into Print', *College & Research Libraries*, **39** (5), (1978), pp. 389–96.

14 Human resources in knowledge management: a case study

The purpose of this chapter is to present a model case report, the final product of a qualitative research study. This report, a fabrication which draws upon several studies including some of our own,[1] exemplifies one method for organizing such a report. It follows conventional qualitative research practice in protecting the privacy and identity of research respondents and of the research setting. To this end, informants' names and other details have been modified.

Introduction

There has been a great deal written about knowledge management over the past few years.[2] Much of this has focused either on technical aspects of knowledge management, such as the information systems involved, or upon the strategies adopted.[3] Current issues of particular concern in the field include the application of complexity and chaos theory to help increase our understanding of the processes involved in knowledge management.[4]

Rather less has been written about management of the key personnel involved, the knowledge managers themselves – in particular, in the area of human resources (HR) – and the cultural contexts within which they operate.[5] Yet, as Scarbrough has shown, implementation of a knowledge management programme may fail if networks of social relationships are not adequately recognized.[6] Indeed, a Dutch study asked a similar question to that posed in this study: 'What types of activities are perceived by professionals working in human resource development (HRD) offices to be relevant to good knowledge management within their own office?'[7] The present study differs from that in examining knowledge management, not in an HRD office but in a knowledge management consultancy firm, and in adopting a qualitative rather than largely quantitative approach.

One of the aims of this case study was to provide an opportunity to explore all of these issues in a real-life situation.

Method

This study was undertaken as part of the author's PhD in knowledge management. It involved a longitudinal, ethnographic case study carried out within a knowledge management firm. To preserve confidentiality, that business is referred to as Knowledge Management Partners (KMP) in this report.

The author met one of the partners in KMP at a professional function and enquired about the possibility of studying the organization. It took a considerable time to obtain permission, which was finally granted on the understanding that the firm's real name would not be used for either the thesis or reports based upon it, and that staff within the organization would also not be referred to using their real names. In addition the senior partner would have the right to see and, if necessary, veto any such subsequent publications (the right to veto was not extended to the thesis itself). Furthermore, the researcher was required to obtain her university's Ethics Committee approval for the project. This also proved time-consuming, as an amended application had to be resubmitted. The Ethics Committee required all interviewees to sign an approved written consent form, and confirmation that transcripts of all interviews would be kept secure.

The researcher was introduced to KMP as a student who would be assisting with some human resources (HR) functions, and formally reporting to the HR manager. She was allocated a shared desk in an open-plan office within the organization, attended several HR staff meetings and some social gatherings (such as a farewell lunch for a colleague), and also attended a small number of other meetings, including one board meeting. As a staff member, albeit temporary and unpaid, she was given access to KMP's intranet, its internal staff e-mail and to its internal documentation.

In addition she interviewed a range of staff from the senior partner to junior staff.[8] Some staff were interviewed on several occasions, and using Yin's terminology [9] could be described as key informants. The fieldwork component of this study involved some five months, with two subsequent short follow-up sessions.

The researcher took brief notes at or immediately following all the meetings she attended, and selectively photocopied or printed some internal documents. All interviews were transcribed by the researcher, and NVivo was used for content analysis. Thus the data were gathered using a variety of methods to provide triangulation.[10] At the conclusion of the study two informants who had been especially helpful were asked to read a draft report on the organization and confirm its accuracy.[11]

KMP and knowledge management

KMP was founded as recently as 1992 but today is a global organization employing over 120 staff. Of these, nearly 100 are expert consultants with a great deal of freedom in their work methods. Typically each consultant belongs to several ad hoc project teams, many but by no means all associated with a particular client. Some large clients have associations with several such teams. KMP is based in a European capital city, occupying one whole floor of a recently restored heritage building in the older part of the CBD (central business district).

Organizational culture in KMP values creativity and innovation, flexibility and hard work rather than formality or hierarchy. KMP has a flat management structure, where most communication is lateral and informal. All staff, whatever their level, address each other by their given names (occasionally nicknames), dress is usually informal except when there is to be a client presentation – and not always even then, and hours are flexible if long. For example, most staff come in for at least some time on both days of the weekend.

Because managing the shared knowledge base of the organization is seen as critical to its continued success and growth, and because of this strong but informal organizational culture, appropriate HR practices were considered essential to attract and retain appropriate staff. During the time the researcher was attached to KMP turnover rates were low by industry standards: four people (equivalent to an annual turnover of approximately 8%). Because she was attached to the HR function, the researcher was able to participate in the recruitment process to replace these four people.

Recruitment

In the past, most of the staff of KMP had been recruited by personal contact with the partners, especially the senior partner. However, with the appointment of KMP's first HR manager a more formal recruitment process was developed. This was intended to complement rather than supersede recruitment through personal networks. Nevertheless, the senior partner commented:

> These days I'm much less likely to come across bright young people we'd like to take on – I'm spending more and more time meeting with senior executives, some of whom we'd definitely *not* wish to consider! I'm happy to leave recruitment to [the HR manager] provided that I still get to meet and assess everyone we're seriously considering.

The HR manager had been appointed from a prominent recruitment agency and maintained some of his ties with that agency. They are contracted to suggest possible new staff to KMP as suitable candidates arise. Consultants with KMP also suggest individuals to contact. A senior consultant said:

> Oh, I can give you an example from last week. I was in a meeting with [a major client] and they had a team which included a new graduate from Northwestern [University]. I was very impressed by him, and asked about him afterwards. When they said he was only with them on short-term contract and wouldn't be staying, I approached him myself and asked him to contact [the HR manager]. He looked like a good bet to me – but I wouldn't want to lose a long-term client by poaching staff from them!

Once identified, the HR manager is responsible for shortlisting potential candidates. This involves assessment against a checklist and then personal interview, sometimes by phone. The HR manager says he is not looking for a particular 'type', rather for exceptionally intelligent and academically well-qualified people who take an unconventional approach to problem solving:

> We're not looking for the 'organization man' here – anything but! We value openness, flexibility and what has been designed as the 'ability to think outside the square'. Tolerance of uncertainty comes pretty high, too – we want risk takers, not risk avoiders.

Less than a third of potential candidates are then reinterviewed by the HR manager and a senior consultant in the candidate's technical area of expertise, occasionally with one or more other staff in the area as well. This is also the stage at which informal checking with past employers and academic mentors is undertaken. The areas covered in the second round interview cover:

- understanding of the area of expertise
- interdisciplinary knowledge
- client focus
- communication skills
- ability to 'fit in'
- commitment to sharing knowledge and expertise.

Following this second, in-depth interview, the surviving candidates make a visit to KMP where they meet a number of staff, including the senior partner, formally and informally. A final interview involves a panel drawn from across the organization – and really chosen more for their availability on the day than their areas of expertise. This is regarded as appropriate because any successful new starter will have to work across the organization.

This relatively unconventional recruitment process eliminates all but about one in ten of those originally suggested. It is less structured and less formal than most, reflecting the culture of KMP itself. However, by including an opportunity for subjective reactions to candidates it is apparent that the process does also recognize the importance of tacit knowledge. The downside is that it is both time-consuming and intensive of staff time. 'We've lost some good prospects who were offered more money elsewhere while we still making up our minds, yes,' said the HR manager.

Training and development

At KMP there are no formal induction programmes, and no formal training is organized. Instead, consultants and others are expected to identify and undertake whatever professional development they feel will be useful to them. The role of HR is thus reduced to one of information disseminator and facilitator, making bookings and so on. As one consultant said:

> If you employ the right people you shouldn't need to send them off for some sort of standardized training. If they're any good they'll be the best people to decide what they need in order to keep up to date. In general, we'd expect people who work with us to be self-starters in training as well as in everything else. Occasionally someone decides they

need to do something which seems rather odd – attend a conference well outside their own area, for example – but we've seen some great ideas come out of that sort of cross-fertilization.

This may work well for continuing professional development, but does not always work so well when a new staff member joins. Of the three new staff who started during the period the researcher was attached to KMP (a fourth started shortly after she left), two were 'thrown straight into a top-priority job: it took me ages to work out which way was up'. One of the terms used by these new staff members to describe what was going on at the time was 'chaos'. The third staff member was introduced to the organization and its members by a mentor, and this appeared to have worked particularly well: the mentor and new staff member formed a strong bond and have since co-operated on two separate projects.

Mentoring is, in fact, a major component of staff development in KMP. Experienced staff mentor juniors, and sometimes a less experienced consultant is appointed leader of a particular project in the knowledge that there is a more experienced person also on the project team. This was described to the researcher as working particularly well when the experienced consultant was very short of time – as is often the case. Mentoring is seen as one way of ensuring knowledge and expertise is shared within the organization.

KMP provides an environment which in some ways is very supportive of the ongoing professional development of its staff. This commitment to professional development might usefully be extended to new staff through a formal mentoring process.[12] Alternatively, there may be some other culturally acceptable way of inducting new staff which avoids the stress a couple of new staff reported.

Organizational culture

Mobility in consulting organizations can be very high. There are several ways of ensuring highly qualified, highly productive staff in areas greatly in demand stay with an organization. Remuneration is only one of these – and by the standards of the consulting industry, pay rates for most of the staff at KMP are not exceptional (although some senior consultants and the partners are well paid).

Asked, 'Why do you stay here?' one young staff member said:

I like it. They're a great bunch here, provided you know your stuff and put in the hard yards when you have to. If I'm working on a project I know I can just get on with it, working around the clock if necessary – and if I need some support, there'll be others who'll work alongside me. If I need to spend some money, buy some software, fly to Spain to meet with the client, I don't have to ask for permission, I just do it. There's a saying, 'It's easier to ask for forgiveness than seek permission', and this place works like that. So far I haven't had to ask for forgiveness!

The freedom to work when and how you wish, as long as this is consistent with project requirements and deadlines, appears greatly valued by everyone. This unusual degree of autonomy and trust given employees extends to working hours, sick leave and holiday entitlements and so on. Formal records of these are not kept. Some staff work around the clock for days and weeks at a time when involved in a major project and then disappear for a month or two before taking on their next task. Others work a more conventional week but, as noted above, almost all drop in to the office whenever they are in town, during the weekend almost as much as during the week. As another consultant said:

> It's good to work with colleagues who trust you to balance your work and your private life as well as you can. If you work 24/7 at some times, you need to take breaks at other times if you expect a wife or family still to be there when the project ends. Too many consultants I know have busted marriages.

Although KMP has what is essentially a flat management structure, it does retain some features of a more formal system. The partners and some senior consultants form a board of management, which meets each week. Matters discussed include possible new consultancies, progress reports from consultants leading current projects, and related matters. Summary notes on these meetings are distributed by e-mail, and monthly financial reports are distributed throughout the organization. Hence all staff are kept fully informed of developments.

Individual projects are undertaken by temporary project teams, each with a leader. Some staff belong to more than one team. Team leaders negotiate commitments from team members, who then have to organize their workload accordingly. Rewards structures are frequently seen as a problem with team-based projects.[13] As a component of individual remuneration at KMP relates to income from the projects a staff member has worked on, there is an incentive to contribute to successful projects. Only areas like HR and IT do not receive project-related income – and staff areas such as these are kept as small as possible, in order to minimize overheads.

In fact, there appears to be some considerable disparity between the pay rates of different consultants. Premiums are paid to those with skills greatly in demand; project leaders are paid a premium; those whose expertise attracts additional work to KMP of course have this recognized; and in general those who have been with KMP longer tend to have negotiated higher base rates. As everyone's pay also includes a component based on the overall success of the enterprise, however, there is also an incentive to share knowledge and expertise whether or not an individual is formally associated with a particular project. Not freely sharing would be regarded as not 'playing the game'.

Peer respect appears to play a large part. People are invited to join a project because of their reputation within the organization, including their reputation for sharing. The senior consultants were described by a junior consultant as 'very approachable, very helpful, especially when you think how busy they are'. The rewards within KMP are not simply financial, then, but also include intangibles such as work flexibility, mentoring and peer respect.

Overall, KMP impresses the outside observer as an organization with a very strong and clearly defined culture of individual initiative coupled with co-operation and sharing.

The role of IT

We regard IT as a facilitator, not as the answer.

(senior partner)

KMP is an organization which communicates via e-mail. Staff are so frequently working odd hours, or overseas, or out of the office for some reason, that no one thinks it unusual to send an e-mail to the person who works at the desk next to them. Asynchronous communication is an accepted part of life. Only formal meetings and social gatherings are invariably face-to-face – and notes on meetings are almost always sent out as e-mail messages.

E-mail thus serves both as communication medium and as a formal record of decisions and activity. For this reason, e-mails are stored on the server rather than on individual desktops. The downside of all this is e-mail overload:

Sometimes I come in and it takes me a couple of hours to work through all my e-mails. When I'm working on a project with short deadlines I'll sometimes leave all non-project e-mail to be dealt with mañana – and sometimes mañana never comes!

(junior consultant)

As noted above, while she was with KMP, the researcher was given access to its intranet and received all organization-wide e-mail messages as well as her own. After she became aware of the e-mail overload problem, towards the end of her attachment, she kept a record of all incoming e-mail. She received 872 non-personal messages in one month, 289 in the busiest week. A fair number of these were sent to all staff, often just 'for information'. No one could hope to read more than a fraction of these messages.

This seems to be a problem which everyone in KMP recognizes and complains about, but no one does anything to resolve – 'A bit like the weather,' as one staff member said. Several project teams have tried using groupware, in particular Lotus Notes, in an attempt to overcome some of these problems, but this seems to have been most successful when the project team has either included outside members who are not part of the internal e-mail system (such as staff from a client) or has been geographically dispersed. The avalanche of e-mail adds considerably to both the stress and the complexity of work at KMP. 'E-mail is our biggest unsolved problem,' said one consultant. In this, they are not alone.[14]

Given that it is a knowledge management organization, it is of considerable interest that KMP has *not* set up a knowledge management database of their own resources or expertise – even though it has developed such systems for some clients. 'We figure we're still small enough to get away with carrying everything in our heads,' said the senior consultant. The mentoring described above certainly helps support this informal knowledge sharing. As the organization continues to grow, however, and as the first generation of partners nears retirement, this decision may need to be reviewed.[15]

Conclusions

KMP is far from a typical organization, though it appears to share many features with other consulting organizations. It was of particular interest to note the areas in which it appeared to follow not standard HR practice, but a practical implementation of knowledge management theory. Such areas include its highly participative recruitment process, its mentoring of staff (though not always for new staff), the emphasis on trust, and its open and lateral communication.

The problems noted above with the induction of new staff and with e-mail overload are widely recognized, but priority has so far been given to the successful completion of the projects from which KMP's income is earned. Internal management issues are of secondary importance.

The longitudinal ethnographic case study design adopted proved particularly successful in this project. It enabled the researcher to see some of the motivations and reality behind senior management descriptions of the processes adopted by the organization studied, and the comments on the full draft report by the two informants have greatly increased its credibility and trustworthiness. She was also relieved that the senior partner agreed to the publication of her findings, including the present one, without requesting any alterations.

The researcher compiled a short report to KMP, which made a number of recommendations to the organization. These included

- the introduction of a formal induction process for all newly appointed staff
- identification of possible mentors for all newly appointed staff
- the near-elimination of e-mails addressed to all staff, 'for information' only
- investigation of the potential of groupware such as Lotus Notes, and of an internal database or databases of resources and expertise, to better support current projects.

The case also suggests that further research in consulting organizations, including but not restricted to firms specializing in knowledge management, would be of value to see to what extent the HR practices observed here are typical of such organizations. In particular, do other organizations adopt similarly unconventional recruiting practices? Do they have similar induction difficulties? Is mentoring, of the ongoing kind observed at KMP, common? Have other consulting firms been able to devise comparable remuneration schemes which support, rather than undermine, a culture of sharing information?

Whatever else it demonstrates, KMP's focus on people rather than systems seems crucial to its continued success in a complex, rapidly changing and even at times chaotic environment.

Acknowledgements

Completion of this research would not have been possible without the full co-operation of KMP and all its staff. I am particularly grateful to all those who gave me their time so generously and answered my questions so openly and honestly, when I could see how busy they were. I am only sorry that confidentiality prevents me from naming them and their organization.

I would also like to acknowledge and thank my doctorial supervisor and his departmental colleagues for their assistance and faith that I would eventually complete and graduate.

Notes

1   This case study was in part suggested by M. Robertson and G. O'M. Hammersley, 'Knowledge Management Practices within a Knowledge-Intensive Firm: The Significance of the People Management Function', *Journal Of European Industrial Training*, **24** (2/3/4), 2000, pp. 241–53. We would like to acknowledge the assistance of Trish Milne of the University of Canberra with its preparation.

2   D. Binney, 'The Knowledge Management Spectrum – Understanding the KM Landscape', *Journal of Knowledge Management*, **5** (1), 2001, pp. 33-42; G. P. Huber, 'Transfer of Knowledge in Knowledge Management Systems: Unexplored Issues and Suggested Studies', *European Journal of Information Systems*, **10** (2), June 2001, pp. 72–9; N. K. Kakabadse, A. Kakabadse and A. Kouzmin, 'Reviewing the Knowledge Management Literature: Towards a Taxonomy'. *Journal of Knowledge Management*, **7** (4), 2003, 75–91; P. Milne, 'Rewards, Recognition and Knowledge Sharing: Seeking a Causal Link', *Australian Academic & Research Libraries*, **32** (4), December 2001, pp. 321–31; H. Scarbrough, J. Swan et al., *Knowledge Management: A Literature Review* (London, Institute of Personnel and Development, 1999). See also websites such as the KM Network (www.brint.com/km/).

3   E. Perez, 'A Second Shot at the Knowledge Management Challenge', *Online*, **26** (6), Nov/Dec 2002, pp. 25–6, 28–9; J. Storey and E. Barnett, 'Knowledge Management Initiatives: Learning from Failure', *Journal of Knowledge Management*, **4** (2), 2000, pp. 145–56.

4   M. W. McElroy, 'Integrating Complexity Theory, Knowledge Management and Organizational Learning', *Journal of Knowledge Management*, **4** (3), 2000, pp. 195–203.

5   D. W. De Long and L. Fahey, 'Diagnosing Cultural Barriers to Knowledge Management', *Academy of Management Executive*, **14** (1), 2000, pp. 113–27; D. Hislop, 'Linking Human Resource Management and Knowledge Management via Commitment', *Employee*

Relations, **25** (2), 2003, pp. 182–202; Robertson and Hammersley, op. cit.

6   H. Scarbrough, 'Knowledge Management, HRM and the Innovation Process', *International Journal of Manpower,* **24** (5), 2003, pp. 501–16.

7   R. Filius, J. A. de Jong and E. C. Roelofs, 'Knowledge Management in the Office: A Comparison of Three Cases', *Journal of Workplace Learning,* **12** (7), 2000, p. 287.

8   M. Brenner, 'Intensive Interviewing'. In *The Research Interview: Uses and Approaches,* ed. M. Brenner, J. Brown and D. Canter (London: Academic, 1985), pp. 147–62.

9   R. K. Yin, *Case Study Research: Design and Methods,* rev edn (Newbury Park, CA: Sage, 1989).

10 E. G. Guba, 'Criteria for Assessing the Trustworthiness of Naturalistic Inquiries', *Educational Communication and Technology,* **29** (2), 1981, p. 85.

11 Ibid., pp. 85–6; Yin, op. cit., pp. 143–6.

12 J. Regan, 'Mentoring Schemes: Raising the Standards', *Library + Information Update,* **2** (4), April 2003, pp. 36-7. L. A. Joia provides an interesting case study of the role of mentoring in knowledge transfer between teachers in disadvantaged areas: 'Assessing Unqualified In-Service Teacher Training in Brazil Using Knowledge Management Theory: A Case Study', *Journal of Knowledge Management,* **6** (1), 2002, pp. 74–86.

13 Milne, op.cit.

14 See, for example, N. Bontis, M. Fearon and M. Hishon, 'The E-Flow Audit: An Evaluation of Knowledge Flow Within and Outside a High-Tech Firm', *Journal of Knowledge Management,* **7** (1), 2003, pp. 6–19.

15 S. D. Galup, R. Dattero and R. C. Hicks, 'Knowledge Management Systems: An Architecture for Active and Passive Knowledge', *Information Resources Management Journal,* **15** (1), Jan–Mar 2002, pp. 22-7; a successful case study is reported by L. Worley, 'The Way We Were, the Way We Live Now: OURBase at Richards Butler', *Legal Information Management,* **2** (3), Autumn 2002, pp. 22–5.

Select bibliography

Adela Clayton

This bibliography is intended only as an indicative guide to a range of materials that usefully supplement and expand this book. It focuses principally on writing about qualitative research in information settings, covering both theoretical contributions and practical examples, but also includes some valuable general texts. It is divided into three sections:

- Theoretical contributions, which should be of value in helping practitioners and students better understand the various aspects of qualitative investigation.
- Items that discuss particular qualitative research methods and issues.
- Practical examples. Here, we have included only a representative sampling of qualitative studies relevant to information work. No such investigation can ever be ideal, but the examples listed in this bibliography usefully illuminate aspects of the qualitative mode of research in this area. As many such research reports also discuss the methodology employed, inevitably there is some degree of overlap between these last two groupings.

For additional material, readers are referred again to the 'Further reading' sections which conclude most chapters, and to the individual items cited in the chapter endnotes.

Theoretical contributions

Bradley, J. R. 'Methodological issues and practices in qualitative research'. *Library Quarterly*, **63** (4), 1993, pp. 431–49.
    Considers methodological issues arising when empirical enquiry is conducted within a qualitative framework, and discusses methodological practices that have arisen in the context of qualitative assumptions. Issues raised include the researcher as interpreter, the emergent nature of qualitative research and trustworthiness in qualitative research. This article appears in a special issue of the *Library Quarterly* devoted to qualitative research.

Burgess, R. G. *In the field: an introduction to field research*, Contemporary social research, 8, London: Routledge, 1991.

An authoritative guide to the problems and procedures associated with data collection and analysis in field research.

Busha, C. H. and Harter, S. P. *Research methods in librarianship*, New York: Academic Press, 1980.

Still useful despite its age, this text includes discussion of the historical method, case study method, comparative librarianship research and content analysis as part of a general text on research in library science.

Chatman, E. A. 'Field research: methodological themes', *Library & Information Science Research*, **6**, 1984, pp. 425–38.

Describes a number of issues related to field research (researcher's role, empathy, reciprocity, etc.) based on the author's own experience of fieldwork.

Creswell, J. W. *Research design: qualitative, quantitative and mixed methods approaches*, 2nd edn, Thousand Oaks, CA: Sage, 2003.

An accessible discussion with many examples and an annotated bibliography at the end of each chapter. The chapter on mixed methods procedures shows readers how to identify types of mixed methods strategy, select data collection and analysis approaches and plan the overall structure of the study.

de Laine, M. *Fieldwork, participation and practice: ethics and dilemmas in qualitative research*, Thousand Oaks, CA: Sage, 2000.

Suitable as text for all types of fieldwork, the author does not just cover basic ethical principles but fully informs readers of the complex issues in contemporary fieldwork.

Denzin, N. K. and Lincoln, Y. S. *Collecting and interpreting qualitative materials*, 3rd edn, Thousand Oaks, CA: Sage, 2003.

Covers basic methods of gathering, analysing and interpreting qualitative empirical materials. Part 1 moves from interviewing to observing, to the use of artefacts, documents and records from the past; to visual, and autoethnographic methods. It then takes up analysis methods, including computer-assisted methodologies, as well as strategies for analysing talk, and text. Includes discussions of critical feminist inquiry and applied ethnography.

Denzin, N. K. and Lincoln, Y. S. *Handbook of qualitative research*, 2nd edn, Thousand Oaks, CA: Sage, 2000.

This very readable book is a collection of readings with authors selected from many disciplines. The handbook examines the various paradigms for doing qualitative work, and a variety of techniques for collecting, analysing, interpreting and reporting findings.

Estabrook, L. S. ed. *Applying research to practice: how to use data collection and research to improve library management decision making*, Urbana-Champaign: University of Illinois, Graduate School of Library and Information Science, 1992.

Proceedings from a conference at the Library Research Center at the University of Illinois, focusing in particular on public libraries. Possibly more successful as an introduction to research methods than in its stated aim of showing how research can improve library management.

Flick, U. *An introduction to qualitative research*, London: Sage, 2001.

An up-to-date generic introduction to qualitative research with a very large bibliography.

Glazier, J. D. and Powell, R. R. eds. *Qualitative research in information management*, Englewood, CO: Libraries Unlimited, 1992.

Contains 14 papers by librarians and others on a range of issues relevant to qualitative research (e.g., visualization, case studies, focus groups, participant observation), in library and information science. Includes an annotated bibliography.

Glesne, C. *Becoming qualitative researchers: an introduction*, 2nd edn, NY: Pearson Education, 1998.

A very competent general introduction to qualitative research for social scientists, containing much sound advice based on the author's own experiences. Many useful examples covering the entire process, from beginning to end.

Golafshani, N. 'Understanding reliability and validity in qualitative research', *The Qualitative Report*, **8** (4), 2003, pp. 597-606, www.nova.edu/ssss/QR/QR8-4/Golafshani.pdf.

From a qualitative point of view reliability, validity and triangulation have to be redefined in order to reflect the multiple ways of establishing truth in qualitative research.

Hernon, P. 'Components of the research process: where do we need to focus attention?', *Journal of Academic Librarianship*, **27** (2), 2001, pp. 81–9.

Overview of the structure of a research project of particular interest to those beginning a first piece of research.

Hittleman, D. R. and Simon, A. J. *Interpreting education research: an introduction for consumers of research*, 3rd edn, Columbus, OH: Prentice Hall, 2002.

This text provides the basic knowledge and skills to read, interpret, evaluate, and write about quantitative and qualitative educational research.

Holliday, A. *Doing and writing qualitative research*, London: Sage, 2001.

Written in a user-friendly manner, providing an excellent summary at the end of each chapter. The chapter 'Writing about data' illustrates the conceptual structure of data becoming evidence for an argument using tables and figures.

Huberman, A. M. and Miles, M. B. *The qualitative researcher's companion*, Thousand Oaks, CA: Sage, 2002.

A valuable source book. Part one has useful chapters on theory building, validity, ethnography and realism, organizational ethnography and data collection. Part two covers methodological perspectives and part three, empirical studies.

Janesick, V. J. '*Stretching' exercises for qualitative researchers*, 2nd edn, Thousand Oaks, CA: Sage, 2003.

An interesting non-traditional handbook for those embarking on qualitative research for the first time. Janesick believes that qualitative researchers should use a set of systematic exercises in order to prepare themselves for tasks such as interviewing and observation. The metaphor of qualitative research as a dance is used throughout. The second edition has new sections on internet sources, narrative techniques and analysis and interpretation of qualitative data.

Mann, C. and Stewart, F. *Internet communication and qualitative research: a handbook for researching online*, Thousand Oaks, CA: Sage, 2000.

Focuses mainly on using the internet as a data gathering tool, for example for focus groups and interviewing, discussing theoretical, methodological, and practical considerations including ethics.

Marshall, C. and Rossman, G. B. *Designing qualitative research*, 3rd edn, Thousand Oaks, CA: Sage, 1999.

A practical guide on how to put together strong, convincing qualitative research proposals: building the conceptual framework and the research; planning time and resources; and defending the value and logic of qualitative research, as well as data collection, recording, managing and analysing.

May, T. *Qualitative research in action*, London: Sage, 2002.

Brings together contributions from both world-leading scholars and younger researchers. It focuses on cutting-edge issues related to the practice of qualitative research in the field.

McCotter, S. S. 'The journey of a beginning researcher', *Qualitative Report*, **6** (2), 2001, www.nova.edu/ssss/QR/QR6-2/mccotter.html.

An outline of the common problems for the novice in qualitative research and some suggested solutions. Problems discussed include how to use and integrate theory with data, being simultaneously a researcher and participant and how to represent participants with integrity and authenticity.

McKenzie, G., Powell, J. and Usher, R. eds. *Understanding social research: perspectives on methodology and practice*, London, Falmer, 1997.

The book is divided into three sections: the nature of enquiry; the nature of disciplines; and research practice, the latter including chapters on qualitative approaches to data collection and analysis, grounded theory, action research and issues in participant observation.

Mehra, B. 'Bias in qualitative research: voices from an online classroom', *Qualitative Report*, **7** (1), 2002, www.nova.edu/ssss/QR/QR7-1/mehra.html.

A reflective paper about the role researcher self and subjectivity play in designing and conducting qualitative research.

Mellon, C. A. *Naturalistic enquiry for library science: methods and applications for research, evaluation and teaching*, Westport, CT: Greenwood, 1990.

Discusses theoretical foundations of this approach and outlines how to conduct such a study, from definition of the project to presentation of results. While including numerous examples from library science, it is based heavily on educational models.

Morse, J. M. and Richards, L. *Read me first for a user's guide to qualitative methods*, London: Sage, 2002.

A good text on qualitative research for the beginner, helpful and easy to understand on the process of producing data using various qualitative methods. A good choice if planning to use NVivo software.

Patton, M. Q. *Qualitative research and evaluation methods*, 3rd edn, Thousand Oaks, CA: Sage, 2002.
Readable text recommended for the beginning researcher, it successfully brings together theory and practice.

Powell, R. R. 'Recent trends in research: a methodological essay', *Library & Information Science Research*, **21** (1), 1999, pp. 91–119.
Begins by reviewing research methods that have been used in library and information science then identifies methods appearing in the qualitative research literature. Briefly considers possible future methodological trends.

Powell, R. R. *Basic research methods for librarians*, 3rd edn, Greenwich, CT: Ablex, 1997.
A general guide to all types of research for librarians, which includes coverage of interviewing, observation and historical research as data collection methods. Also includes chapters on writing proposals and research reports.

Rossman, G. B. and Rallis, S. F. *Learning in the field: an introduction to qualitative research*, Thousand Oaks, CA: Sage, 1998.
A helpful introductory book for qualitative researchers. There are examples of interviews, field notes, analytic memos and final projects, along with commentary from the authors about the strengths and weaknesses of the data and analysis.

Scarbrough, E. and Tanenbaum, E. *Research strategies in the social sciences: a guide to new approaches*, Oxford: Oxford University Press, 1998.
An overview of the effect on social research of the use of computing technologies and new analytic strategies.

Schram, T. H. *Conceptualizing qualitative inquiry: mindwork for fieldwork in education and the social sciences*, Columbus, OH: Prentice-Hall, 2003.
A framework within which students can learn how to ask informed questions and uncover informative answers. Chapter topics cover engaging the problem and purpose, establishing a perspective, constructing a conceptual context, forming research questions, deciding about traditions, getting into place for fieldwork, establishing an inquiry's integrity, and writing a proposal.

Slater, M. ed. *Research methods in library and information studies*, London: Library Association Publishing, 1990.
Slater offers a useful overview on qualitative research, covering in abbreviated form such issues as the quantitative–qualitative distinction, various data gathering techniques (interviews, group discussion, questionnaires), non-verbal behaviour, observation, reporting, content analysis and games-playing.

Stern, P. C. and Kalof, L. *Evaluating social science research*, 2nd edn, New York: Oxford University Press, 1996.
Provides methods for thinking critically about claims of factual knowledge and drawing appropriate conclusions.

Strauss, A. and Corbin, J. *Basics of qualitative research: techniques and procedures for developing grounded theory*, 2nd edn, London: Sage, 1998.
Contains practical advice and technical expertise for researchers in analysing

and interpreting their collected data, and ultimately building theory from it.

Sutton, B. 'The rationale for qualitative research: a review of principles and theoretical foundations', *Library Quarterly*, **63** (4), 1993, pp. 411–30.

Surveys some of the theoretical principles underlying qualitative research methods, particularly in the social sciences, and discusses some of the methodological issues raised by those principles. The four themes that form the basis of discussion are: contextualization, an approach to social scientific observation that takes into account the environment in which the observational event takes place; understanding; pluralism; and expression.

Tenni, A., Smyth, C. and Boucher, C. 'The researcher as autobiographer: analysing data written about oneself', *Qualitative Report*, **8** (1), 2003, www.nova.edu/ssss/QR/QR8-1/tenni.html.

The authors suggest a number of strategies that a researcher can employ to analyse such data including collaborative analysis, forms of grounded theory and alternative forms of representation such as poetry, art and drama. They also discuss the use of frameworks such as psychodynamic theories, feminist theories and critical theories.

Westbrook, L. 'Qualitative research methods: a review of major stages, data analysis techniques, and quality controls', *Library & Information Science Research*, **16**, 1994, pp. 241–54.

Examines basic tenets of qualitative research, and especially their value to library and information science research. Focuses on the following components of the qualitative approach: research problem, data gathering, content analysis, theory development and validity techniques.

Wilson, T. *'Information science' and research methods*, 2002, http://informationr. net/tdw/publ/papers/slovak02.html.

Considers problems of defining 'information science' as a specific discipline and how information requires social scientific research methods to be applied to its investigation. Sets out a new taxonomy for social research methods.

Wolcott, H. F. *Writing up qualitative research*, 2nd edn, Qualitative research methods, 20, Thousand Oaks, CA: Sage, 2001.

While referring to writing in general, the focus is on reporting on qualitative, descriptive or naturalistic research in the social sciences. Discusses getting going and keeping going, linking with the work of others, tightening up, finishing up and getting published.

Wolcott, H. F. *The art of fieldwork*, 2nd edn, Walnut Creek, CA: Altamira Press, 2004.

Believing that the increasing dominance of a scientific perspective in fieldwork has led to an overemphasis on method, rigour, objectivity, efficiency, reliability and generalizability, Wolcott promotes the artistic aspects of fieldwork: intuition, uncertainty, meaning, intimacy, holism and aesthetics. Practical and sensible advice to novices and experienced researchers alike.

Particular methodologies and issues
Case studies

Clayton, P. 'No easy option: case study research in libraries', *Australian Academic & Research Libraries*, **26** (2), 1995, pp. 69–75.
Discusses when case study methodology may be appropriate in information organizations, its advantages and disadvantages, and ways in which to improve reliability and validity.

Fidel, R. 'The case study method: a case study', *Library & Information Science Research*, **6**, 1984, pp. 273-88.
Outlines the steps in undertaking a case study of online searching (study design, subject selection, data gathering, etc.) and summarizes a range of methodological problems encountered.

Tellis, W. 'Introduction to case study', *Qualitative Report*, **3** (2), 1997, www.nova.edu/ssss/QR/QR3-2/tellis1.html.
Covers the history of case study methodology, some of the applications and specific research protocols.

Travers, M. *Qualitative research through case studies*, Thousand Oaks, CA: Sage 2001.
Provides an overview of some of the diverse approaches that are currently available within the qualitative tradition. Includes interpretive approaches such as grounded theory, dramaturgical analysis, ethnomethodology and conversation analysis and political approaches such as critical discourse analysis, feminism and postmodern ethnography. Each chapter introduces the theoretical assumptions of the tradition through discussing a number of case studies. There are also practical hints on designing undergraduate projects, exercises and a guide to further reading. Should be of special value to those beginning to research.

Yin, R. K. *Case study research, design and methods*, 3rd edn, Thousand Oaks, CA: Sage, 2002.
The classic work on the case study method.

Discourse analysis

Frohmann, B. 'Discourse analysis as a research method in library and information science', *Library & Information Science Research*, **16**, 1994, pp. 119–38.
Introduces discourse analysis developed by Foucault et al. and shows how it can be applied as a useful research method in librarianship, especially with reference to analysis of the ways in which information, its uses and users are discursively constructed.

Ethnography

Atkinson, P. [et al.] eds. *Handbook of ethnography*, London: Sage, 2001.
Provides a critical guide to principles and practice by internationally known experts from a wide range of disciplines.

Emerson, R. L., Fretz, R. I. and Shaw, L. L. *Writing ethnographic field notes*, Chicago: Chicago University Press, 1995.

Covers the process of how one goes about collecting and writing ethnographic data. The book begins with theoretical issues, then moves into jotting, full field notes, how to analyse fieldnotes and write a full ethnography. Provides practical advice illustrated by samples collected by the authors and their students.

LeCompte, B. K. and Schensul, J. J. *Analyzing and interpreting ethnographic data*, Ethnographer's toolkit 5, Walnut Creek, CA: Altamira, 1999.

For the novice researcher. Case studies, checklists, key points to remember, and additional resources to consult are all included. Examples are from a limited field.

Sade-Beck, L. 'Internet ethnography: online and offline', *International Journal of Qualitative Methods*, **3** (2), 2004, www.ualberta.ca/~iiqm/backissues/3_2/pdf/sadebeck.pdf.

This article proposes a new methodology for qualitative research on the internet, based on the integration of qualitative data-gathering methodologies both online and offline.

Schensul, S. L., Schensul, J. J. and LeCompte, B. K. *Essential ethnographic methods: observations, interviews and questionnaires*, Ethnographer's toolkit 2, Walnut Creek, CA: Altamira, 1999.

Good introductory material on ethnographic fieldwork techniques: participant and non-participant observation, interviewing, and ethnographically informed survey research, including systematically administered structured interviews and questionnaires. The methods are given in relation to theoretical models. Includes chapters on sampling and on validity and reliability.

Focus groups

Bader, G. E. and Rossi, C. A. *Focus groups: a step by step guide*, 3rd edn, San Diego, CA: Bader Group, 2002.

This brief and clearly written monograph provides a very practical overview of how to set up and use focus groups. The emphasis is on involving employees in organizational change.

Barbour, R. S. and Kitzinger, J. eds. *Developing focus group research: politics, theory and practice*, Thousand Oaks, CA: Sage, 1999.

Experienced researchers from a range of fields discuss different ways of designing, conducting and analysing focus group research. They examine sampling strategies; the implications of combining focus groups with other methods; accessing views of 'minority' groups; their contribution to participatory or feminist research; use of software packages; discourse analysis; and the epistemological and political underpinnings of research. Good mix of theory and practice.

Chase, L. and Alvarez, J. 'Internet research: the role of the focus group', *Library & Information Science Research*, **22** (4), 2000, pp. 357–69.

Discusses similarities and differences of face-to-face and online focus group methods though a review of research studies.

Drabenstott, K. M. 'Focused group interviews'. In *Qualitative research in information management,* eds. J. D. Glazier and R. R. Powell, pp. 85–104. Englewood, CO: Libraries Unlimited, 1992.

Discusses the development of focus groups as a research technique and its use in library research projects, with particular reference to the author's experience of this method.

Goulding, A. 'Joking, being aggressive and shutting people up: the use of focus groups in LIS research', *Education for Information,* **15**, 1997, pp. 331–41.

Argues that focus groups have great potential for data gathering and discusses what focus groups are, why focus groups should be considered an appropriate research tool in library and information services, the advantages of using focus groups, the practicalities of running a focus group session, and the type of data generated in focus groups and methods of analysis.

Krueger, R. and Casey, M. A. *Focus groups: a practical guide for applied research,* 3rd edn, Newbury Park, CA: Sage, 2000.

The book aims to describe what focus groups are, provide a how-to guide, illustrate with real-life examples and provide a toolkit of methods and techniques. It is suitable for undergraduate research or market research students, but lacks the theoretical underpinning necessary for the more experienced researcher.

Von Seggern, M. and Young, N. J. 'The focus group method in libraries: issues relating to process and data analysis', *Reference Services Review,* **31** (3), 2003, pp. 272–84.

Provides a recent overview of the use of focus group in libraries and includes a useful bibliography.

Grounded theory

Dey, I. *Grounding grounded theory: guidelines for qualitative inquiry,* San Diego: Academic Press, 1999.

Though a small volume, contains a surprising amount of theoretical and practical material. There is a strong emphasis on the process of theorizing from grounded data.

Glaser, B. G. and Strauss, A. L. *The discovery of grounded theory: strategies for qualitative research,* Chicago: Aldine, 1967.

A classic work. The authors regard grounded theory as a general theory of scientific method concerned with the generation, elaboration, and validation of social science theory.

Historical

Duff, W. M. and Cherry, J. M. 'Use of historical documents in a digital world:

LIVERPOOL JOHN MOORES UNIVERSITY
Aldham Roberts L.R.C.
TEL. 051 231 3701/3634

comparisons with original materials and microfiche', *Information Research*, **6** (1), 2000, http://informationr.net/ir/6-1/paper86.html.

Included a survey of users, focus group sessions and server log analysis.

Tosh, J. *The pursuit of history: aims, methods and new directions in the study of modern history*, 3rd edn, London: Longman, 2002.

Excellent introduction to the practice of history which takes an even-handed approach, looking at issues such as oral, visual and written history. Accessible and enthusiastic, encouraging readers to be more reflective.

Interviewing

Bampton, R. and Cowton, C. J. 'The e-interview', *Forum: Qualitative Social Research*, **3** (2), 2002, http://qualitative-research.net/fqs-texte/2-02/2-02bamptoncowton-e.htm#g4.

Based on recent experience of interviewing by e-mail, the authors describe the principal characteristics of the 'e-interview'. Paying particular attention to issues relating to time, space and technology, the paper identifies the possible strengths and weaknesses of the e-interview. It discusses the potential of the e-interview as a research tool, perhaps as a complement to more established methods.

Gubrium, J. F. and Holstein, J. A. eds. *Handbook of interview research: context and method*, Thousand Oaks, CA: Sage, 2002.

This encyclopaedic volume is an authoritative and comprehensive compilation on interviewing. The book is divided into six sections: Forms of interviewing; Distinctive respondents; Auspices of interviewing (that is, the circumstances under which interviewing may be carried out for reasons other than academic research); Technical issues (ranging from internet interviewing to the 'reluctant respondent'); Analytic strategies (analysing the data); and Reflection and representation.

Minichiello, V., Aroni, R., Timewell, E. and Alexander, L. *In-depth interviewing: researching people: principles, techniques, analysis*, 2nd edn, Melbourne: Longman Cheshire, 1995.

Drawing on detailed Australian research examples, this work uses the methodological technique of in-depth interviewing as a focal point to illuminate the whole process of qualitative research from literature review to writing up, going beyond a 'how to' approach in order to explore relevant social, political, ethical and theoretical issues as they arise.

Rubin, H. J and Rubin, I. S. *Qualitative interviewing: the art of hearing data*, 2nd edn, Thousand Oaks, CA: Sage, 2004.

This user-friendly text explains how to obtain detailed information through open-ended depth interviewing.

Talja, S. 'Analyzing qualitative interview data: the discourse analytic method', *Library & Information Science Research*, **21** (4), 1999, pp. 459–77.

This method aims to recognize cultural contexts.

Weiss, R. S. *Learning from strangers: the art and method of qualitative interview studies*, New York: Free Press, 1994.
Weiss includes lengthy excerpts from actual interview transcripts, with detailed commentary on what worked well and what did not. Has excellent advice on developing interview questions, selecting interviewees, analysing interview data and writing the final report.

Nominal group technique

Gaskin, S. 'A guide to nominal group technique (NGT) in focus-group research', *Journal of Geography in Higher Education*, **27** (3), 2003, pp. 342–7.
This article briefly describes the use of nominal group technique to elicit information from a small group. Covers the different stages of NGT sequentially and provides a short case study on the use of NGT in a recent geography and environmental sciences pedagogic research project. Also considers the appropriate use of NGT and covers some of the technique's weaknesses. Concludes with recommendations for practitioners.

NVivo

Bazeley, P. and Richards, L. *The NVivo qualitative project book*, London: Sage, 2001.
Gives basic steps for creating and conducting a real project with real data, using the new-generation software package, QSR NVivo. The software tools are introduced only as needed and explained in the framework of what is being asked. An enclosed CD-ROM provides demonstration software.
Richards, L. *The NVivo qualitative project book*, London: Sage, 1999.
Suggests way to integrate thinking about the project and data with practical ways that NVivo can facilitate the process. The tools are introduced only as needed and explained in the framework of what is being asked.
Walsh, M. 'Teaching qualitative analysis using QSR NVivo', *Qualitative Report*, **8** (2), 2003, pp. 251–6, www.nova.edu.au/ssss/QR/QR8-2/.
The author recounts her own experiences and challenges using QSR NVivo. Includes students' reflections on how technology helps advance the analysis process. Strengths and weaknesses of the software are discussed.

Observation

Labaree, R. V. 'The risk of "going observationalist": negotiating the hidden dilemmas of being an insider participant observer', *Qualitative Research*, **2** (1), 2002, pp. 97–122, http://QRJ.sagepub.com/cgi/reprint/2/1/97.
Based on a review of the literature and the author's own experiences, this article develops a framework for understanding the hidden dilemmas of being an insider participant observer. The article discusses these dilemmas and identifies issues

that need more careful evaluation and analysis within the field of qualitative inquiry.

Phenomenological

Groenewald, T. 'A phenomenological research design illustrated', *International Journal of Qualitative Methods*, **3** (1), 2004, www.ualberta.ca/~iiqm/backissues/3_1/html/groenewald.html.
Covers the core principles of this design and, by means of a specific study, illustrates the phenomenological methodology. Includes a brief overview of phenomenology, the research paradigm of the specific study, the location of the data, and explains the data-gathering and data-storage methods. Unstructured in-depth phenomenological interviews supplemented by memoing, essays by participants, a focus group discussion and field notes were used.

Use of technology

Bauer, M. W. and Gaskell, G. eds. *Qualitative researching with text, image and sound: a practical handbook*, London: Sage, 2000.
The book has four main sections: constructing a research corpus; analytic approaches for text, image and sound; computer assistance; and issues of good practice.

Gibbs, G. R., Friese, S. and Mangabeira, W. C. 'The use of new technology in qualitative research', *Forum: Qualitative Social Research*, **3** (2), 2002, www.qualitative-research.net/fqs-texte/2-02/2-02hrsg-e.htm.
An overview of the ways that the new technologies are affecting the generation, collection and analysis of qualitative data. Video and photographic images, audio recordings and the internet are considered as well as the use of digital technology for computer-assisted qualitative data analysis (CAQDAS).

Rosenstein, B. 'Video use in social science research and program evaluation', *International Journal of Qualitative Methods*, **1** (3), 2002, www.ualberta.ca/~ijqm/english/engframeset.html.
A review of the literature shows that the use of video technology for research falls into three areas: observation (including data collection and analysis), a mechanism for giving feedback, and a means for distance learning and consulting via videoconferencing. The article concludes with a discussion of epistemological methodological issues and the ethics involved in such a technologically advanced medium.

Spiers, J. A. 'Tech tips: Using video management/analysis technology in qualitative research', *International Journal of Qualitative Methods*, **3** (1), 2004. Available at http://www.ualberta.ca/~iiqm/backissues/3_1/pdf/spiersvideo.pdf.
Presents tips on how to use video in qualitative research. The author states that, though there are many, the work done in qualitative research does not require complex and powerful computer programs for working with video programs.

For this work, simple editing software is sufficient. An easy and efficient method of transcribing video clips is also presented.

Other issues

Barry, C. A. 'The research activity timeline: a qualitative tool for information research'. *Library & Information Science Research*, **19** (2), 1997, pp. 153–79.
This qualitative data collection and analysis technique was developed to investigate traditional and electronic information-seeking activity. The seven stages are outlined in detail and demonstrated using the results of a project. Various methodological issues are discussed.

Hubbell, L. D. 'False starts, suspicious interviewees and nearly impossible tasks: some reflections on the difficulty of conducting field research abroad', *Qualitative Report*, **8** (2), 2003, pp. 195–209, www.nova.edu/ssss/QR/QR8-2/hubbell.pdf.
The author discusses the problems encountered in conducting research in a number of different countries. Problems included gaining access to interviewees, establishing rapport with interviewees from different societies, and having one's intentions questioned.

Wolfinger, N. H. 'On writing fieldnotes: collection strategies and background expectancies', *Qualitative Research*, **2** (1), 2002, pp. 85–96.
This article uses fieldnotes from various sources to show that, irrespective of any formal strategies for note-taking, researchers' tacit knowledge and expectations often play a major role in determining which observations are worthy of annotation. A greater understanding of these dynamics could complement existing trends in reflexive ethnography by increasing insight into the note-taking process.

Examples of qualitative research
Mixed method

Cooper, M. 'Perspectives on qualitative research with quantitative implications: studies in information management', *Journal of Education for Library and Information Science*, **31** (2), 1990, pp. 105–12.
A study of the relationship between libraries and computer centres, and of emerging models of information management infrastructure. Used a qualitative survey to precede a quantitative, arguing that both together gave better results.

Frick, E. 'Qualitative evaluation of user education programs: the best choice?', *Research Strategies*, **8** (1), 1990, pp. 4–13.
Most evaluations of user education programmes use quantitative methods. This article discussed qualitative evaluation and its use in user education, stressing that choice between quantitative and qualitative approaches will depend on the purposes for which evaluation is being undertaken.

Wildemuth, B. M. 'Post-positivist research: two examples of methodological pluralism', *Library Quarterly*, **63** (4), 1993, pp. 450–68.

Discusses both an exploratory study of end-user computing, based on interviews analysed using a grounded theory approach, and a study of end-user searching behaviour undertaken using search scenarios. Argues that the choice of method should depend on the research question, and that both approaches used in this study have value.

Case studies

Hellström, T., Kemlin, P. and Malmquist, U. 'Knowledge and competence management at Ericsson: decentalization and organizational fit', *Journal of Knowledge Management*, **4** (2), 2000, pp. 99–110.

In this cross-sectional case study the researchers used a series of semi-structured interviews to identify organizational needs.

Filius, R., de Jong, J. A. and Roelofs, E. C. 'Knowledge management in the office: a comparison of three cases', *Journal of Workplace Learning*, **12** (7), 2000, pp. 286–95.

Effectiveness of knowledge management in the three offices was studied using structured questionnaires and interviews with four HRD professionals in each office.

Haricombe, L. J. 'Confirming qualitative and quantitative methodologies by studying the effects of an academic boycott on academics in South Africa', *Library Quarterly*, **63** (4), 1993, pp. 508–27.

A case study of triangulation, which compared a mail survey with interview data. Both approaches provided valuable information, with the interviews especially useful in illuminating the psychological effects on academic staff.

Joia, L. A. 'Assessing unqualified in-service teacher training in Brazil using knowledge management theory: a case study', *Journal of Knowledge Management*, **6** (1), 2002, pp. 74–86.

In an article which seeks to analyse the key factors for successful implementation of government to government (G2G) projects, multiple case study explanatory methodology based on two recent real-life cases was adopted. From these case studies, a heuristic model is proposed for successful implementation of G2G endeavours.

Jones, K., Kinnell, M. and Usherwood, B. 'The development of self-assessment tool-kits for the library and information sector', *Journal of Documentation*, **56** (2), 2000, pp. 119–35.

The researchers developed and evaluated a technique using action research involving three case study library authorities.

Marcella, R. and Baxter, G. 'Citizenship information service provision in the United Kingdom: a study of 27 case agencies', *Journal of Librarianship and Information Science*, **32** (1), 2000, pp. 9–25.

Reports results of 27 case study visits to UK public libraries, Citizens Advice

Bureaux and other advice agencies to examine existing levels of citizenship information provision within these organizations. The project used interviews and examination of these organizations' collections of citizenship and community information.

Robertson, M. and Hammerlsey, G. O. 'Knowledge management practices within a knowledge-intensive firm: the significance of the people management dimension', *Journal of European Industrial Training*, **24**, 2000, pp. 241–53.

Using case study methodology people management practices of a specialist consulting firm were studied in relation to their role in facilitating knowledge management .

Storey, J. and Barnett, E. 'Knowledge management initiatives: learning from failure', *Journal of Knowledge Management*, **3** (2), 2000, pp. 145–56.

Case study method was used to analyse the social influences on knowledge management following the implementation of an IT-based knowledge management program.

Widén-Wulff, G. 'Business information culture: a qualitative study of the information culture in the Finnish insurance business', *Information Research*, **5** (3), 2000, http://informationr.net/5-3/paper77.html.

Used 40 in-depth interviews analysed through the multiple case study method. The analysis was conducted in five stages considering information environment, information as resource, work processes, innovation and business success.

Focus groups

Dennison, R. F., Jackson, J., Leighton, H. V. and Sullivan, K. 'Web page design and successful use: a focus group study', *Internet Reference Services Quarterly*, **8** (3), 2003, pp. 17–27.

Two focus groups were asked to use web pages that incorporated the elements under examination. While the users' preferences were noted, the research team was more interested in which design elements affected the users' ability to successfully find the information they were asked to locate.

Grounded theory

Ellis, D. 'Modeling the information-seeking patterns of academic researchers: a grounded theory approach', *Library Quarterly*, **63** (4), October 1993, pp. 469–86.

Based on a series of studies undertaken at Sheffield University, the author discusses methodological issues including analysis, comparison, validity, data recording, coding and selection.

Yoong, P. and Pauleen, D. 'Generating and analysing data for applied research on emerging technologies: a grounded action learning approach', *Information Research*, **9** (4), 2004, http://InformationR.net/ir/9-4/paper195.html.

This study aims to assist in finding new research approaches that can generate accessible and relevant data for research on the emerging technologies. Describes two case studies in which the researchers used a grounded action learning approach to study the nature of e-facilitation for face-to-face and for distributed electronic meetings. The grounded action learning approach combines two research methodologies, grounded theory and action learning.

Historical

Baggs, C. '"The whole tragedy of penury": the South Wales Miner's Institute Libraries during the Depression', *Libraries and Culture*, **39** (2), 2004, pp. 115–36. During the economic depression of the late 1920s Welsh miners' institute libraries experienced increasing financial difficulties and turned to external bodies, including public libraries, social service agencies and government-funded schemes, for assistance. This prolonged their existence but undermined the very independence that made them unique.

Boadle, D. 'The historian as archival collector: an Australian local study', *Australian Academic & Research Libraries*, **34** (1), 2003, pp. 14–31. An Australian study focusing on the writing of local historian Keith Swan and the archival records he created.

Hubbard, E. A. 'Library service to unions: a historical overview', *Library Trends*, **50** (3), 2002, www.findarticles.com/p/articles/mi_m1387/is_1_51/ai_94596901/pg_1. This article briefly reviews the evolution of public libraries in the USA, the origins of the currents union movement, and the role of the AFL-CIO/ALA Joint Committee on Library Service to Labor Groups. The article further defines a number of misunderstandings and lack of trust between libraries and organized labour.

Interviews

Dewdney, P. and Harris, R. 'Community information needs: the case of wife assault', *Library & Information Science Research*, 14, 1992, pp. 5-29. Uses interviews with women and service agencies to examine relationships between community needs for information about wife assault and information response offered through social service networks.

Jacobs, N. A. 'Students' perceptions of the library service at the University of Sussex: practical quantitative and qualitative use in an academic library', *Journal of Documentation*, **52** (2), June 1996, pp. 139–62. A qualitative research strategy was used to investigate puzzling responses to a quantitative user survey of book availability in a student reserve collection. Semi-structured interviews were analysed using the NUD*IST software package. The article includes the interview schedules and a detailed discussion of the use of NUD*IST.

McManus, D. and Loughridge, B. 'Corporate information, institutional culture and knowledge management: a UK university library perspective', *New Library*

World, **103**, 2002, pp. 320–7.

A small-scale pilot interview based survey of senior information professionals provides some reasons for the perceived unpopularity of knowledge management in universities.

Zafeiriou, G. 'Managing conflict and reaching consensus in text-based computer conferencing: the students' perspective', *Education for Information*, **21** (2/3), 2003, pp. 97–111.

The study looked at conflict in a higher education online context. Fifty semi-structured interviews were the main tool of data collection. A grounded theory approach, as developed by Strauss and Corbin, was adopted for the analysis, which also used the Atlas.ti qualitative data software. A discussion of the findings in relation to the existing literature is included.

Nominal group technique

Duggan, E. W. and Thachenkary, C. S. 'Supporting the JAD facilitator with the nominal group technique', *Journal of Organizational and End User Computing*, **16** (2), 2004, pp. 1–19.

This study was in the area of systems development requirements (SDR). Joint application development (JAD) was introduced in the late 1970s to solve many of the problems system users experienced with the conventional methods used in SDR. JAD sessions are susceptible to the problems which reduce the effectiveness of groups and outcomes are also critically dependent on excellent facilitation for minimizing dysfunctional group behaviours. The nominal group technique (NGT) was designed to reduce the impact of negative group dynamics. An integration of JAD and NGT was tested empirically in a laboratory experiment and appeared to outperform JAD alone.

Havelka, D. 'A user-oriented model of factors that affect information requirements determination process quality', *Information Resources Management Journal*, **16** (4), 2003, pp. 15–32.

This study aimed to identify factors that affect the process quality of the information requirements determination (IRD) process from a user perspective. A nominal group process was used with three groups of users that have had experience with the IRD process. The study found 33 factors critical to IRD process quality.

Jones, S. C. 'Using the Nominal Group Technique to select the most appropriate topics for postgraduate research students'seminars', *Journal of University Teaching and Learning Practice*, **1** (1), 2004, pp. 20–34, http://jutlp.uow.edu.au/ 2004_v01_i01/pdf/jones_001.pdf

This project at the University of Wollongong used a two-stage evaluation process, nominal groups with a subset of postgraduate research students followed by a survey based on the groups of all students.

Observation

Chatman, E. A. 'Life in a small world: applicability of gratification theory to information-seeking behavior', *Journal of the American Society for Information Science*, **42**, 1991, pp. 438–49.

Applies gratification theory to the information-seeking behaviour of a lower working class population (janitors), finding that the subjects were not active information seekers outside their familiar social milieu.

Cooper, J., Lewis, R. and Urquhart, C. 'Using participant or non-participant observation to explain information behaviour', *Information Research*, **9** (4), 2004, http://InformationR.net/ir/9-4/paper184.html.

Examines lessons learned during non-participant observation of hospital pharmacists, and participant observation with dependent older people living in their own homes. Describes the methods used in both studies, and discusses the ethical issues involved in gaining access to the subjects. Both studies indicated the fundamental need for trust between the observer and the research subjects.

Dewdney, P. 'Recording the reference interview: a field experiment'. In *Qualitative research in information management,* eds. J. D. Glazier and R. R. Powell, pp. 122–50, Englewood, CO: Libraries Unlimited, 1992.

Describes a study in which audiotape recording was used as a method of structured observation in order to discover how librarians interacted with public library users, and shows that such technology not only helps document observed behaviour but also enhances the observer's capacity for systematic attention to detail and accurate recall.

Echavarria, T. et al. 'Encouraging research through electronic mentoring: a case study', *College & Research Libraries*, **56** (4), 1995, pp. 352–61.

Reports on a US experiment using e-mail to create mentoring relationships focusing on library science research, and includes first-hand accounts of participant experiences.

Merchant, L. and Hepworth, M. 'Information literacy of teachers and pupils in secondary schools', *Journal of Librarianship and Information Science*, **34** (2), 2002, pp. 81–9.

Research involved observation of ten teachers and 40 pupils in the classroom, complemented by observation of pupils' behaviour in the school library and computing facilities.

Whitlatch, J. B. 'Unobtrusive studies and the quality of academic library reference services', *College & Research Libraries*, **50** (2), 1989, pp. 181–94.

Explores content validity and assumptions regarding unobtrusive studies by using empirical data from an obtrusive study of reference performance, and finds that improvements are desirable before conducting more unobtrusive studies of reference performance.

Index